iPad® For Seniors

FOR DUMMIES®

A Wiley Brand

8th Edition

by Nancy C. Muir

iPad® For Seniors For Dummies®, 8th Edition

Published by: **John Wiley & Sons, Inc.,** 111 River Street, Hoboken, NJ 07030-5774, www.wiley.com

Copyright © 2016 by John Wiley & Sons, Inc., Hoboken, New Jersey

Published simultaneously in Canada

No part of this publication may be reproduced, stored in a retrieval system or transmitted in any form or by any means, electronic, mechanical, photocopying, recording, scanning or otherwise, except as permitted under Sections 107 or 108 of the 1976 United States Copyright Act, without the prior written permission of the Publisher. Requests to the Publisher for permission should be addressed to the Permissions Department, John Wiley & Sons, Inc., 111 River Street, Hoboken, NJ 07030, (201) 748-6011, fax (201) 748-6008, or online at http://www.wiley.com/go/permissions.

Trademarks: Wiley, For Dummies, the Dummies Man logo, Dummies.com, Making Everything Easier, and related trade dress are trademarks or registered trademarks of John Wiley & Sons, Inc. and may not be used without written permission. iPad is a registered trademark of Apple. All other trademarks are the property of their respective owners. John Wiley & Sons, Inc. is not associated with any product or vendor mentioned in this book.

For general information on our other products and services, please contact our Customer Care Department within the U.S. at 877-762-2974, outside the U.S. at 317-572-3993, or fax 317-572-4002. For technical support, please visit www.wiley.com/techsupport.

Wiley publishes in a variety of print and electronic formats and by print-on-demand. Some material included with standard print versions of this book may not be included in e-books or in print-on-demand. If this book refers to media such as a CD or DVD that is not included in the version you purchased, you may download this material at http://booksupport.wiley.com. For more information about Wiley products, visit www.wiley.com.

Library of Congress Control Number: 2015956623

ISBN 978-1-119-13779-5 (pbk); ISBN 978-1-119-14135-8 (ebk); ISBN 978-1-119-14134-1 (ebk)

Manufactured in the United States of America

10 9 8 7 6 5 4 3 2 1

Contents at a Glance

Table of Contents

*I*f you bought this book (or are even thinking about buying it), you've probably already made the decision to buy an iPad. The iPad is designed to be simple to use, but still, you can spend hours exploring the preinstalled apps, finding out how to change settings, and figuring out how to sync the device to your computer or through iTunes or iCloud. I've invested those hours so that you don't have to — and I've added advice and tips for getting the most out of your iPad.

This book helps you get going with the iPad quickly and painlessly so that you can move directly to the fun part.

About This Book

This book is written specifically for mature people like you, folks who may be relatively new to using a tablet device and want to discover the basics of buying an iPad, working with its preinstalled apps, and getting on the Internet. In writing this book, I've tried to consider the types of activities that might interest someone who is 50 years old or older and picking up an iPad for the first time.

Foolish Assumptions

This book is organized by sets of tasks. These tasks start from the beginning, assuming that you've never laid your hands on an iPad, and guide you through basic steps in nontechnical language.

This book was written about the iPad Pro (with a 12.9 inch display), iPad Air 2 (the 9.7-inch model), and iPad mini 4 (the 7.9-inch model). Most material is relevant whether you have an iPad second-generation or later, though I strongly recommend that you update to the latest operating system, iOS 9, which is quick and easy to do (see Chapter 2). iOS 9 is the operating system I based this book on.

This book covers both the Wi-Fi–only and the Wi-Fi and 3G/4G iPad features. Examples that involve iTunes are based on version 12.2 of that software.

Icons Used in This Book

There are two icons used in this book to alert you to special content:

 Tip icons point out insights or helpful suggestions related to tasks in the step lists.

 This icon is used to highlight features of the latest iPad models or iOS 9 that are new and exciting, in case you're moving up from earlier versions.

Beyond the Book

I've provided additional information about iPad and iOS 9 online to help you on your way:

➠ **Cheat Sheet:** Check out www.dummies.com/cheatsheet/ipadforseniors to help you figure out various iPad General settings and settings for email and contacts that will come in handy on a regular basis.

➡ **Online articles:** On several of the pages that open each of this book's parts, you'll find links to what the folks at *For Dummies* call Web Extras, which expand on features that I've discussed in that particular section. You'll find them at `www.dummies.com/extras/ipadforseniors`. There, I've given you a listing of free apps to get you going with your iPad at no cost, info about using Apple Music, and a handy list of Siri commands.

Where to Go from Here

Dive in and get started! You can work through this book from beginning to end, or simply open a chapter to solve a problem or acquire a specific new skill whenever you need it. The steps in every task quickly get you to where you want to go, without a lot of technical explanation.

Note: At the time I wrote this book, all the information it contained was accurate. Apple may introduce new iPad models and new versions of the iOS and iTunes between book editions. If you've bought a new iPad and its hardware, user interface, or version of iTunes looks a little different, be sure to check out what Apple has to say at `www.apple.com/ipad`. You'll no doubt find updates on the company's latest releases. Also, if you don't set up iCloud to automatically update your iPad, perform updates to the operating system on a regular basis, as described in Chapter 2.

When a change is very substantial, I may add an update or bonus information that you can download at my website for this book, `www.ipadmadeclear.com`.

Part I
Making the iPad Yours

Visit www.dummies.com for more great content online.

Buying Your iPad

*Y*ou've read about it. You're so intrigued that you've decided to get your own iPad to have fun, explore the online world, read e-books, organize your photos, play games, and more.

You've made a good decision because the iPad redefines the computing experience in an exciting new way. It's also an absolutely perfect fit for many seniors.

In this chapter, you discover the different types of iPad models and their relative advantages, as well as where to buy this magical device. After you have one in your hands, I help you explore what's in the box and give you an overview of the little buttons and slots you'll encounter; luckily, the iPad has very few of them.

Get ready to . . .

Discover What's New in iOS 9 and the New iPads

Apple's iPad gets its features from a combination of hardware and its software operating system (called *iOS*; the term is short for *iPhone Operating System,* in case you want to impress your friends). The current operating system is iOS 9, though small updates appear all the time, so by the time you're reading this book, you might have 9.2, 9.3, or 9.4!

If you've seen an older iPad in action, or if you own one, it's helpful to understand which new features the latest iPad devices bring to the table (all of which are covered in more detail throughout this book).

Three iPads are now being offered: iPad mini 4, iPad Air 2, and iPad Pro. The Pro is the newest addition to the line, with a large 12.9-inch screen, an optional attached keyboard accessory, and an optional stylus with fancy sensors for better control drawing and performing tasks on the screen. iPad Air 2 is left over from last year's line-up, and iPad mini 4 brings some tweaks to the quality and performance of the iPad mini 3, which is no longer available.

In addition to the features of previous iPads, the latest iPad models offer

⇒ **Design:** For iPad Air 2 and the iPad mini 4, Apple has made them a bit lighter and thinner than earlier models and made improvements to screen and camera quality. iPad mini 4 has a fully laminated display with antireflective coating, just like iPad Air 2 and iPad Pro. iPad Air 2 weighs .96 pounds, iPad mini 4 weighs .65 pounds, and the big brother of them all, iPad Pro, weighs 1.57 pounds, which is still impressive given the overall dimensions of the display.

⇒ **An improved chip:** The 64-bit A8X processor in the iPad Air 2 increases the processor and graphics speeds accomplished by the A8 chip on the previous-generation iPad Air. The iPad mini 4 has advanced to an A8 processor. iPad Pro sports the best processor of the bunch, an A9X, which makes it the fastest performer of the trio.

→ **Better Wi-Fi:** Two-antennae, dual-channel Wi-Fi and the use of MIMO (multiple-input, multiple output) technology allows for much faster wireless connections. In iPad Air 2, support of the latest Wi-Fi standard, 802.11 ac, ups the ante on Wi-Fi performance. Note that the iPad mini 4 doesn't support this standard.

→ **Motion Coprocessor:** This coprocessor processes game features like the gyroscope and accelerometer. On iPad Air 2 and iPad mini 4, there's an M8 motion coprocessor. The iPad Pro offers a slightly faster M9 motion coprocessor.

→ **Photos and Video Recording:** Video recording features added to the iPad mini 4 include the addition of Slo-mo mode for video recording and Burst mode for taking and optimizing a series of pictures.

→ **Touch ID:** This security feature is now included on all iPad models (it was missing on iPad mini 2). Essentially, sensors in the Home button allow you to train the iPad to recognize your fingerprint and grant you access to not only your iPad with a finger press, but also allow you to use the Apple Pay feature to buy items without having to enter your payment information every time.

→ **A barometer sensor:** Now on all three iPad models, this sensor makes it possible for your iPad to sense air pressure and weather around you. This one's especially cool when hiking a mountain where the weather may change as you climb.

→ **Apple Pencil and 3D Touch:** With iPad Pro, some exciting new hardware features include the ability to use the optional Apple Pencil stylus to interact with the screen. In addition, the 3D Touch feature (sometimes referred to as Multi-Touch) allows for three levels of pressure on the screen. For example, the lightest tap on an object selects it; medium pressure displays a preview (called Peek by Apple); the heaviest pressure opens the item (called Pop).

⟶ **Keyboard options:** iPad Pro has a full size onscreen keyboard. Additionally, you can buy an attachable physical keyboard, which you hook up using a Smart Connector connection, making it much easier to get work or complex tasks done.

⟶ **Live Photos:** Using the 3D Touch feature, you can press harder on a photo on the screen and it "plays" like a short video. Essentially, the Camera app captures 1.5 seconds on either side of the moment when you capture the photo, so anything that moved, such as water flowing in a stream, will seem to move when you press the still photo.

 Throughout this book, I highlight features that are available only on certain iPad models, so you can probably use much of the information in this book even if you own an earlier version of the iPad.

Almost any iPad device except the original iPad can use most features of iOS 9 if you update the operating system (discussed in detail in Chapter 2); this book is based on version 9 of the iOS. This update to the operating system adds a few new features, including

⟶ **The News app:** This new app is an intelligent news aggregator, which means that it gathers news stories from various sources in one place. It's intelligent because it "learns" to present you with stories that are similar to other content you've viewed. See Chapter 21 for more about how News works.

➡ **More integrated Notes:** The Notes app gets a facelift with iOS 9, with the ability to add photos, maps, and URLs to notes. Additionally, you can create instant checklists and even sketch in your notes. You can also share items to Notes using the Share feature in apps such as Photos. See Chapter 20 for more about Notes.

➡ **Improvements to the Maps app:** With iOS 9, Maps gets a Transit view for finding information about public transit in select cities around the world. Also, the Nearby feature provides suggestions of nearby businesses and services, such as restaurants, bank ATMs, and gas stations.

➡ **Improved Siri suggestions and search:** Siri, iPhone's personal assistant feature, can now offer suggestions of items you might be interested in even before you ask. For example, if you read a newspaper the same time every morning, Siri might suggest the publication to you. Siri can even search for a photo or video based on the date and location where you took the photo. See Chapter 19 for details about using Siri.

➡ **Stronger passcodes and two-factor authentication:** With iOS 9, longer passcodes provide more security, while two-factor authentication helps your iPad make sure you're you. With this feature, when you try to access any accounts or information from a new device, you're asked to retrieve a code from another device via a text message or phone call to sign in, in addition to your account information.

➡ **Car Play:** Car Play is a new feature that is largely still on the drawing board, because car manufacturers are only now planning to build it into their car models. If you buy a car down the road with Car Play, it will allow you to control several features, use apps, and play content from your iPad from a graphical screen built into the dashboard.

Choose the Right iPad for You

The most obvious differences among iPad models is their thickness and weight, with the Pro being biggest, then iPad Air 2, and finally the smallest, iPad mini 4 (see **Figure 1-1**). All three models come in three colors: space gray, silver, or gold.

Figure 1-1

All three models come in Wi-Fi only for accessing a Wi-Fi network, or 3G/4G for connecting to the Internet through a cellular network as your cell phone does. The iPad models also differ slightly in available memory and price based on that memory:

➡ **iPad Pro:** $799 for 32 GB and $949 for 128 GB.

➡ **iPad Air 2:** $499 for 16 GB; $599 for 64 GB; $699 for 128 GB.

➡ **iPad mini 4:** $399 for 16 GB; $499 for 64 GB; $599 for 128 GB. Comparable Wi-Fi plus Cellular models cost about $130 more for each model.

Finally, there are variations in screen quality and resolution, camera quality, and so on. Logically, the bigger the iPad, the bigger the price and higher the quality.

Read on as I explain some of these variations in more detail.

Decide How Much Memory Is Enough

Storage capacity is a measure of how much information — for example, movies, photos, and software applications (or *apps*) — you can store on a computing device. Capacity can also affect your iPad's performance when handling tasks such as streaming favorite TV shows from the World Wide Web or downloading music.

 Streaming refers to watching video content from the web (or from other devices) rather than playing a file stored on your iPad. You can enjoy a lot of material online without ever downloading its full content to your iPad's memory — and given that every iPad model has a relatively small amount of capacity, that's not a bad idea. See Chapters 11 and 13 for more about getting your music and movies online.

Your storage capacity options are 16, 32, 64, or 128 gigabytes (GB) depending on the model. You must choose the right amount for your needs, because you can't open the unit and add storage. Additionally, you can't insert a *flash drive* (also known as a *USB stick*) to add backup capacity because the iPad has no USB port — or CD/DVD drive, for that matter. However, Apple has thoughtfully provided iCloud, a service you can use to save space by backing up content to the Internet (you can read more about that in Chapter 3).

 With an Apple Digital AV Adapter accessory, you can plug into the Lightning Connector slot to attach a MicroSD or USB–enabled device to add an external hard drive for additional storage capacity. ViewSonic offers several HDMI projectors; DVDO offers an HD Travel Kit for smartphones and tablets; and Belkin has introduced a line of tools for HDTV streaming. See Chapter 13 for more about using these AV features.

So how much capacity is enough for your iPad? Here's a rule of thumb: If you like lots of media, such as movies or TV shows, and you want to store them on your iPad (rather than experiencing or accessing this content online on sites such as Hulu or Netflix), you might need 64GB or 128GB. For most people who manage a reasonable number of photos, download some music, and watch heavy-duty media such as movies online, 64GB is probably sufficient. If you simply want to check email, browse the web, read e-books, and write short notes to yourself, 16GB *might* be enough.

 Do you have a clue how big a gigabyte (GB) is? Consider this: Just about any computer you buy today comes with a minimum of 250–500GB of storage. Computers have to tackle larger tasks than iPads do, so that number makes sense. The iPad, which uses a technology called *flash* for memory storage, is meant (to a great extent) to help you experience online media and email; it doesn't have to store much and in fact pulls lots of content from online. In the world of memory, 16GB for any kind of storage is puny if you keep lots of content and graphics on the device.

Choose Wi-Fi Only or Wi-Fi + Cellular

Because the iPad is great for browsing online, shopping online, emailing, and so on, having an Internet connection for it is important. One feature that makes the iPad's price and performance variable is whether your model is Wi-Fi only or Wi-Fi + Cellular (3G/4G). Wi-Fi and 3G/4G are used to connect to the Internet.

You use *Wi-Fi* to connect to a wireless network at home or at locations such as your local coffee shop, a grocery store, or an airport that offers Wi-Fi. This type of network uses short-range radio to connect to the Internet; its range is reasonably limited, so if you leave home or walk out of the coffee shop, you can't use it anymore. (These limitations may change, however, as some towns are installing communitywide Wi-Fi networks.)

The 3G and 4G cellular technologies allow an iPad to connect to the Internet via a widespread cellular-phone network. You use it in much the same way that you make calls from just about anywhere with your cellphone. 4G may not always be available in every location. You'll still connect to the Internet via 3G when 4G service isn't available, but without the advantage of the super-fast 4G technology.

Getting a Wi-Fi + Cellular iPad costs an additional $130, but it also includes GPS, which pinpoints your location so that you can get more accurate driving directions. You have to buy an iPad model that fits your data connection provider — either AT&T, Sprint, T-Mobile, or Verizon in the United States.

Also, to use your 3G/4G network, you have to pay a monthly fee (in the U.K., you can connect through EE). The good news is that no carrier requires a long-term contract, which you probably had to have when you bought your cellphone and its service plan. You can pay for a connection during the month you visit your grandkids, for example, and get rid of it when you arrive home. Features, data allowance (which relates to accessing email or downloading items from the Internet, for example), and prices vary by carrier and could change at any time so visit each carrier's website to see what it offers. Note that if you intend to *stream* videos (watch them on your iPad from the Internet), you can eat through your data plan allowance quickly.

 Go to these links for more information about iPad data plans: AT&T is at www.att.com/shop/ wireless/devices/ipad.jsp; Verizon is at www.verizonwireless.com/landingpages/ ipad; T-Mobile's address is www.t-mobile.com; and Sprint is at http://sprint.com.

So how do you choose? If you want to wander around the woods or town — or take long drives with your iPad continually connected to the Internet to get step-by-step navigation info from the Maps app — get Wi-Fi + Cellular and pay the price. If you'll use your iPad mainly at home or via a Wi-Fi *hotspot* (a location where Wi-Fi access to the Internet is available, such as an Internet cafe), then don't bother with 3G/4G. Frankly, you can find *lots* of hotspots out there, at libraries, restaurants, hotels, airports, and more.

If you have a Wi-Fi–only iPad, you can use the hotspot feature on a smartphone, which allows the iPad to use your phone's 3G or 4G connection to go online if you pay for a higher-data-use plan that supports hotspot use with your phone service carrier. Check out the features of your phone to turn on the hotspot feature.

Because 3G and 4G iPads are also GPS (Global Positioning System) devices, they know where you are and can act as a navigation system to get you from here to there. The Wi-Fi–only model uses a digital compass and triangulation method for locating your current position, which is less accurate; with no constant Internet connection, it won't help you get around town. If getting accurate directions is one iPad feature that excites you, get 3G/4G and then see Chapter 15 for more about the Maps feature.

Understand What You Need to Use Your iPad

Before you head off to buy your iPad, you should know what other devices, connections, and accounts you'll need to work with it optimally.

At a bare minimum, you need to be able to connect to the Internet to take advantage of most iPad features. If you have an Apple ID you also have an iCloud account, Apple's online storage service, to store and share content online, and you can use a computer to download photos, music, or applications from non-Apple online sources (such as stores, sharing sites, or your local library) and transfer them to your iPad through a process called *syncing*. You can also use a computer or iCloud to register your iPad the first time you start it, although you can have the folks at the Apple Store handle registration for you if you have an Apple Store nearby.

Can you use your iPad without owning a computer and just use public Wi-Fi hotspots to go online (or a 3G/4G connection, if you have such a model)? Yes. To go online using a Wi-Fi–only iPad and to use many

of its built-in features at home, however, you need to have a home Wi-Fi network available. You also need to use iCloud or sync to your computer to get updates for the iPad operating system.

For syncing with a computer, Apple's *iPad User Guide* recommends that you have

⟼ A Mac or PC with a USB 2.0 port and one of the following operating systems:

- Mac OS X version 10.6.8 or later

- Windows 10, 8, 7, Windows Vista, or Windows XP Home or Professional with Service Pack 3 or later

⟼ iTunes 11 or later, available at `www.itunes.com/download`

⟼ An Apple ID and iTunes Store account

⟼ Internet access

⟼ An iCloud account

Apple has set up its iTunes software and the iCloud service to give you two ways to manage content for your iPad — including movies, music, or photos you've downloaded — and specify how to sync your calendar and contact information. There are a lot of tech terms to absorb here (iCloud, iTunes, syncing, and so on). Don't worry: Chapter 3 covers those settings in more detail.

Know Where to Buy Your iPad

As of this writing, you can buy an iPad at the Apple Store; at brick-and-mortar stores such as Best Buy, Walmart, Sam's Club, and Target; and at online sites such as MacMall.com. You can also buy 3G/4G models (models that require an account with a phone service provider) from Sprint, AT&T, T-Mobile, and Verizon, as well as at the Apple Store.

Apple Stores aren't on every corner, so if visiting one isn't an option (or you just prefer to go it alone), you can go to the Apple Store website (`http://store.apple.com/shop/buy-iPad/ipad-air`) and order an iPad to be shipped to you — even get it engraved, if you want. Typically, standard shipping is free, and if there's a problem, Apple's customer service reps will help you solve the problem or replace your iPad. Additionally, smaller stores that sell electronics can have an Apple Specialist designation that allows them to carry and sell Apple products. Check your local stores for this.

Consider iPad Accessories

At present, Apple offers a few accessories that you may want to check out when you purchase your iPad (or purchase down the road), including

- **iPad Smart Case/Smart Cover:** Your iPad isn't cheap, and unlike a laptop computer, it has an exposed screen that can be damaged if you drop or scratch it. Investing in the iPad Smart Case or Smart Cover is a good idea if you intend to take your iPad out of your house — or if you have a cat or grandchildren. The iPad Smart Cover (see **Figure 1-2**) ranges from $39.95 to $129.95 from third-party sources depending on design and material.

- **Printers:** There are printers from HP, Brother, Canon, and Epson that support the wireless AirPrint feature. As of this writing, prices range from $129 to $399.

- **Smart Keyboard:** You can buy an attachable keyboard for your iPad Pro for $169, which will make working with productivity apps much easier. This keyboard connects to your iPad to provide power and transmit data between the devices. Also, a Bluetooth keyboard is available as part of the $99.95 case.

Figure 1-2

➡ **Apple Pencil:** For $99, you can buy the highly sophisticated stylus for use with the iPad Pro. The Apple Pencil makes it easy to draw on your iPad screen or manage complex interactions more precisely.

➡ **Belkin Express Dock:** The iPad is light and thin, which is great, but holding it all the time can get tedious. The Belkin Dock lets you prop up the device so that you can view it hands-free and then charge the battery and sync to your computer. At about $60, it's a good investment for ease and comfort. Be sure to get one that matches your iPad model.

➡ **Apple Digital AV Adapter:** To connect devices to output high-definition media, you can buy this adapter for about $40 and use it with an HDMI cable. More and more devices that use this technology are coming out, such as projectors and TVs.

⟶ **Stands:** Apple offers the Twelve South HoverBar Stand for iPad that costs $99.99 and attaches your iPad to your computer.

 Several companies produce iPad accessories, such as cases, and more will undoubtedly pop up, so feel free to do an online search for different items and prices.

 Don't bother buying a wireless mouse to connect with your iPad via Bluetooth; the iPad recognizes your finger as its primary input device, and mice need not apply. However, you can use a stylus to tap your input.

Explore What's in the Box

After you fork over your hard-earned money for your iPad, you'll be holding one box. Besides your iPad and a small documentation package, here's a rundown of what you'll find when you take off the shrink wrap and open the box:

⟶ **iPad:** Your iPad is covered in a thick plastic sleeve-thingie that you can take off and toss (unless you think there's a chance that you'll return the device, in which case you may want to keep all packaging for 14 days — Apple's standard return period).

⟶ **Documentation** (and I use the term loosely): Notice, under the iPad itself, a small, white envelope about the size of a half-dozen index cards. Open it and you'll find

- A *single sheet titled iPad Info:* This pamphlet is essentially small print (that you mostly don't need to read) from agencies like the Federal Communications Commission (FCC).

- A *label sheet:* This sheet has two white Apple logos on it. (Apple has provided these for years with its products as a form of cheap advertising when

users place stickers on places like their computers or car rear windows.)

- *A small card:* This card displays a picture of the iPad and callouts to its buttons on one side, and the other side contains brief instructions for setting it up and information about where to find out more.

⟶ **A Lightning-to-USB cable (fourth-generation iPad and later and all iPad mini models) or Dock Connector-to-USB cable (all earlier iPad models):** Use this cord (see **Figure 1-3**) to connect the iPad to your computer, or use it with the last item in the box: the USB Power Adapter.

⟶ **10W USB Power Adapter:** The power adapter (refer to Figure 1-3) attaches to the Lightning-to-USB cable so that you can plug it into the wall and charge the battery.

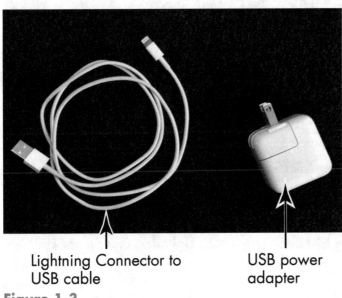

Lightning Connector to
USB cable

USB power
adapter

Figure 1-3

That's it. That's all you'll find in the box. It's kind of a study in Zen-like simplicity.

Take a First Look at the Gadget

The little card contained in the documentation that comes with your iPad gives you a picture of the iPad with callouts to the buttons you'll find on it. In this task, I give you a bit more information about those buttons and other physical features of the iPad. **Figure 1-4** shows you where each of these items is located on an iPad Air 2. The Pro model also has a Smart Connector slot in addition to items shown here.

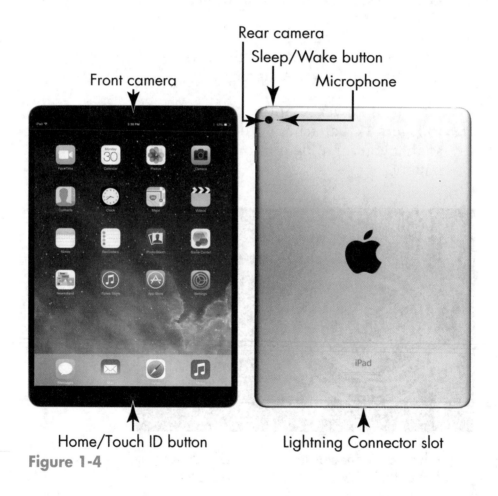

Figure 1-4

Here's the rundown on what the various hardware features are and what they do:

➡ **(The all-important) Home/Touch ID button:** On the iPad, press this button to go back to the Home screen to find just about anything. The Home screen displays all your installed and preinstalled apps and gives you access to your iPad settings. No matter where you are or what you're doing, press the Home button, and you're back at home base. You can also double-press the Home button to pull up a scrolling list of apps so you can quickly move from one app to another. (Apple refers to this as multitasking.) If you press and hold the Home button, you open Siri, the iPhone voice assistant. Finally, on the newest iPads, the Home button contains a fingerprint reader used with the Touch ID feature.

➡ **Sleep/Wake button:** You can use this button (whose functionality I cover in more detail in Chapter 2) to power up your iPad, put it in Sleep mode, wake it up, or power it down.

➡ **Lightning Connector slot:** Plug in the Lightning Connector at the USB end to the power adapter to charge your battery or use it without the power adapter to sync your iPad with your computer (which you find out more about in Chapter 3).

➡ **Cameras:** iPads (except for the original iPad) offer front- and rear-facing cameras, which you can use to shoot photos or video. The rear one is on the top-right corner (if you're looking at the front of the iPad), and you need to be careful not to put your thumb over it when taking shots. (I have several very nice photos of my fingers already.)

➡ **(Tiny, mighty) Speakers:** One nice surprise when I first got my iPad was hearing what a great little stereo sound system it has and how much sound can come from these tiny speakers. The speakers are located along one side of the iPad Air 2 and iPad mini 4. With iPad Pro, you get four speakers, two on either side, which provide the best sound of all the models.

➡ **Volume:** Tap the volume switch, called a *rocker*, up for more volume and down for less. You can use this rocker as a camera shutter button when the camera is activated.

➡ **Headphone jack and microphone:** If you want to listen to your music in private, you can plug in a 3.5mm mini-jack headphone (including an iPhone headset, if you have one, which gives you bidirectional sound). A tiny microphone makes it possible to speak into your iPad to deliver commands or enter content using the Siri personal-assistant feature. Using Siri, you can do things such as make phone calls using the Internet, use video-calling services, dictate your keyboard input, or work with other apps that accept audio input.

Looking Over the Home Screen

I won't kid you: You may have a slight learning curve ahead of you: Touchscreen tablets like the iPad are different from your desktop or laptop. That's mainly because of its Multi-Touch screen and onscreen keyboard — no mouse necessary. The iPad doesn't have a Windows or Mac operating system: It does have a modified iPhone operating system (iOS), so some of the methods you may have used on computers before (such as right-clicking) don't work in quite the same way on the touchscreen.

The good news is that getting anything done on the iPad is simple after you know the ropes. In fact, using your fingers instead of a mouse to do things onscreen is a very intuitive way to communicate with your computing device.

In this chapter, you turn on your iPad and register it and then take your first look at the Home screen. You also practice using the onscreen keyboard, see how to interact with the touchscreen in various ways, get pointers on working with cameras, and get an overview of built-in applications (called *apps*) and the Control Center.

Get ready to . . .

Have a soft cloth handy, like the one you might use to clean your eyeglasses. Despite a screen that's been treated to repel oils, you're about to deposit a ton of fingerprints on your iPad — one downside of a touchscreen device.

See What You Need to Use the iPad

You need to be able, at a minimum, to connect to the Internet to take advantage of most iPad features, which you can do by using a Wi-Fi network (a network you set up in your own home or access in a public place such as a library) or by paying a fee and using a phone provider's network if you bought a Wi-Fi + Cellular iPad model. You may want to have a computer so that you can connect your iPad to it to download photos, videos, music, or applications and then transfer them to or from your iPad through a process called *syncing*. An Apple service called iCloud syncs content from all your Apple iOS devices, such as iPhone, and your Mac and/or PC wirelessly, so anything you buy on your iPhone, for example, will automatically be delivered to your iPad. In addition, you can sync without connecting a cable to a computer by using a wireless Wi-Fi connection to your computer.

You can register your iPad the first time you start it by using iCloud or by syncing with your computer via a cable, although you can have the folks at the Apple Store handle registration for you if you have an Apple Store nearby.

Can you use the iPad if you don't own a computer and you use public Wi-Fi hotspots to go online (or a 3G/4G connection, if you have one of those models)? Yes. However, to be able to go online using a Wi-Fi–only iPad and to use many of its built-in features at home, you need to have a Wi-Fi network available.

Apple has set up both iCloud and its iTunes software to help you manage content for your iPad — which includes the movies, TV shows, music, or photos you've downloaded — and specify from where it should transfer your calendar and contact information. Chapter 3 covers these settings in more detail.

Turn On the iPad for the First Time

When you're ready to get going with your new toy, be sure you're within range of a Wi-Fi network that you can connect with, and then hold the iPad with one hand on either side, oriented like a pad of paper. Plug the Lightning-to-USB cable that came with your device into your iPad and plug the other end into a USB port on your computer just in case you lose your battery charge during the setup process.

Now follow these steps to set up and register your iPad:

1. Press and hold the Sleep/Wake button on the top of your iPad until the Apple logo appears.

In another moment, a screen appears with a cheery Hello on it.

2. Slide your finger to the right on the screen where it says Slide to Set Up.

3. Follow the series of prompts to make choices about your language and location, using iCloud (Apple's online sharing service), and so on.

4. After you deal with all the setup screens, a Welcome to iPad screen appears; tap Get Started to display the Home screen.

 If you set up iCloud when registering or after registering (see Chapter 3), updates to your operating system will be downloaded to your iPad without plugging it into a computer running iTunes. Apple refers to this feature as *PC Free*, simply meaning that your device has been liberated from having to use a physical connection to a computer to get upgrades.

Meet the Multi-Touch Screen

When the first iPad Home screen appears (see **Figure 2-1**), you see a pretty background and two sets of icons. One set appears in the Dock, along the bottom of the screen. The *Dock* contains the Messages, Mail,

Figure 2-1

Safari, and Music app icons by default, though you can add up to two other apps to it. The Dock appears on every Home screen (you can create up to 10 additional Home screens by populating them with additional apps to fill them.

Another set of icons appears above the Dock. (I cover all these icons in the "Take Inventory of Preinstalled Apps" task, later in this chapter.) Different icons appear in this area on each Home screen, but this Home screen contains most of the preinstalled apps. You can add new apps to populate as many as 11 Home screens and move apps from one Home screen to another (see Chapter 9 for more about this). You can also nest apps in folders, which theoretically gives you the possibility of storing limitless apps on your iPad, limited only by your tablet's memory.

 Treat the iPad screen carefully. It's made of glass and will smudge when you touch it (and will break if you throw it against the wall).

The iPad uses *touchscreen technology*. When you swipe your finger across the screen or tap it, you're providing input to the device just as you use a mouse or keyboard with your computer. You hear more about the touchscreen in the next task, but for now, go ahead and play with it for a few minutes; really, you can't hurt anything. Use the pads of your fingertips (not your fingernails), and follow these steps:

1. Tap the Settings icon. The various settings (which you read more about throughout this book) appear, as shown in **Figure** 2-2.

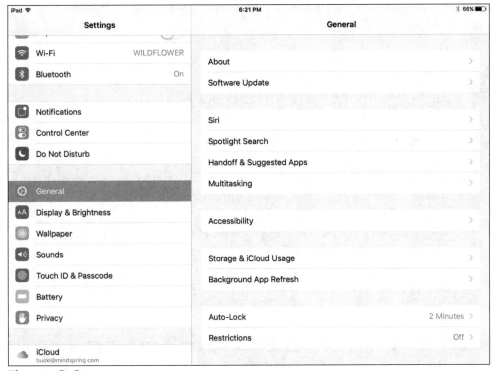

Figure 2-2

2. To return to the Home screen, press the Home button.

3. Swipe a finger or two from right to left on the screen. This action moves you to the next Home screen. Note that the little dots at the bottom of the screen, above the Dock icons, indicate which Home screen is displayed.

4. To experience the screen rotation feature, hold the iPad firmly with the Home button on the side and turn it sideways. The screen flips to vertical orientation. To flip the screen back, just turn the device so it's oriented horizontally again.

5. Drag your finger down from the top of the screen to reveal Notification Center, which contains items such as reminders, calendar entries, and so on (covered in Chapter 17); drag up from the bottom of the Home screen to hide Notification Center and to display Control Center, which contains the commonly used controls and tools discussed later in this chapter.

 You can customize the Home screen by changing its *wallpaper* (background picture) and brightness. You can read about making these changes in Chapter 4.

Hello Tap-and-Swipe

You can use several methods to get around and get things done on the iPad by using its Multi-Touch screen, including

➡ **Tap once.** To open an application on the Home screen, choose a field (such as a search field), select an item in a list, select an arrow to move back or forward one screen, or follow an online link, tap the item once with your finger.

➡ **Tap twice.** Use this method to enlarge or reduce the display of a web page (see Chapter 5 for more about using the Safari web browser) or to zoom in or out in the Maps app.

➡ **Pinch and expand.** As an alternative to the tap-twice method, you can pinch your fingers together or move them apart (expand) on the screen when you're looking at photos, maps, web pages (see **Figure 2-3**), or email messages to quickly reduce or enlarge them, respectively.

Figure 2-3

 You can use a three-finger tap to zoom your screen to be even larger or use multitasking gestures to swipe with four or five fingers (see the "Explore Multitasking Gestures" task later in this chapter). This method is handy if you have vision challenges. Go to Chapter 4 to discover how to turn on this feature by using Accessibility settings.

➠ **Drag to scroll (known as *swiping*).** When you press your finger to the screen and drag to the right or left, the screen moves (see **Figure 2-4**). Swiping to the left on the Home screen, for example, moves you to the next Home screen. Swiping up while reading an online newspaper moves you down the page; swiping down moves you back up the page.

Report: Court orders former Egyptian President Hosni Mubarak freed

By **Karl Penhaul and Laura Smith-Spark**, CNN
updated 1:35 PM EDT, Wed August 21 2013

Ousted Egyptian President Hosni Mubarak is wheeled out of an ambulance following a hearing in Cairo on April 13, 2013.

Figure 2-4

➡ **Flick.** To scroll more quickly on a page, quickly flick your finger on the screen in the direction in which you want to move.

Notice that when you rock your iPad backward or forward, the background moves as well, in what is called *the parallax feature.* You can disable this feature if it makes you seasick. Tap Settings ⇨ General ⇨ Accessibility and then if the Reduce Motion setting is set to on, tap it and turn off the setting.

➡ **Tap the status bar.** To move quickly to the top of a list, web page, or email message, tap the status bar at the top of the iPad screen.

➡ **Touch and hold.** If you're using Notes or Mail or any other application that lets you select text, or if you're on a web page, pressing and holding text selects a word and displays editing tools you can use to select, cut or copy, and paste the text.

Try these methods now by following these steps:

1. Tap the Safari button in the Dock at the bottom of any iPad Home screen to display the web browser. (You may be asked to enter your network password to access the network.)

2. Tap a link (typically, colored text or a button or image) to move to another page.

3. Double-tap the page to enlarge it; then pinch your fingers together onscreen to reduce it.

4. Drag one finger around the page to scroll up, down, or side to side.

5. Flick your finger quickly on the page to scroll more quickly.

6. Press and hold your finger — iOS's equivalent to a right-click — on black text that isn't a link (links usually are blue and take you to another location on the web). The word is selected, and the toolbar containing Copy/Define/Share tools is displayed with relevant options, as shown in **Figure 2-5**. (You can use this tool to get a definition of a word or copy it.)

7. Press and hold your finger on a link or an image. A contextual menu appears, with commands you select to open the link or picture, open it in a new tab, add it to your Reading List (see Chapter 5), or copy it. If you tap and hold an image, the menu also offers the Save Image command.

8. Position your fingers slightly apart on the screen and then pinch your fingers together on the screen to reduce the page. With your fingers pinched together on the screen move them apart to enlarge the page.

9. Press the Home button to go back to the Home screen.

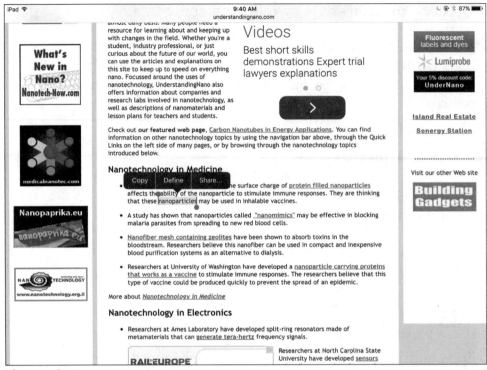

Figure 2-5

Using Apple Pencil

If you dug deep into your pockets and bought the new iPad Pro model, you can buy a Smart Keyboard and Apple Pencil, if you like. The Apple Pencil provides a method of interacting with the touchscreen that is more precise than using your finger. The iPad Pro screen detects the position of the Pencil tip, as well as the angle and force applied to it. These abilities mean that the Pencil is great for drawing in various apps. You can draw thinner or thicker lines depending on how you press the Pencil to the screen. An Apple Pencil will set you back $99, as of this writing.

Display and Use the Onscreen Keyboard

1. The built-in iPad keyboard appears whenever you're in a text-entry location, such as a search field or an email message. Tap the Notes icon on the Home screen to open this easy-to-use notepad and try out the keyboard.

2. Tap the note page, or if you've already entered notes, tap one to display the page; then tap anywhere on the note. The onscreen keyboard appears.

3. Type a few words, using the keyboard. To make the keyboard display as wide as possible, rotate your iPad to landscape (horizontal) orientation, as shown in **Figure 2-6.**

Figure 2-6

4. If you make a mistake while using the keyboard — and you will when you first use it — press the Delete key (it's in the top-right corner of the keyboard, with the little *x* on it) to delete text to the left of the insertion point.

5. To create a new paragraph, press the Return key just as you would on a computer keyboard.

6. To type numbers and symbols, press the number key (labeled *.?123*) on either side of the spacebar (refer to Figure 2-6). The characters on the keyboard change. If you type a number and then tap the spacebar, the keyboard returns to the letter keyboard automatically. To return to the letter keyboard at any time, simply tap one of the letter keys (labeled *ABC*) on either side of the spacebar.

7. Use the Shift keys (thick upward-pointing arrows in the bottom-left and bottom-right corners of the keyboard) just as you would on a regular keyboard to type uppercase letters. Tapping a Shift key once causes just the next letter you type to be capitalized.

8. Double-tap the Shift key to turn on the Caps Lock feature so that all letters you type are capitalized until you turn the feature off. Tap the Shift key once to turn off Caps Lock. (You have to turn this feature on by opening the Settings app and, in the General pane, tapping Keyboard.)

9. To type a variation on a symbol (such as to see alternative currency symbols when you press the dollar sign on the numeric keyboard), hold down the key; a set of alternative symbols appears (see **Figure 2-7**). Note that this trick works only with certain symbols.

Figure 2-7

10. Tap the Dictation key (refer to Figure 2-6; it has a micro-phone symbol on it) to activate the Dictation feature (not available on the original iPad or the iPad 2) and then speak your input. Tap the Dictation key again (or tap in a note) to turn off the Dictation feature. (This feature works in several apps, such as Mail, Notes, and Maps. You must also be connected to the Internet for it to work.)

11. Tap the Emoji button (a smiley face symbol to the left of the Dictation button) to display and select from a set of smiley symbols to insert in your document. Tap tabs along the bottom to display other graphic icon sets such as pictures from nature or city skylines.

12. To hide the keyboard, tap the Keyboard key in the bottom-right corner.

13. Press the Home button to return to the Home screen.

You can undock the keyboard to move it around the screen. To do this, tap and hold the Keyboard key on the keyboard, and from the pop-up menu that appears, choose Undock. Now, by dragging the Keyboard key up or down, you can move the keyboard up and down on the screen. To dock the keyboard at the bottom of the screen again, tap and hold the Keyboard key, and choose Dock from the pop-up menu.

 With the latest version of the Notes app, you can display a shortcut keyboard using the General/Keyboard settings that allows you to create a checklist, choose a font style, insert a photo, or create a drawing within your note. The onscreen keyboard also uses a feature called QuickType to provide suggestions above the keyboard as you type. See Chapter 20 for more about using the Notes app.

 To type a period and space, just double-tap the spacebar. If you want to add punctuation, such as a comma, and then return immediately to the letter keyboard, simply tap the *123* key and then drag up to the punctuation you want to use.

 You can buy a Smart Keyboard to go with an iPad Pro for $169. This physical keyboard from Apple attaches to your iPad and allows both power and data exchange. The connection for your keyboard is magnetic, so it's a snap to put it and the iPad together.

Use the Split Keyboard

1. The *split keyboard* feature allows you to split the keyboard so that each side appears nearer the edge of the iPad screen. For those who are into texting or typing with thumbs, this feature makes it easier to reach all the keys from the sides of the device, useful if you're holding your iPad with both hands. Open an application such as Notes where you can use the onscreen keyboard.

2. Tap in an entry field or page that displays the onscreen keyboard.

3. Place two fingers in the middle of the onscreen keyboard, and spread them left and right. The keyboard splits, as shown in **Figure 2-8.** (Note this feature can be finicky so you might have to try it a few times.)

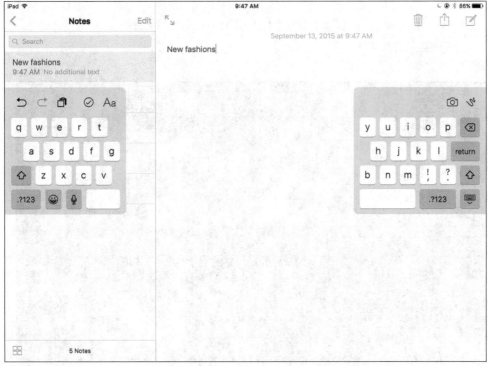

Figure 2-8

4. Now hold the iPad with a hand on either side and practice using your thumbs to enter text.

5. To rejoin the keyboard, place two fingers on each side of the keyboard and swipe to join them again.

 When the keyboard is docked and merged at the bottom of your screen, you can also simply drag the Keyboard key upward. This action undocks and splits the keyboard. To revert this action, drag the Keyboard key downward. The keyboard is docked and merged.

Flick to Search

1. The Spotlight Search feature of the iPad helps you find
suggestions from the Internet, Music, iTunes, and the
App Store, as well as suggestions for nearby locations,
photos, music, emails, contacts, movies, and more. Swipe
down on any Home screen (but not from the very top or
bottom of the screen) to reveal the Search feature.

2. Tap in the Search iPad field (see **Figure 2-9**). The
keyboard appears.

Figure 2-9

3. Begin entering a search term. In **Figure 2-10,** if I type the
letter C, the search result displays any contacts, built-in
apps, music, and videos you've downloaded, as well as
items created in Notes that begin with a C. As you continue to type a search term, the results narrow to match it.

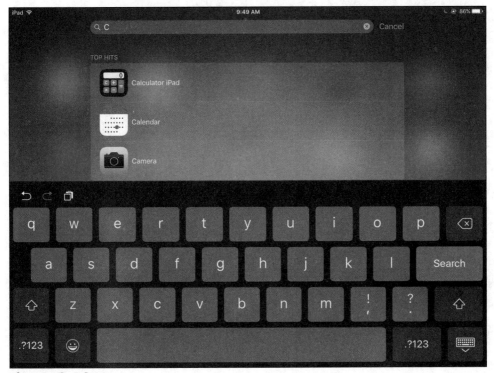

Figure 2-10

4. Scroll down to the bottom of the search results and tap
Search Web, Search App Store, or Search Maps to check
results from those sources.

5. Tap an item in the search results to open it in the corresponding app or player.

Update the Operating System to iOS 9

1. This book is based on the latest version of the iPad operating system at the time of writing: iOS 9. To be sure you
have the latest and greatest features, update your iPad to
the latest iOS now (and periodically, to receive minor
upgrades to iOS 9 or future versions of the iOS). If you've
set up an iCloud account on your iPad, updates happen
automatically; otherwise, you can update over a Wi-Fi or
3G/4G connection by tapping Settings ➪ General ➪ Software
Update (see **Figure 2-11**).

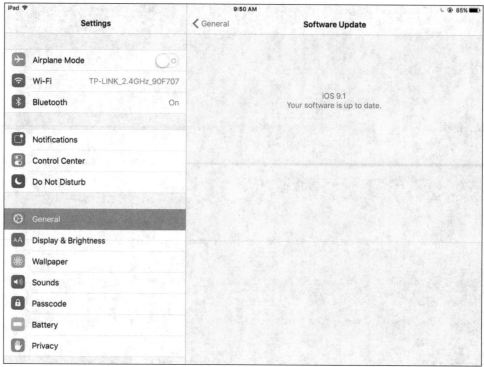

Figure 2-11

2. Read the note above the Check for Update button to see whether your iOS is up to date. If it isn't, click the Check for Update button. iPad searches for the latest iOS version and performs the update.

 A new iOS version may introduce new features for your iPad. If a new iOS appears after you buy this book, go to the website www.ipadmadeclear.com for updates on new features introduced in major updates.

Learn Multitasking Basics

1. *Multitasking* lets you easily switch from one app to another without closing the first one and returning to the Home screen. You can accomplish this task by previewing all open apps and jumping from one to another, and quit

an app by simply swiping upward. First, open two or
more apps.

2. Double-press the Home button.

3. On the app switcher screen that appears (see **Figure 2-12**),
flick to scroll to the left or right to locate another app that
you want to move to.

4. Tap an app to open it.

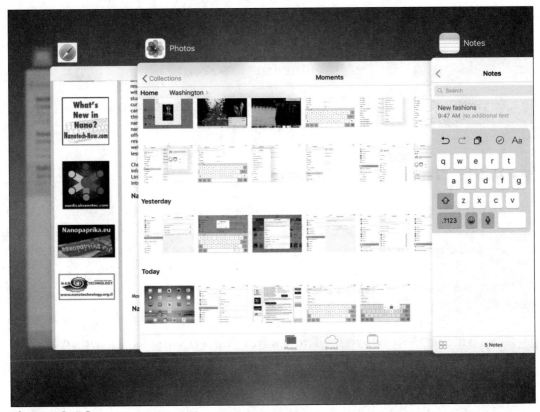

Figure 2-12

 Tap the Home button to remove the multitasking bar
from the Home screen and return to the app you
were working in.

Explore Multitasking Gestures

Multitasking involves jumping from one app to another. The Multitasking Gestures feature allows you to use four or five fingers to multitask. You can turn on these gestures by tapping Settings on the Home screen and then, in the General pane, tapping the On/Off switch for Multitasking Gestures.

Here are the three multitasking gestures you can use:

⟹ Swipe up with four or five fingers on any Home screen to reveal the app switcher.

⟹ Swipe down with four or five fingers to remove the app switcher from the Home screen.

⟹ With an app open, swipe left or right with four or five fingers to move to another app.

Examine the iPad Cameras

iPad has front- and back-facing cameras, with the latest versions of iPad Air 2 and iPad mini 4 introducing a higher-quality front-facing iSight camera for making FaceTime video calls. You can use the cameras to take still photos (covered in detail in Chapter 12) or shoot videos (covered in Chapter 13).

For now, take a quick look at your camera by tapping the Camera icon on the Home screen. The Camera app opens, as shown in **Figure 2-13**.

You can use the controls on the screen to

⟹ Take a picture or start recording a video.

⟹ Turn the Time-Lapse feature on or off.

⟹ Change from still-camera to video-camera operation by using the Camera/Video slider.

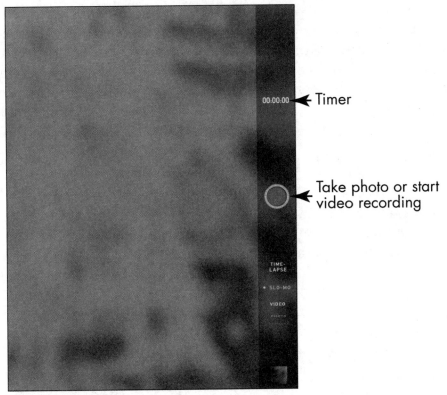

Timer

Take photo or start
video recording

Figure 2-13

⟶ Choose a 3- or 10-second delay with the new Timed
Photos button

⟶ Use the Pano setting to shoot panoramic photos.

⟶ Select the Square option to shoot a format popular
on Instagram photo sharing service.

⟶ Tap the Camera icon at the top of the right panel to
switch from the front and rear camera views.

⟶ Open previously captured images or videos.

When you view a photo or video, you can share it by posting it to Facebook or Flickr or send it by using AirDrop in a tweet, message, or email. You can also print the image, use it as wallpaper (your Home screen or lock screen background image), assign it to a contact, or run a slideshow. See Chapters 12 and 13 for more detail about using the iPad cameras.

Explore the Status Bar

Across the top of the iPad screen is the *status bar* (see **Figure 2-14**). Tiny icons in this area can provide useful information such as the time, battery level, and wireless-connection status. **Table 2-1** lists some of the most common items you find on the status bar.

Figure 2-14

Table 2-1 Common Status Bar Icons

Icon	*Name*	*What It Indicates*
	Activity	A task is in progress — a web page is loading, for example.
	Battery Life	The charge percentage remaining in the battery. The indicator changes to a lightning bolt when the battery is charging.
	Bluetooth	Bluetooth service is on and paired with a wireless device.
	Screen Orientation Lock	The screen is locked and doesn't rotate when you turn the iPad.
12:07 PM	Time	You guessed it: You see the time.
	Wi-Fi	You're connected to a Wi-Fi network.

If you have GPS, 3G, 4G, or Bluetooth service or a connection to a virtual private network (VPN), a corresponding symbol appears on the status bar whenever one of these features is active. The GPS and 3G/4G icons appear only on 3G- or 4G-enabled iPad models. (If you can't even conceive of what a VPN is, my advice is not to worry about it.)

Take Inventory of Preinstalled Apps

The iPad comes with certain functionality and applications — or *apps*, for short — preinstalled. When you look at the Home screen, you see icons for each app. This task gives you an overview of what each app does. (You can find out more about every one of them as you read different chapters of this book.) From left to right, the icons in the Dock (refer to the "Meet the Multi-Touch Screen" task earlier in this chapter) are

➠ **Messages:** For those who have been waiting for instant messaging on iPad, the iMessage feature comes to the rescue. Using the Messages app, you can engage in live text- and image-based conversations with others via their phones or other devices that use messaging. You can also send video or audio messages.

➠ **Mail:** You use this application to access mail accounts that you've set up for the iPad. When you do, your email is displayed without your having to browse to the site or sign in. Then you can use tools to move among a few preset mail folders, read and reply to mail, and download attached photos to your iPad. Read more about email accounts in Chapter 6.

➠ **Safari:** You use the Safari web browser (see **Figure 2-15**) to navigate on the Internet, create and save bookmarks of favorite sites, and add web clips to your Home screen so that you can quickly visit favorite sites from there. You may have used this web browser (or another such as Internet Explorer) on your desktop computer.

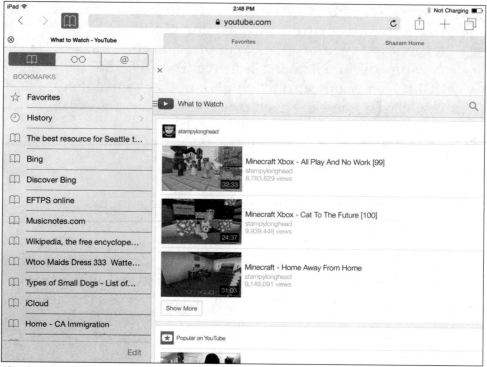

Figure 2-15

⟼ **Music:** Music is the name of your audio media player. Though its main function is to play music, you can use it to play podcasts or audiobooks as well.

Apps with icons above the Dock and closer to the top of the Home screen include

⟼ **FaceTime:** The FaceTime video-calling app lets you use the iPad cameras (not present on the original iPad) to talk face-to-face with someone who has an iPad 2 or later. Chapter 7 fills you in on FaceTime features.

⟼ **Calendar:** Use this handy onscreen daybook to set up appointments and send alerts to remind you about them.

⟶ **Photos:** The photo application in iPad helps you organize pictures in folders, email photos to others, use a photo as your iPad wallpaper, and assign pictures to contact records. You can also run slideshows of your photos, open albums, pinch or unpinch to shrink or expand photos, and scroll photos with a simple swipe. You can use the Photo Stream feature via iCloud to share photos among your friends. Photos displays images by collections, including Years and Moments, and offers filters you can apply to pictures you've taken to achieve different effects (see **Figure 2-16**).

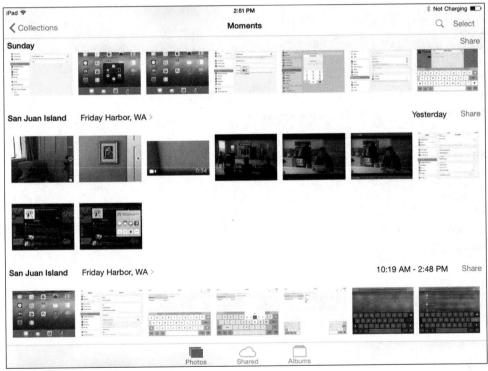

Figure 2-16

⟫ **Camera:** As you may have read earlier in this chapter, the Camera app is central control for the still and video cameras built into the iPad 2 and later. In addition, the FaceTime app uses your iPad camera to make and receive FaceTime (video) calls.

⟫ **Contacts:** In this address-book feature (see **Figure 2-17**), you can enter contact information (including photos, if you like, from your Photos or Cameras app) and share contact information by email. You can also use the search feature to find your contacts easily.

Figure 2-17

⟫ **Clock:** This app allows you to display clocks from around the world, set alarms, and use timer and stopwatch features.

➠ **Maps:** In this cool Apple mapping program, you can view classic maps or aerial views of addresses; find directions from one place to another by car or foot; and view your maps in 3-D. You can even get your directions read out loud by a spoken narration feature.

➠ **Videos:** This media player is similar to Music but specializes in playing videos and offers a few features specific to this type of media, such as chapter breakdowns and information about a movie's plot and cast.

➠ **Notes:** Enter text or cut and paste text from a website into this simple notepad app. You can't do much except save notes or email them; the app has no features for formatting text or inserting objects. You'll find Notes handy, though, for taking simple notes on the fly.

➠ **Reminders:** This useful app centralizes all your calendar entries and alerts to keep you on schedule, and also allows you to create to-do lists.

➠ **Photo Booth:** This fun photo effects app, which has been supplied with Mac computers for some time, lets you add effects to photos you take with your iPad camera in weird and wonderful ways.

 ➠ **News:** This app, new with iOS 9, is a news aggregator. You can select news sources and the News app displays top stories from those sources.

➠ **Game Center:** The Game Center app helps you browse games in the App Store and track scores when you play games with other people online. You can add friends and challenge one another to beat best scores. See Chapter 14 for more about Game Center.

➡ **iTunes Store:** Tapping this icon takes you to the iTunes Store, where you can shop 'til you drop (or until your iPad battery runs out of juice) for music, movies, TV shows, audiobooks, and podcasts and then download them directly to your iPad. (See Chapter 8 for more about how iTunes works.)

➡ **App Store:** At the online App Store, you can buy and download applications that enable you to do everything from playing games to building business presentations. Some of these apps are even free!

➡ **iBooks:** This is an outstanding *e-reader* app similar to the Amazon Kindle. To work with the iBooks e-reader application, go to Chapter 10.

➡ **Settings:** Settings isn't exactly an app, but it's an icon you should know about, anyway: It's the central location on the iPad where you can specify settings for various functions and perform administrative tasks such as setting up email accounts or creating a password.

➡ **Podcasts:** On the second Home screen in portrait orientation (or the first Home screen in landscape), in the Extras folder, you'll find the Podcasts app for playing audio broadcasts, and iTunes U offering access to tons of online courses.

Also, note that some free apps such as Pages and the Calculator appear on your second Home screen.

Discover Control Center

1. Control Center is a one-stop screen for common features and settings, such as connecting to a network, increasing screen brightness or volume, and turning Bluetooth on or off. To display Control Center, swipe up from the bottom edge of the screen.

2. At the bottom of the screen that appears, tap a button or slider to access or adjust a setting (see **Figure 2-18**).

3. Swipe the top of Control Center down to hide it.

Figure 2-18

Understand Touch ID

In previous versions of the iPad, you had to set a password to protect the contents of your iPad from others and input that password every time your tablet went to sleep. More recent iPads sport a feature called Touch ID that was previously only available on iPhones. Touch ID allows you to unlock your phone by tapping your finger on the redesigned Home button. That button now contains a sophisticated fingerprint sensor. Because your fingerprint is unique, this is one of the most foolproof ways to protect your data.

You have to educate the iPad about your fingerprint on your finger of choice by going into Settings, tapping Touch ID & Passcode, entering your passcode, and choosing what to use Touch ID for: iPad Unlock, Apple Pay (Apple's electronic wallet service), or App & iTunes Stores payments. Then, if you did not set up a fingerprint previously or want to add another one, tap Add a Fingerprint. Follow the instructions and press your finger on the Home button several times to allow Touch ID to sense and record your fingerprint. With the iPad Unlock option turned on, press the power button to go to the lock screen and tap the Home button. The iPad unlocks. If you chose the option for using Touch ID with Apple Pay or purchasing an item in the Apple stores, you'll simply touch your finger to the Home button rather than entering your Apple ID and password to complete a purchase.

Touch ID also works with secure apps and with the iTunes Store. Instead of entering your Apple ID and password every time you want to buy something, when prompted, just lightly press your finger on the Home button. Easy!

Lock the iPad, Turn It Off, and Unlock It

Earlier in this chapter, I mention how simple it is to turn on the power to your iPad. Now it's time to put it to *sleep* (a state in which the screen goes black, though you can quickly wake up the iPad) or to turn off the power to give your new toy a rest. Here are the procedures you can use:

➡ **Press the Sleep/Wake button.** The iPad goes to sleep: The screen goes black and is locked.

 If you bought a Smart Cover or Smart Case with your iPad or a third-party case with Smart Cover functionality, you can just fold the cover over the front of the screen, and the iPad goes to sleep; open the cover to wake up the iPad. (See Chapter 1 for more about iPad accessories.)

➡️ **Press the Home button.** The iPad wakes up (assuming you don't have a Touch ID or fingerprint access method set up). Swipe the onscreen arrow on the Slide to Unlock bar at the bottom of the screen to unlock the iPad.

➡️ **On any app or Home screen, press and hold the Sleep/Wake button until the Slide to Power Off bar appears at the top of the screen; then swipe the bar.** You've just turned off your iPad.

 The iPad automatically enters sleep mode after a few minutes of inactivity. You can change the time interval at which it sleeps by adjusting the Auto-Lock feature in Settings. See this book's companion Cheat Sheet at www.dummies.com/cheatsheet/ ipadforseniors to review tables of various settings.

Getting Going

*Y*our first step in getting to work with the iPad is making sure that its battery is charged. Next, if you want to find free or paid content for your iPad from Apple, from movies to music to e-books to audiobooks, you may want to open an iTunes account.

You can use the wireless sync feature to exchange content over a wireless network.

If you prefer, you can take advantage of the iCloud Library from Apple to store and share all kinds of content and data to all your Apple devices — wirelessly. Also, edits you make to documents in iCloud can be detected by iOS devices and Macs running OS X Yosemite or later whether or not they are compatible with the viewing app.

You can pick up where you left off reading, listening, or watching content from one device to another with a feature called Handoff.

Chapter

3

Get ready to . . .

Charge the Battery

1. My iPad showed up in the box almost fully charged, and let's hope yours did, too. Because all batteries run down eventually, one of your first priorities is to know how to recharge your iPad battery. Go get your iPad and its Lightning-to-USB cable (iPad fourth generation and later, and iPad mini) and the Apple USB power adapter.

2. Gently plug the USB end of the Lightning-to-USB cable (or the Dock Connector-to-USB cable, for old models) into the USB power adapter.

3. Plug the other end of the cord (see **Figure** 3-1) into the Lightning Connector (or Dock Connector) slot on the iPad.

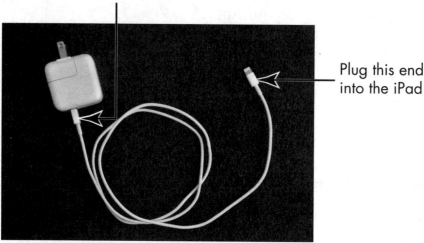

Attach the USB Connector to the power adapter

Plug this end into the iPad

Figure 3-1

4. Unfold the two metal prongs on the power adapter (refer to Figure 3-1) so that they extend from it at a 90-degree angle; then plug the adapter into an electrical outlet.

Power adapters for early versions of the iPad or other Apple devices (such as the iPhone and iPod) don't work with your fourth- generation or later iPad. Adapters are available from Apple and other companies, however.

Sign into an iTunes Account

1. To be able to buy or download free items from the iTunes Store or the App Store on your iPad, you must sign into an iTunes account. First, tap Settings on your iPad.

2. Click iTunes & App Store; assuming you're not signed in with an Apple ID, the screen shown in **Figure 3-2** appears.

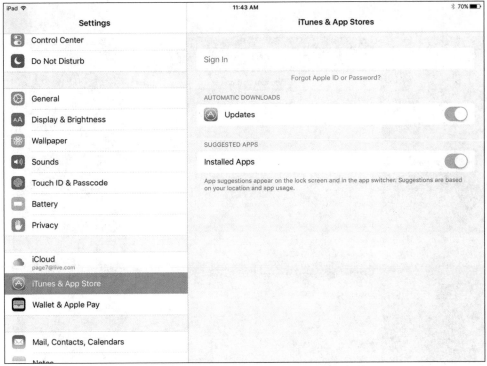

Figure 3-2

3. Tap Sign In, enter your Apple ID and password, and then tap Sign In again (see **Figure 3-3**).

Apple ID Sign In

page7@live.com

Password

Cancel   Sign In

Figure 3-3

4. A screen appears asking for verification. Click OK. In the Account Settings screen that follows (see **Figure** 3-4), fill in any required information fields to verify your payment method and then click the Done button. A screen appears, confirming that your account information has been saved.

Figure 3-4

Though it should be quite safe, if you prefer not to leave your credit card info with Apple, one option is to buy an iTunes gift card and provide that as your payment information. You can replenish the card periodically through the Apple Store.

Sync Wirelessly

1. You can use the iTunes Wi-Fi Sync setting to allow cordless syncing if you're within range of a Wi-Fi network that has a computer connected to it with iTunes installed (to install iTunes on your computer, go to www.apple.com/itunes/download). To use this setting you should have set up an Apple ID and chosen to sync with iTunes when you first set up your iPad. Then, with your iPad connected to your computer using the Lightening-to-USB Cable and iTunes open, on your computer, select your iPad in the Devices list. On the Summary tab of iTunes, click Sync with This iPad over Wi-Fi, and then click Apply. You only need to make this setting once. Disconnect your iPad from your computer.

2. Next, on your iPad tap Settings ➪ General ➪ iTunes Wi-Fi Sync.

3. In the pane shown in **Figure 3-5**, tap Sync Now to manually sync with a computer connected to the same Wi-Fi network.

 If you have your iPad set up to sync wirelessly to your Mac or PC, and both devices are within range of the same Wi-Fi network, the iPad appears in your iTunes Devices list. Selecting iPad on your Devices list allows you to sync and manage syncing from within iTunes.

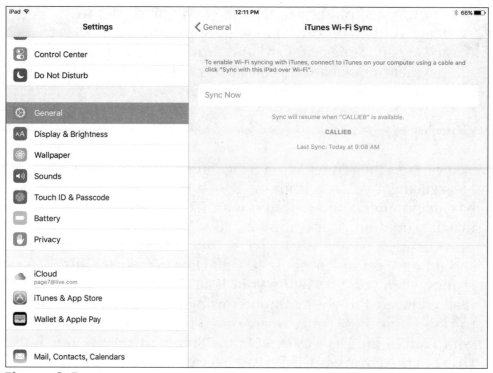

Figure 3-5

 You can click any item on the left side of the iTunes window to handle settings for syncing items such as movies, music, and apps. In the Apps category, you can also choose to remove certain apps from your Home screens. You can also tap the list of items On My Device on the left side to view and even play contents.

Understand iCloud

There's an alternative to backing up content with iTunes. iCloud is a service that allows you to back up all your content and certain settings (such as bookmarks) to online storage. (However, note that some content, such as videos, isn't backed up, so consider an occasional backup of content to your computer or an external storage device attached to your computer such as a USB stick, as well.) That content and those settings are pushed automatically to all your Apple devices through a wireless connection.

All you need to do is create an iCloud account (go to `www.icloud.com` and click Create Yours Now), which is free, and then make settings on your devices to specify which types of content you want pushed to each device. After you've done that, any content you create (except video) or purchase on one device — such as music, apps, books, and TV shows, as well as documents created in Apple's iWork apps, photos, and so on — can be synced among your devices automatically.

When you get an iCloud account, you get 5GB of free storage. Content that you purchase through Apple (such as apps, books, music, and TV shows) won't be counted against your storage. If you want additional storage, you can buy an upgrade from one of your devices. 50GB costs $0.99 cents per month, 200GB is $3.99 per month, 500GB is $9.99 a month, and one terabyte is $19.99 a month. Most people do just fine with the free 5GB of storage.

To upgrade your storage, tap Settings ⇨ iCloud ⇨ Storage ⇨ Manage Storage. In the pane that appears, tap Change Storage Plan. Tap the amount you need and then tap Buy. You can also choose Buy More Storage under Manage Storage if you are willing to pay more to get a greater storage amount.

 If you change your mind, you can get in touch with Apple within 15 days to cancel your upgrade.

 If you pay $24.99 a year for the iTunes Match service, you can sync almost any amount of music in your iTunes library to your devices, which may be a less expensive way to go than paying for added iCloud storage. Tap Match in iTunes or visit `www.apple.com/itunes/itunes-match` for more information.

Turn on iCloud Backup

Before you can use iCloud, you need an iCloud account, which is tied to the Apple ID you probably already have. You can turn on iCloud when you first set up your iPad, or you can use the Settings app on your iPad to sign up with your Apple ID and turn on the Backup feature.

1. When you first set up your iPad (except for an original iPad), in the sequence of screens that appears, tap Use iCloud.

2. In the next screen, tap Back Up to iCloud. In the next screen, shown in **Figure 3-6**, enter your Apple ID and password.

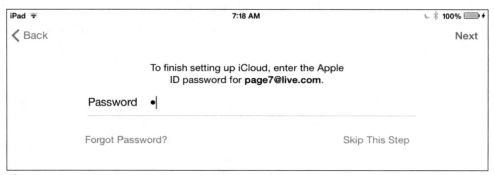

Figure 3-6

Your account is now set up based on the Apple ID you entered earlier in the setup sequence.

Here are the steps for setting up iCloud Backup on your iPad:

1. Tap Settings ➪ iCloud ➪ Backup (see Figure 3-7).

2. Tap the On/Off switch to turn on iCloud Backup.

Figure 3-7

Make iCloud Sync Settings

When you have an iCloud account up and running (see the preceding task), you have to specify which types of content should be synced with your iPad via iCloud. Note that the content you purchase and download from the iTunes Store will be synced among your devices automatically via iCloud in a process Apple calls *connectivity*.

1. Tap Settings ⇨ iCloud.

2. In the iCloud Settings pane, shown in **Figure 3-8**, tap the On/Off switch for any item that's turned off that you want to turn on (or vice versa). You can sync Photos, Mail, Contacts, Calendars, Reminders, Safari Bookmarks, Notes, News, Backup, Keychain (a service that syncs all your passwords in the Safari browser across all Macs, PCs, and Apple devices), and Find My iPad.

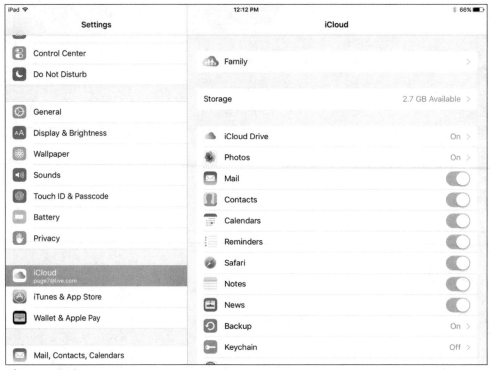

Figure 3-8

3. To enable automatic downloads of music, apps, and books, tap iTunes & App Store in Settings (see **Figure 3-9**).

4. Tap the On/Off switch for Music, Apps, Books, or Updates to set up automatic downloads of any of this content to your iPad via iCloud.

> If you want to allow iCloud to provide a service for locating a lost or stolen iPad, tap the On/Off switch in the Find My iPad field to activate it. This service helps you locate, send a message to, or delete content from your iPad if it falls into other hands.

> If you need help with any of these features, you can always find and download the Apple manual in the iBooks Store (it's a free book).

Figure 3-9

Making Your iPad More Accessible

*i*Pad users are all different; some face visual, motor, or hearing challenges. If you're one of these folks, you'll be glad to hear that the iPad offers some handy accessibility features.

To make your screen easier to read, you can adjust the brightness or change wallpaper. You can also set up the VoiceOver feature to read onscreen elements out loud. Then you can turn a slew of features on or off, including Zoom, Invert Colors, Speak Selection, Large Type, and more.

If hearing is your challenge, you can do the obvious thing and adjust the system volume. The iPad also has settings for mono audio (useful when you're wearing headphones) and using an LED flash when an alert sounds. Features that help you deal with physical and motor challenges include AssistiveTouch for those who have difficulty using the iPad touchscreen, Switch Control for working with adaptive accessories, and the Home Button and Call Audio Routing settings that allow you to adjust how quickly you have to tap the iPad screen to work with features.

Finally, the Guided Access feature provides help for those who have difficulty focusing on one task. It also provides a handy mode for showing presentations of content in settings where you don't want users to flit off to other apps, as in school or a public kiosk.

Set Brightness

1. Especially when you're using the iPad as an e-reader, you may find that a slightly less-bright screen reduces strain on your eyes. To adjust screen brightness, tap the Settings icon on the Home screen.

2. Tap Display & Brightness.

3. To control brightness manually, tap the Auto-Brightness On/Off switch (see **Figure 4-1**) to turn off this feature.

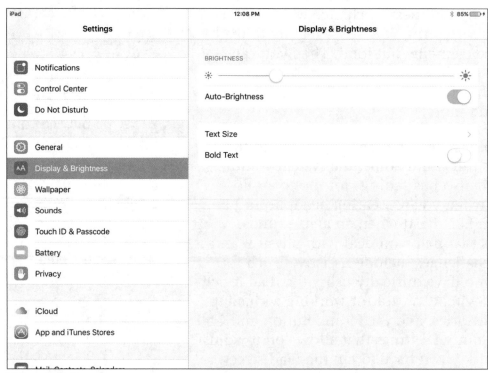

Figure 4-1

4. Tap and drag the Brightness slider (refer to Figure 4-1) to the right to make the screen brighter or to the left to make it dimmer.

5. Press the Home button to close Settings.

 If glare from the screen is a problem for you, consider getting a *screen protector*. This thin film not only protects your screen from damage, but also reduces glare.

 In the iBooks e-reader app, you can set a sepia tone for the page, which might be easier on your eyes. See Chapter 10 for more about using iBooks.

Change the Wallpaper

1. The default iPad's background image may be pretty, but it may not be the best for you. Choosing different wallpaper may help you see all the icons on your Home screen. Start by tapping the Settings icon on the Home screen.

2. In Settings, tap Wallpaper (refer to Figure 4-1).

3. In the Wallpaper settings that appear, tap Choose a New Wallpaper and then tap a wallpaper category. Tap either Dynamic or Stills, shown in **Figure 4-2**, to view your choices, and tap a sample to select it. Alternatively, on the initial wallpaper screen, tap an album in the Photos section, locate a picture to use as your wallpaper, and tap it.

4. In the preview that appears (see **Figure 4-3**), tap Set Lock Screen, Set Home Screen, or Set Both if you want to use the image for the Lock screen and Home screen. You can also tap Perspective Zoom to turn that feature on or off. When turned on, Perspective Zoom makes images move slightly as you move your iPad.

5. Press the Home button to return to your Home screen, where the new wallpaper is set as the background.

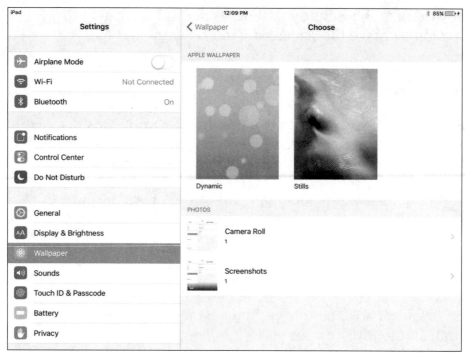

Figure 4-2

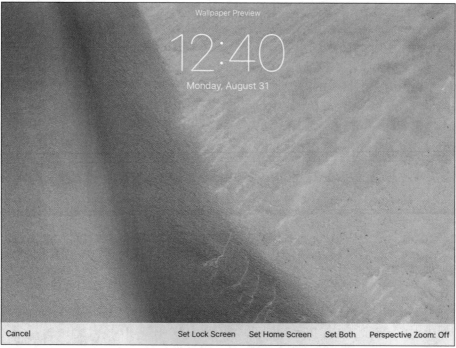

Figure 4-3

Set Up VoiceOver

1. VoiceOver reads the names of screen elements and settings to you, but it also changes the way you provide input to the iPad. In Notes, for example, you can have VoiceOver read the name of the Notes buttons to you, and when you enter notes, it reads words or characters you've entered. It can also tell you whether features such as Auto-Correction are on. To turn on this feature, tap the Settings icon on the Home screen. Tap General and then tap Accessibility.

2. In the Accessibility pane, shown in **Figure** 4-4, tap the VoiceOver On/Off switch to display the VoiceOver pane.

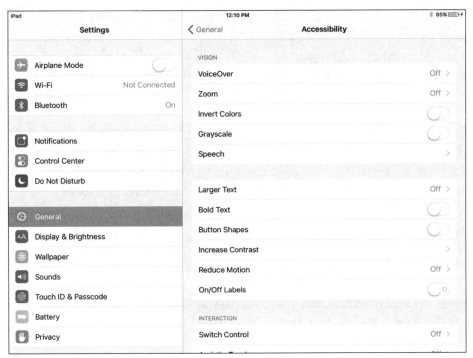

Figure 4-4

3. In the VoiceOver pane, shown in **Figure 4-5**, tap the VoiceOver On/Off switch to turn on this feature. The first time you use it, you will see a message that lets you know that enabling VoiceOver changes the gestures that you use with iPad. Double-tap OK to proceed.

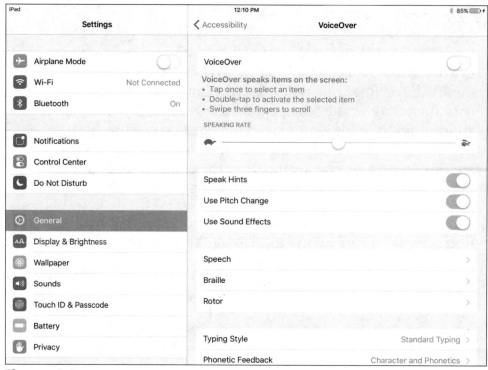

Figure 4-5

When VoiceOver is on, you first tap to select an item such as a button, which causes VoiceOver to read the name of the item to you; then you double-tap the item to activate its function.

4. Tap the VoiceOver Practice button to select it and then double-tap the button to open VoiceOver Practice. (Double-tapping replaces the tapping action when VoiceOver is turned on.) Practice using gestures such as pinching or flicking left, and VoiceOver tells you what action each gesture initiates.

5. Tap the Done button and then double-tap the same button to return to the VoiceOver settings.

6. Tap the Speak Hints field On/Off switch, and then double-tap the same button. VoiceOver speaks the name of each tapped item.

7. If you want VoiceOver to read words or characters to you (in the Notes app, for example), scroll down and tap and then double-tap Typing Feedback.

8. In the Typing Feedback settings, tap and then double-tap to select the option you prefer. The Words option causes VoiceOver to read words to you but not characters, such as the dollar sign ($). The Characters and Words option causes VoiceOver to read both, and so on.

9. Press the Home button to return to the Home screen. Read the next task to find out how to navigate your iPad after you've turned on VoiceOver.

 You can change the language that VoiceOver speaks. In the General category of Settings, choose International and then Language, and select another language. This action, however, also changes the language used for labels on Home-screen icons and various settings and fields on the iPad.

 You can use the Accessibility Shortcut setting to toggle the VoiceOver, Zoom, Switch Control, AssistiveTouch, Grayscale, and Invert Colors features rapidly. In the Accessibility category of Settings, tap Accessibility Shortcut. In the setting that appears in the right pane, choose what you want a triple-press of the Home button to activate. Now a triple-press of the Home button opens the option you selected in this dialog (such as Zoom or Invert Colors, for example) wherever you go in iPad.

Use VoiceOver

After VoiceOver is turned on, you need to figure out how to use it. I won't kid you — using it is awkward at first, but you'll get the hang of it! Here are the main onscreen gestures you should know how to use:

⇢ **Tap an item to select it.** VoiceOver speaks the item's name.

⇒ **Double-tap the selected item.** This action activates the item.

⇒ **Flick three fingers.** It takes three fingers to scroll around a page when VoiceOver is turned on.

Table 4-1 provides additional gestures that help you use VoiceOver. I suggest that if you want to use this feature often, you read the VoiceOver section of the *iPad User Guide* (see Chapter 3), which goes into a great deal of detail about the ins and outs of using VoiceOver. You'll find the *iPad User Guide* by downloading it through the iBooks Store or going to `https://help.apple.com/ipad/9/`.

Table 4-1	VoiceOver Gestures
Gesture	*Effect*
Flick right or left.	Select the next or preceding item.
Tap with two fingers.	Stop speaking the current item.
Flick two fingers up.	Read everything from the top of the screen.
Flick two fingers down.	Read everything from the current position.
Flick three fingers up or down.	Scroll one page at a time.
Flick three fingers right or left.	Go to the next or preceding page.
Tap three fingers.	Speak the scroll status (for example, line 20 of 100).
Flick four fingers up or down.	Go to the first or last element on a page.

 If tapping with two or three fingers is difficult for you, try tapping with one finger of one hand and one or two fingers of the other hand. When you're double- or triple-tapping, you have to perform these gestures as quickly as you can to make them work.

 Check out some of the settings for VoiceOver, including Braille, Language Rotor (for making language choices), a setting for navigating images, and a setting that directs the iPad to read notifications to you.

Make Additional Vision Settings

Several vision features are simple on/off settings, so rather than give you the steps to get to those settings repeatedly, I provide this useful bullet list of additional features you can turn on or off after you tap Settings ➪ General ➪ Accessibility:

➡ **Zoom:** The Zoom feature enlarges the contents displayed on the iPad's screen when you double-tap the screen with three fingers. The Zoom feature works almost everywhere on the iPad: in Photos, on web pages, on your Home screens, in Mail, in Music, and in Videos. Give it a try!

➡ **Invert Colors:** The Invert Colors setting reverses colors on your screen so that white backgrounds are black and black text is white.

 The Invert Colors feature works well in some places and not so well in others. In the Photos app, for example, pictures appear almost like photo negatives. Your Home screen image will likewise look a bit strange. And don't even think of playing a video with this feature turned on! However, if you need help reading text, White on Black can be useful in several apps.

➡ **Larger Text:** If having larger text in apps such as Contacts, Mail, and Notes would be helpful to you, you can turn on the Larger Type feature and choose the text size that works best for you.

➡ **Bold Text:** Turning on this setting first restarts your iPad (after asking you for permission to do so) and then causes text in various apps and in Settings to be bold. This setting is a handy one, as text in the iOS 7 and 8 redesign was simplified (meaning it got thinner!).

⟱➡ **Increase Contrast:** Use these three settings to add greater contrast to backgrounds in some areas of the iPad and apps, which should improve visibility.

⟱➡ **Reduce Motion:** If you turned on this setting but would rather have it off, tap this accessibility feature and then tap the On/Off switch to turn off the parallax effect, which causes the background of your Home screens to appear to float as you move the iPad around.

⟱➡ **On/Off Labels:** If you have trouble making out colors, and so have trouble telling when an On/Off switch is On (green) or Off (white), use the On/Off Labels setting to add a circle to the right of a setting when it's off and a white vertical line to a setting when it's on (see **Figure 4-6**).

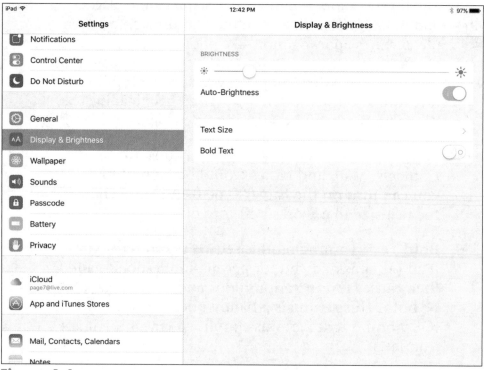

Figure 4-6

Adjust the Volume

1. Though individual apps such as Music and Video have their own volume settings, you can set your iPad system volume for your ringer and alerts as well to help you better hear what's going on. To start, tap Settings ⇨ Sounds.

2. In the Sounds pane that appears (see **Figure** 4-7), tap and drag the Ringer and Alerts slider to the right to increase the volume of these audible attention-grabbers or to the left to lower the volume.

3. Press the Home button to display the Home screen.

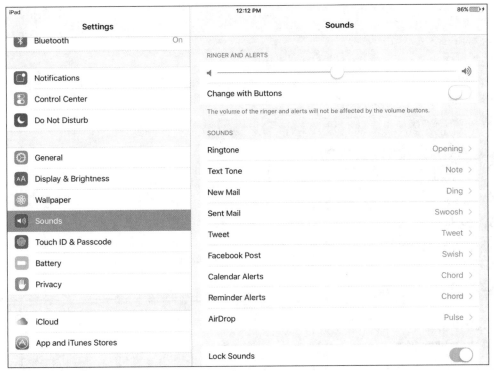

Figure 4-7

 In the Sounds pane, you can turn on or off the sounds that the iPad makes when certain events occur (such as new mail or Calendar alerts). These sounds are turned on by default.

Set Up Subtitles and Captioning

1. Closed captioning and subtitles help folks with hearing challenges enjoy entertainment and educational content. Tap Settings on the Home screen, tap General, and then tap Accessibility. On the Accessibility Settings screen (refer to Figure 4-4), scroll down to the Media section and tap Subtitles & Captioning.

2. On the Subtitles & Captioning screen, shown in **Figure** 4-8, tap the On/Off switch to turn on Closed Captions + SDH (Subtitles for the Deaf and Hard of Hearing). If you'd like, you can also tap Style and choose a text style for the captions.

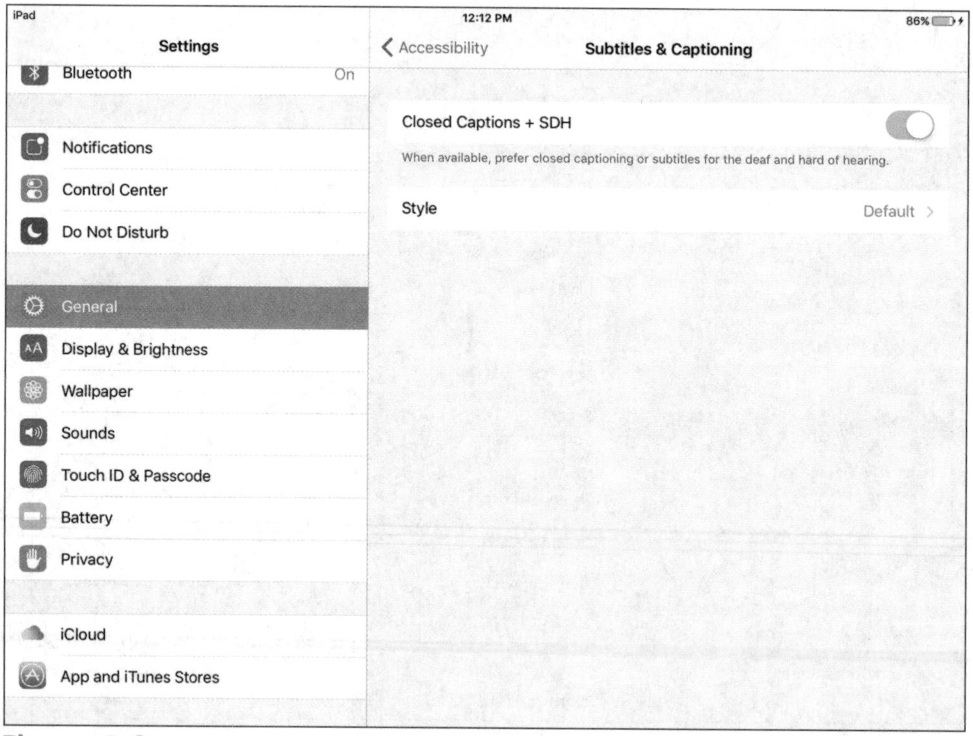

iPad		12:12 PM	86% ▭ ⚡

Settings   ‹ Accessibility   **Subtitles & Captioning**

* Bluetooth — On
* Notifications
* Control Center
* Do Not Disturb
* ⚙ General
* AA Display & Brightness
* Wallpaper
* Sounds
* Touch ID & Passcode
* Battery
* Privacy
* iCloud
* App and iTunes Stores

Closed Captions + SDH

When available, prefer closed captioning or subtitles for the deaf and hard of hearing.

Style   Default ›

Figure 4-8

3. Tap the Style setting and choose the Default style, Large Text, Classic, which looks like a typewriter font, or Create a New Style to personalize the font, size, and color for your captions.

Manage Mono Audio

Using the stereo effect in headphones or a headset breaks up sounds so that you hear a portion in one ear and a portion in the other ear, simulating the way that your ears process sounds. If there's only one channel of sound, that sound is sent to both ears.

If you're hard of hearing or deaf in one ear, however, you're picking up only a portion of the sound in your hearing ear, which can be frustrating. If you have such hearing challenges and want to use the iPad with a headset connected, you should turn on Mono Audio. When that accessibility setting is turned on, all sound is combined and distributed to both ears. You can get to Mono Audio settings in the Accessibility settings under Hearing.

Turn On and Work with AssistiveTouch

1. The AssistiveTouch Control Panel helps those who have challenges working with a touchscreen or who have to use some kind of assistive device for providing input. To turn on AssistiveTouch, tap Settings on the Home screen; then tap General ⇨ Accessibility.

2. In the Accessibility pane, scroll down to tap AssistiveTouch.

3. In the pane that appears, tap the On/Off switch for AssistiveTouch to turn it on (see **Figure 4-9**). A gray square, called the AssistiveTouch button, appears on the screen. This square button now appears in the same location in whatever Home screen or app you display on your iPad, although you can move it around the screen using your finger.

4. Tap the Home button to display the Home screen and then tap the AssistiveTouch button to display its options, shown in **Figure 4-10**. You can tap Device or Custom on the panel to see additional choices, tap Siri to activate the

personal-assistant feature, tap Notification Center or Control Center to display those panels, or tap Home to go directly to the Home screen.

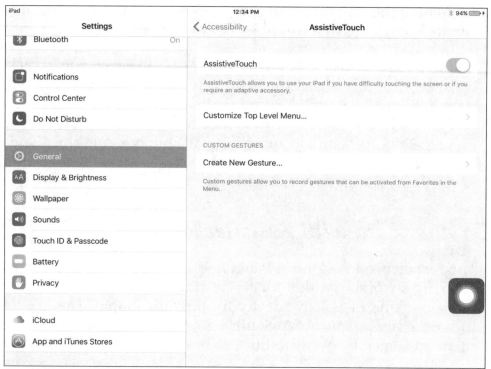

Figure 4-9

Figure 4-10

Table 4-2 shows the major options available in AssistiveTouch and their purposes.

Table 4-2	AssistiveTouch Controls
Control	**Purpose**
Siri	Activates the Siri feature, which allows you to speak questions and make requests of your iPad.
Custom	Displays a set of gestures with only the Pinch gesture preset; you can tap any of the other blank squares to add your own favorite gestures.
Device	Allows you to rotate the screen, lock the screen, turn the volume up or down, mute or unmute sound, or shake the iPad to undo an action by using the presets in this option.
Home	Sends you to the Home screen.
Notification Center	Displays the Notification Center.
Control Center	Displays the Control Center.

 In addition to using Siri, don't forget about using the Dictation key on the onscreen keyboard to speak text entries and basic keyboard commands.

Manage Home Click Speed

Sometimes, if you have dexterity challenges, it's hard to double-press or triple-press the Home button fast enough to make an effect. Choose the Slow or Slowest setting when you tap this setting to allow you a bit more time to make that second or third tap. Follow these steps:

1. Tap Settings ⇨ General ⇨ Accessibility.

2. Scroll down and tap Home Button.

3. Tap the Slow or Slowest setting to change how rapidly you have to double-press or triple-press the Home button to initiate an action.

If you have certain adaptive accessories, you can use head gestures to control your iPad, highlighting features in sequence and then selecting one. Use the Switch Control feature in the Accessibility Settings screen to turn this mode on and configure settings.

Focus Learning with Guided Access

1. Guided Access is a feature you can use to limit a user's access to the iPad to a single app and even limit access to that app to certain features. This feature is useful in several settings, ranging from a classroom to use by someone with attention deficit disorder and even to a public setting (such as a kiosk) where you don't want users to be able to open other apps. To activate it, start by tapping Settings ➪ General ➪ Accessibility ➪ Guided Access.

2. On the screen that appears (see **Figure 4-11**), tap the Guided Access On/Off button to turn the feature on.

3. Tap Passcode Settings and then tap Set Guided Access Passcode to activate a passcode so that those using an app can't return to the Home screen to access other apps. In the Set Passcode dialog that appears (see **Figure 4-12**), enter a passcode, using the numeric pad. Enter the number again when you're prompted.

4. Press the Home button to return to the Home screen.

5. Tap an app to open it.

6. Triple-press the Home button. Several buttons appear at the bottom of the screen including a Hardware Buttons Options button.

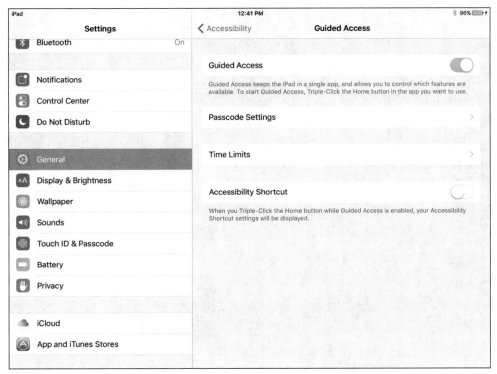

Figure 4-11

7. Tap the Hardware Buttons Options button to display these settings:

- **Sleep/Wake Button:** You can put your iPad to sleep or wake it up with a triple-press of the Home button.

- **Volume Buttons:** Tap Always On or Always Off. If you don't want users to be able to adjust volume by using the volume toggle on the side of the iPad, for example, use the Volume Buttons setting.

- **Motion:** Turn this setting off if you don't want users to disable the motion sensors — for example, so that users can't play a race car driving game.

- **Keyboards:** Use this setting to prohibit people using this app from entering text using the keyboard.

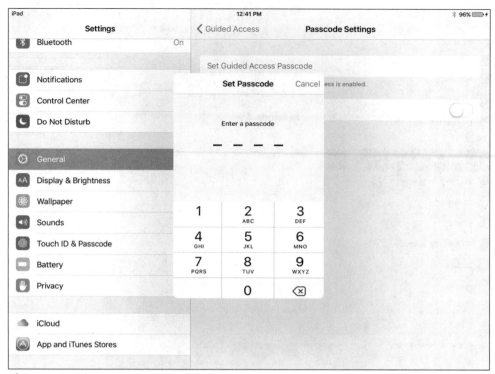

Figure 4-12

8. Another setting that's displayed to the right of Options is **Touch**. If you don't want users to be able to use the touchscreen, turn this off. You can also set a **Time Limit** for users to be able to work with this app.

9. To begin Guided Access tap Start in the upper-right corner; triple-press the Home button and then enter your passcode (if you set one in Step 3) to return to the Home screen.

Part II
Taking the Leap Online

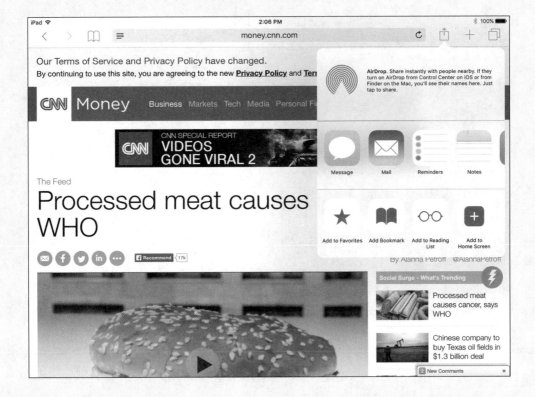

Visit www.dummies.com/extras/ipadforseniors for information about several recommended free (or almost free) apps.

Browsing the Internet with Safari

Getting on the Internet with your iPad is easy thanks to its Wi-Fi or, depending on your model, 3G or 4G capabilities. After you're online, the preinstalled browser (software that helps you navigate the Internet's contents), *Safari*, is your ticket to a wide world of information, entertainment, education, and more. Safari will look familiar to you if you've used it on a PC or Mac device before, though the way you move around it on the iPad touchscreen may be new to you. If you've never used Safari, in this chapter, I take you by the hand and show you all its ins and outs.

In this chapter, you discover how to connect your iPad to the Internet, navigate among web pages, and use iCloud tabs to share your browsing among devices. Along the way, you see how to place a bookmark for a favorite site or place a web clip on your Home screen. Tab view lets you view all your open web pages as thumbnails. You can also view your browsing history, save online images to your photo library, post photos to certain sites from within Safari, or email or tweet a hotlink to a friend. A Sidebar design lists your Bookmarks, Reading List, and Shared Links. You explore the Safari Reader and Safari Reading List features, and see how to keep yourself safer while you're online by using Private Browsing. Finally, you review the simple steps involved in printing what you find online.

Connect to the Internet

How you connect to the Internet depends on which iPad model you own:

➡ The Wi-Fi–only iPad connects to the Internet only via a Wi-Fi network, logically enough. You can set up this type of network in your own home by using your computer and some equipment from your Internet service provider. You can also connect over public Wi-Fi networks, referred to as *hotspots*. You'll probably be surprised to discover how many hotspots your town or city has: Look for Internet cafes, coffee shops, hotels, libraries, and transportation centers such as airports or bus stations, for example. Many of these businesses display signs alerting you to their free Wi-Fi.

➡ If you own a 3G– or 4G–enabled iPad, you can still use a Wi-Fi connection (in fact, when one is available, the iPad defaults to using Wi-Fi to save money), but you can also use the paid data network provided by AT&T, Verizon, T-Mobile, or Sprint to connect from just about anywhere you can get cellphone coverage via a cellular network.

If you have a 3G or 4G model, you don't have to do anything; with a contract for coverage, the connection is made automatically wherever cellular service is available, just as it is on your cellphone. To connect to a Wi-Fi network, you have to complete a few steps once for each network.

1. Tap the Settings icon on the Home screen and then tap Wi-Fi.

2. Make sure that Wi-Fi is set to On (see **Figure** 5-1), and choose a network to connect to. Network names should appear automatically when you're in range of networks. When you're in range of a public hotspot, if access to several nearby networks is available, you may see a message asking you to tap a network name to select it.

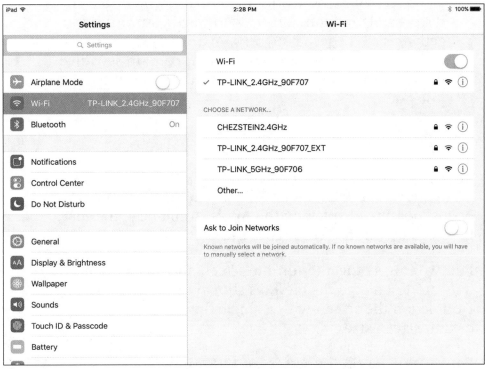

Figure 5-1

3. After you select a network (or if only one network is available), you may see a message asking for your password. Ask the owner of the hotspot (such as a hotel desk clerk or business owner) for this password, or, if you're connecting to your home network, enter your home network password.

4. Tap the Join button, and you're connected. Your iPad will automatically reconnect to this Wi-Fi network in the future when you come in range of it.

 See Chapter 1 for more about the capabilities of different iPad models and the costs associated with 3G and 4G.

 Free public Wi-Fi networks typically don't require a password, or the password is posted prominently for all to see. These networks are *unsecured*, however, so it's possible for someone else to track your online activities over these networks. Avoid accessing financial accounts or sending emails that contain sensitive information when you're connected to a public hotspot.

Explore Safari

1. After you're connected to a network, tap the Safari icon on the dock at the bottom of the Home screen. Safari opens, possibly displaying the Apple home page the first time you go online (see **Figure 5-2**).

2. Put two fingers together on the screen and swipe them outward to enlarge the view, as shown in **Figure 5-3**. Double-tap the screen with a single finger to restore the default screen size.

3. Put your finger on the screen and flick upward to scroll the page contents and view additional contents lower on the page.

4. To return to the top of the web page, put your finger on the screen and drag downward, or tap the status bar at the top of the screen.

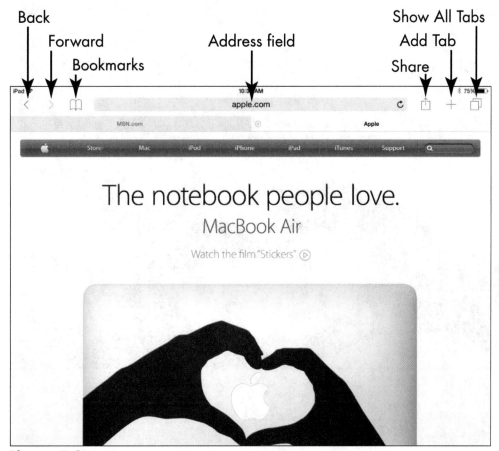

Figure 5-2

 Using the expand or pinch method to enlarge or shrink, respectively, a web page on your screen allows you to view what's displayed at various sizes, giving you more flexibility than the double-tap method.

 When you enlarge the display, you gain more control using two fingers to drag the screen from left to right or from top to bottom. On a reduced display, one finger works fine for making these gestures.

iPad 🔊   10:39 AM   ⚡ 74% 🔋

apple.com

The notebook people love.

Figure 5-3

Navigate among Web Pages

1. With Safari open, tap the Address field below the status bar. The onscreen keyboard appears (see **Figure** 5-4).

2. To clear the Address field, if necessary, tap the X button at its far right or tap the Delete key on the keyboard.

3. Enter a web address. You can enter this website: www.ipadmadeclear.com.

4. Tap the Go key on the keyboard (refer to Figure 5-4). The website that you entered appears.

• If for some reason the page doesn't appear, tap the Reload icon at the right end of the Address field.

Figure 5-4

• If Safari is loading a web page, and you change your mind about viewing the page, you can tap the Stop button (the X icon), which appears at the right end of the Address field during this process, to stop loading the page.

5. Tap the Back button (<) to go to the last page you displayed.

6. Tap the Forward button (>) to go forward to the page you came from when you tapped Back.

7. To follow a link to another web page (links typically are colored text or graphics), tap the link with your finger. To view the destination web address of the link before you tap it, just touch and hold the link. A contextual menu appears, displaying the address at the top, as shown in **Figure 5-5**.

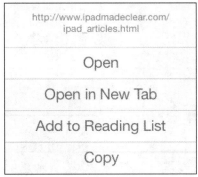

Figure 5-5

 By default, AutoFill is turned on, causing entries that you make in fields such as Address to display possibly matching entries automatically. You can turn off AutoFill by tapping Settings ⇨ Safari ⇨ AutoFill and then turn the Use Contact Info switch to Off.

 QuickType is a feature that supports predictive text in the onscreen keyboard. This means that iPad identifies what you probably intend to type from text you've already entered and makes a suggestion to save you time typing. Tap a suggestion and iPad enters it for you.

Use Tabbed Browsing

1. Safari includes a feature called *tabbed browsing,* which allows you to have several websites open at the same time on separate tabs so that you can move among those sites easily. To add a tab, tap the Add Tab button (shaped like a + symbol) near the top-right corner of the screen (refer to Figure 5-2). A new tab appears with your favorites and frequently visited sites.

2. To add a new page (meaning that you're opening a new website), tap one of the favorites or frequently used sites displayed onscreen (see **Figure 5-6**), or tap the Address field that appears. (Note you can get to a new page

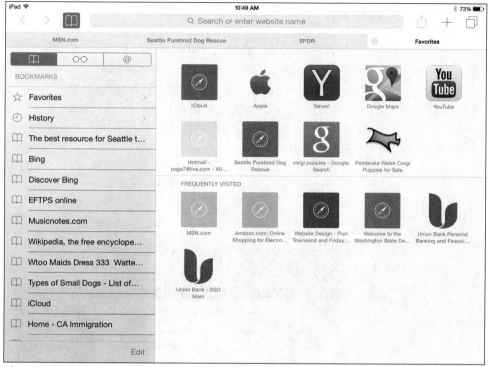

Figure 5-6

simply by tapping the Address field on any site but you will leave that site when you do.) Enter a website address and then tap the Go key.

3. Switch among open sites by tapping another tab, or tap the Show All Tabs button to see all open web pages. Tap a page to go to it, or tap Done to close All Tabs view.

4. To close a tab, scroll to locate the tab and then tap the Close button on the left side of the tab.

 When you're using tabbed browsing, you can place not only a site on a tab, but also a search results screen. If you recently searched for something, those search results are in your Recent Searches list. Also, if you're displaying a search results page when you tap the plus (+) sign to add a tab, the first ten suggested sites in the results are listed for you to choose among.

View Browsing History

1. As you move around the web, your browser keeps a record of your browsing history. This record can be handy when you want to visit a site that you viewed previously but whose address you've forgotten. With Safari open, tap the Bookmarks icon. The Bookmarks Sidebar slides in, as shown in **Figure** 5-7.

Figure 5-7

2. On the Bookmarks list, tap the History option.

3. In the History list that appears, tap a date, if one is available, and then tap a site to navigate to it (see **Figure** 5-8).

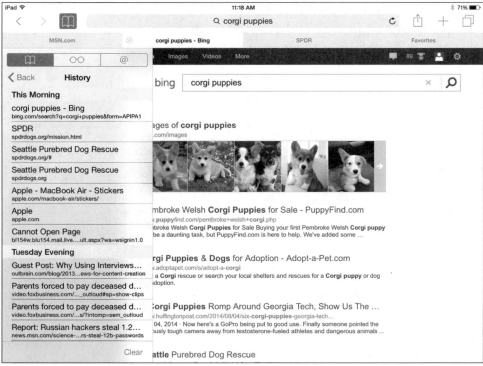

Figure 5-8

 To clear the history, tap the Clear button in the bottom-right corner of the Sidebar (refer to Figure 5-8). This button is useful when you don't want your spouse or grandchildren to see where you've been browsing for birthday or holiday presents!

 You can tap and hold the Back button to quickly display your browsing history for the currently displayed tab during the current browsing session.

Search the Web

1. If you don't know the address of the site that you want to visit (or if you want to research a topic and find other information online), get acquainted with Safari's Search feature on the iPad. By default, Safari uses the Google search engine. With Safari open, tap the Address field. The onscreen keyboard appears.

2. Tap one of the suggested sites that appear, or enter a search word or phrase (which, with Safari's unified smart search field, can be a topic or a web address).

3. Tap the Go key on your keyboard (see **Figure 5-9**).

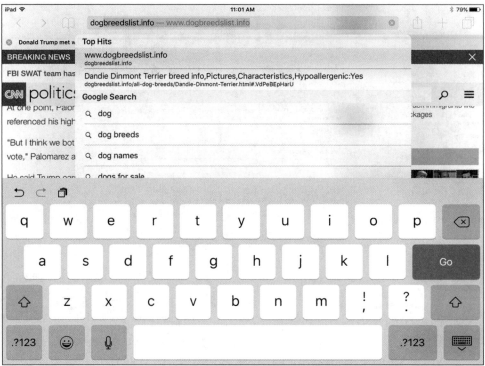

Figure 5-9

4. In the search results, tap a link to visit that site.

  To change your default search engine from Google to Yahoo!, DuckDuckGo, or Bing, in Settings, tap Safari and then tap Search Engine. Tap Yahoo!, DuckDuckGo, or Bing, and your default search engine changes.

  You can browse for specific items such as web images or videos by tapping the corresponding link at the top of the Google results screen. Also, tap the More button in this list to see additional options to narrow your results, such as searching for books or shopping sources related to the subject.

Add and Use Bookmarks

 1. Bookmarks enable you to save favorite sites so you can easily visit them again. With a site that you want to bookmark displayed, tap the Share button in the top right of the screen.

2. On the menu that appears (see **Figure 5-10**), tap Add Bookmark. The Add Bookmark dialog appears.

Figure 5-10

3. In the Add Bookmark dialog, shown in **Figure 5-11,** edit the name of the bookmark, if you want to. To do so, tap the name of the site and then use the onscreen keyboard to edit its name.

To set your default location for saved bookmarks, tap Location and then tap Bookmarks. Tapping Favorites adds saved bookmarks to the Favorites list.

Figure 5-11

4. Specify which folder you want to save the bookmark to by tapping an item under Location. By default, new bookmarks are added to the Favorites folder, so that they appear in the Favorites section of the Bookmarks menu.

5. Tap the Save button.

 6. To go to the bookmark, tap the Bookmarks button near the top left of the screen (shaped like a little book).

7. On the Bookmarks list that appears (see **Figure 5-12**), tap the bookmarked site that you want to visit.

> If you want to sync your bookmarks on your iPad browser with those on your computer, connect your iPad to your computer, tap iPad, and make sure that the Sync Safari Bookmarks setting on the Info tab of iTunes is activated.

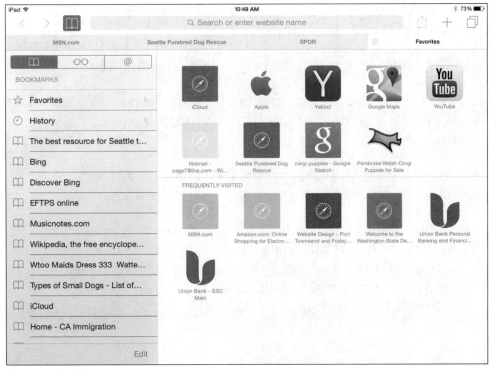

Figure 5-12

 When you tap the Bookmarks button, you can tap Edit and then use the New Folder option to create folders in addition to the existing Favorites folder to organize your bookmarks. When you next add a bookmark, you can choose the folder to which you want to add the new bookmark.

Save Links and Web Pages to the Safari Reading List

The Safari Reading List provides a way to save web pages with content you want to read later so that you can easily visit those saved pages again. You can save not only links to sites, but also the sites themselves, so you can read the content even when you're offline. Where a bookmark takes you to a live, updated page, adding an item to the Reading List simply saves a static copy of the item when you added it to the Reading List. In Safari, you can scroll from one item to the next easily.

1. With a site that you want to add to your Reading List displayed, tap the Share button.

2. On the popover that appears, tap Add to Reading List.

3. To view your Reading List, tap the Bookmarks button and then tap the Reading List tab (the tab sports a pair of reading glasses).

4. On the Reading List that appears (see **Figure 5-13**), tap the content you want to revisit and resume reading.

> If you want to see both Reading List material that you've read and material that you haven't read, tap Show All near the bottom of the Reading List. To see only the material that you haven't read, tap Show Unread (refer to Figure 5-13).

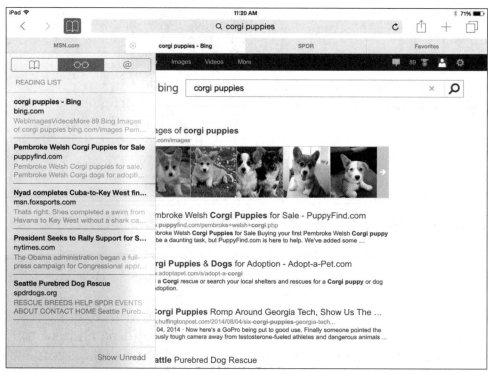

Figure 5-13

To save an image to your Reading List, tap and hold the image until a menu appears; then tap Add to Reading List (this is available only for some images). To delete an item, with the Reading List displayed, swipe left over the item; a Delete button appears. Tap this button to delete the item from the Reading List.

Enjoy Reading with Safari Reader

The Safari Reader feature gives you an e-reader type of experience right within your browser, removing other stories and links as well as those distracting advertisements. When you're on a website, reading content, such as an article, Safari displays the Reader button at the left side of the Address field.

1. Tap the Reader button (see **Figure 5-14**). The content appears in Reader format (see **Figure 5-15**).

Reader button

Figure 5-14

Figure 5-15

2. Scroll down the page. The entire content is contained in one long page.

3. When you finish reading the material, just tap the Reader button in the Address field again to return to the material's source.

Add Web Clips to the Home Screen

1. The *web clips* feature allows you to save a website as an icon on your Home screen so that you can go to the site at any time with one tap. With Safari open and displaying the site that you want to add, tap the Share button.

2. On the menu that appears (refer to Figure 5-10), tap Add to Home Screen.

3. In the Add to Home dialog that appears (see
Figure 5-16), you can edit the name of the site to be
more descriptive, if you like. To do so, tap the name of
the site and use the onscreen keyboard to edit its name.

Figure 5-16

4. Tap the Add button. The site is added to your Home
screen.

 You can have as many as 11 Home screens on your
iPad to accommodate all the web clips and apps you
download (you can save an unlimited number of
apps within folders). If you want to delete an item
from your Home screen for any reason, press and
hold the icon on the Home screen until all items on
the screen start to jiggle and Delete icons appear in

the top-left corner on all items except the preinstalled apps. Tap the Delete icon on each item you want to delete, and it's gone. (To get rid of the jiggle, press the Home button.)

Save an Image to Your Photo Library

1. Display a web page that contains an image you want to copy.

2. Press and hold the image. The menu shown in **Figure 5-17** appears. Note that options on this menu for an image that doesn't contain a link to another location on the web are only Save Image and Copy.

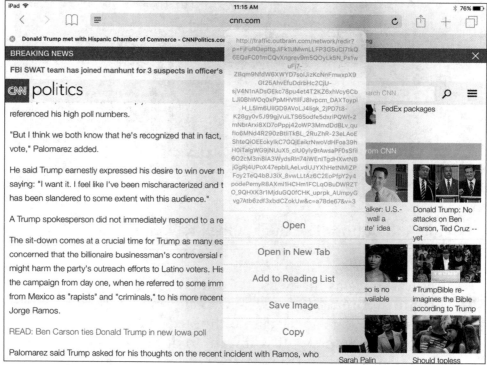

Figure 5-17

3. Tap the Save Image option (refer to Figure 5-17). The image is saved to your Photos gallery.

 Be careful about copying images from the Internet and using them for business or promotional activities. Most images are copyrighted, and you may violate the copyright even if you simply use an image in, say, a brochure for your association or a flyer for your community group. Note that some search engines' advanced search settings offer the option of browsing only for images that aren't copyrighted.

Post Photos from Safari

1. You can post photos to sites such as eBay, Craigslist, and Facebook from within Safari. For this example, go to Facebook and sign in. (To follow this example, you have to have downloaded the Facebook for iPad app and created a Facebook account.)

2. Tap Add Photos/Video, Upload Image/Video, or a link. (On Facebook, you might have to verify that you wish to upload a photo or video rather than create a photo album.)

3. Tap the appropriate source for the image, such as an album in your Photos gallery or iCloud Drive.

4. Tap a photo on your iPad (see **Figure 5-18**).

5. Tap Done or Post, depending on the service, to post the photo or video.

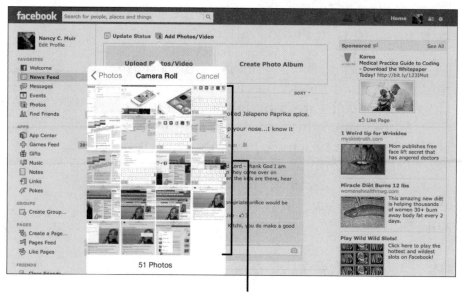

Tap a photo to upload

Figure 5-18

Send a Link

1. If you find a great site that you want to share, you can do so easily by sending a link in an email. (This also works for sending a site via Message, Twitter, or Facebook, or even saving a link to Reminders or Notes.) With Safari open and displaying the site that you want to share, tap the Share button.

2. On the popover that appears (refer to Figure 5-10), tap Mail.

3. On the message form that appears, which contains the link (see **Figure 5-19**), enter a recipient's email address, a subject, and your message.

4. Tap Send, and the email containing the link is sent.

Figure 5-19

 The email is sent from the default email account you set up on your iPad. For more about setting up an email account, see Chapter 6.

 To tweet the link by using your Twitter account, in Step 2 of this task, tap Twitter, enter your tweet in the form that appears, and then tap Send. For more about using Twitter with the iPad, see Chapter 7. You can also choose AirDrop (fourth-generation iPad and later) from the same pop-up menu to share with someone in your immediate vicinity who has an AirDrop-enabled device.

Make Private Browsing and Cookie Settings

Apple has provided some privacy settings for Safari that you should consider using. *Private Browsing* automatically removes items from the download list, stops Safari from using AutoFill to save information used to complete your entries in the search or address fields as you type, and erases some browsing history information. You turn Private Browsing mode on or off by tapping the multiple tabs view (the button in the top right corner of Safari) and tapping Private.

The Block Cookies setting allows you to stop the downloading of *cookies* (small files that document your browsing history so that you can be recognized by a site the next time you go to or move within that site) to your iPad.

You can control both Block Cookies and Do Not Track settings by tapping Safari in the Settings app. In the Privacy & Security section, tap Do Not Track to turn that feature on or off (see **Figure 5-20**). Tap Block Cookies, and choose never to allow cookies to be saved, always save cookies, or allow or block only cookies from the current website or visited third-party and advertiser sites.

 You can also tap the Clear History and Website Data setting (refer to Figure 5-20) to clear your browsing history, saved cookies, and other data manually.

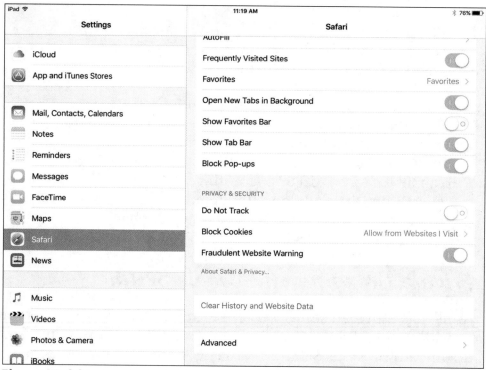

Figure 5-20

Print a Web Page

1. If you have a wireless printer that supports Apple's AirPrint technology (most manufacturers, including Brother, Canon, Epson, Hewlett-Packard, and Lexmark, include AirPrint printers in their product lines), you can print web content via a wireless connection. With Safari open and displaying the site that you want to print, tap the Share button.

 The Mac applications Printopia and handyPrint make any shared or network printer on your home network visible to your iPad. Printopia has more features but costs you, whereas handyPrint is free.

2. On the pop-up menu that appears, scroll to the right on the bottom list of buttons and then tap Print.

3. In the Printer Options dialog that appears (see **Figure 5-21**), tap Select Printer. Then, in the list of printers that appears, tap the name of your wireless printer.

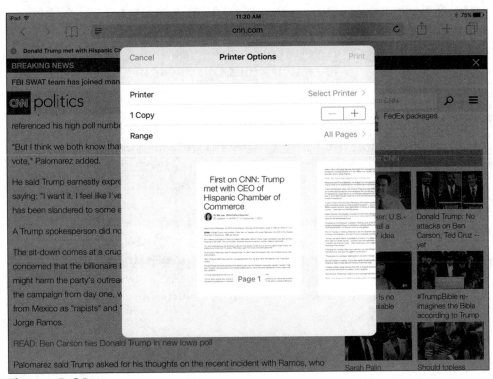

Figure 5-21

4. Tap the plus or minus button in the Copy field to adjust the number of copies to print.

5. If you only want to print certain pages, tap Range and select the pages to print.

6. Tap Print to print the displayed page.

 If you don't have an AirPrint–compatible wireless printer or don't want to use an app to print wirelessly, just email a link to the web page to yourself, open the link on your computer, and print the page from there.

Understand iCloud Tabs

The iCloud Tabs feature allows you to access all browsing history among your different Apple devices from any device. If you begin to research a project on your iPad before you leave home, you can then pick up where you left off as you sit in a waiting room with your iPhone.

1. Tap Settings and then tap iCloud; check to make sure that iPad is using the same iCloud account as your other devices. You may also have to go to iCloud settings and tap Safari to turn it on if it's off and merge Safari and iCloud.

2. Open Safari on another device and tap the Show/Hide Tabs button. Scroll down to see a list of every device using your iCloud account in the bottom-left corner. All items in your iPad's browsing history are displayed on the other devices.

Working with Email in Mail

Staying in touch with others by using email is a great way to use your iPad. You can access an existing account by using the handy Mail app supplied with your iPad or sign in to your email account by using the Safari browser (see Chapter 5). In this chapter, you take a look at using Mail, which involves adding one or more existing email accounts by way of iPad Settings. Then you can use Mail to write, format, retrieve, and forward messages from one or more accounts.

Mail offers the capability to mark the messages you've read, delete messages, organize your messages in folders, and use the handy search feature. You're notified when that special person sends you an email.

iOS 9 includes a feature that makes jumping between a draft email and your Inbox possible; the capability to quickly swipe to mark an email as read or flag it for future action; and the capability to create an event from information about a reservation, flight number, or phone number within an email.

In this chapter, you read all about Mail and its various features.

Get ready to . . .

Add an iCloud, Gmail, Yahoo!, AOL, or Microsoft Outlook.com Account

1. You can add one or more email accounts, including the email account associated with your iCloud account, by using iPad Settings. If you have an account with iCloud, Microsoft Exchange (mostly used for business accounts), Google, Yahoo!, AOL, or Outlook.com (this includes Microsoft accounts from Live, Hotmail, and so on), iPad pretty much automates setup. To set up the iPad to retrieve messages from your email account at one of these popular providers, tap Settings ⇨ Mail, Contacts, Calendars. The settings shown in **Figure 6-1** appear.

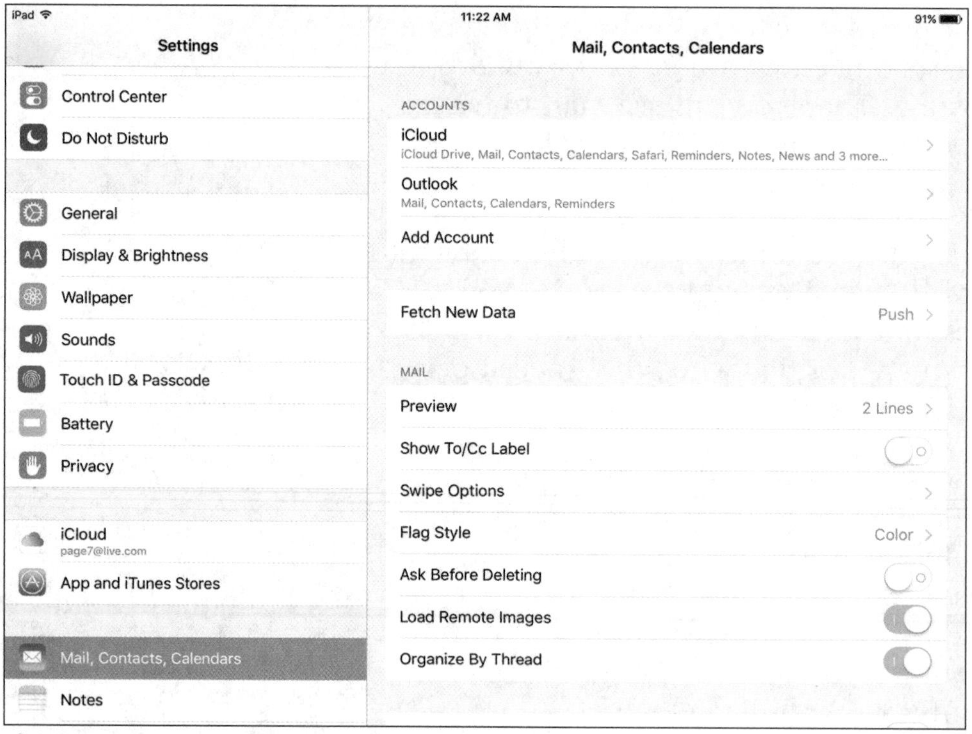

iPad 🛜	11:22 AM	91% 🔋
Settings	**Mail, Contacts, Calendars**	

Control Center
Do Not Disturb

General
Display & Brightness
Wallpaper
Sounds
Touch ID & Passcode
Battery
Privacy

iCloud
page7@live.com
App and iTunes Stores

Mail, Contacts, Calendars
Notes

ACCOUNTS

iCloud
iCloud Drive, Mail, Contacts, Calendars, Safari, Reminders, Notes, News and 3 more... >

Outlook
Mail, Contacts, Calendars, Reminders >

Add Account >

Fetch New Data   Push >

MAIL

Preview   2 Lines >
Show To/Cc Label   ⚪
Swipe Options   >
Flag Style   Color >
Ask Before Deleting   ⚪
Load Remote Images   🔵
Organize By Thread   🔵

Figure 6-1

2. Tap Add Account. The options shown in **Figure** 6-2 appear.

Figure 6-2

3. Tap iCloud, Exchange, Google, Yahoo!, AOL, Exchange, or Outlook.com.

4. Enter your account information in the form that appears (see **Figure** 6-3) and tap Sign In or, for AOL and Outlook accounts, tap Next.

5. After the iPad takes a moment to verify your account information, tap any On/Off switch to have Mail, Contacts, Calendars, Notes, or Reminders from that account synced with the iPad.

6. When you're done, tap Save. The account is saved, and you can now open it by using Mail.

Figure 6-3

Set Up a POP3 or IMAP Email Account

1. You can also set up most popular email accounts, such as those available through EarthLink or a cable provider's service, by obtaining the host name from the provider. To set up an existing account with a provider other than iCloud, Gmail, Outlook.com, Yahoo!, or AOL, you have to enter the account settings yourself. First, tap Settings ⇨ Mail, Contacts, Calendars.

2. Tap Add Account in the top-right corner of the screen that appears.

3. On the screen that appears (refer to Figure 6-2), tap Other.

4. On the screen shown in **Figure 6-4**, tap Add Mail Account.

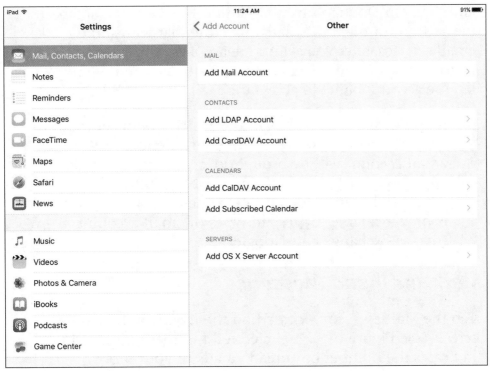

Figure 6-4

5. In the next form, enter your name and an account address, password, and description; then tap Next. The iPad takes a moment to verify your account and then returns you to the Mail, Contacts, Calendars page, where your new account is displayed.

 If you have a less-mainstream email service, you may have to enter what's called the mail server protocol (protocols are either POP3 or IMAP; ask your email provider for this information) and your password. The iPad probably will add the outgoing mail server (SMTP) information for you, but if it doesn't, you may have to enter it yourself. Your Internet service provider (ISP) can provide this information as well.

6. To make sure that the Account field is set to On for receiving email, tap the account name on the Mail, Contacts, Calendars pane of Settings (refer to Figure 6-1). In the settings that appear, tap the On/Off switch for the Mail field and then tap Done to save the setting. Now you can access the account through the Mail app. Note that with some email services, after you set up the account, you have to go to Settings ⇨ Mail, Contacts, and Calendars and then tap the account name to access the Mail On/Off slider.

 If you turn on Calendars in the Mail account settings, any information you've put in your calendar in that email account will be brought over into the Calendar app on your iPad and reflected in Notification Center (discussed in more detail in Chapter 17). This option is only available for certain types of email accounts such as Exchange and Google.

Open Mail and Read Messages

1. Tap the Mail app icon, located on the Dock on the Home screen (see **Figure 6-5**). A circled red number on the icon indicates the number of unread emails in your Inbox.

Figure 6-5

2. In the Mail app, if the Inbox you want isn't displayed, tap Mailboxes (or the specific name of the mailbox that's displayed) in the top-left corner (see **Figure 6-6**) to display your list of Inboxes. Then tap the Inbox whose contents you want to display.

Figure 6-6

3. Tap a message to read it. It opens (see **Figure 6-7**).

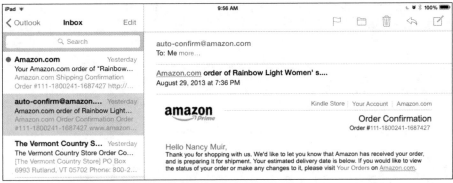

Figure 6-7

4. If you need to scroll to see the entire message, just place your finger on the screen and flick upward to scroll down.

 You can swipe right while reading a message in portrait orientation to open the Inbox list of messages and then swipe left to hide the list.

You can tap the Next (downward arrow) or Previous (upward arrow) button (top-left corner of the message in portrait orientation) to move to the next or previous message.

 Email messages that you haven't read are marked with a blue circle in your Inbox (refer to Figure 6-6). After you read a message, the blue circle disappears. You can mark a read message as unread to help remind you to read it again later. With your messages displayed, swipe to the right on a message and then tap Mark as Unread.

Reply to or Forward Email

1. With an email message open (see the preceding task), tap the Reply/Forward button, which looks like a left-facing arrow (refer to Figure 6-7).

2. Tap Reply, Reply All (if the email has multiple recipients), or Forward in the menu that appears (see **Figure 6-8**).

Reply/Forward button

Figure 6-8

3. Take one of the following actions:

- Tap Reply to respond to the sender of the message, or if the message had other recipients, tap Reply All to respond to the sender and to all recipients. The Reply Message form, shown in **Figure 6-9**, appears. Enter a message.

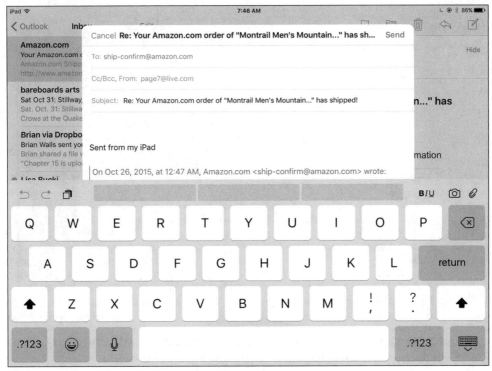

Figure 6-9

- Tap Forward to send the message to somebody other than the sender. The form shown in **Figure 6-10** appears. Enter a recipient in the To: field, tap in the message body, and enter a message.

4. Tap Send. The message is sent.

 If you want to copy an address from the To: field to the Cc or Bcc field, tap and hold the address, and drag it to the other field.

Figure 6-10

If you tap Forward to send the message to somebody else, and the original message had an attachment, you're offered the option of including or not including the attachment.

Create and Send a New Message

1. With Mail open, tap the New Message icon (it looks like a piece of paper with a pen on it). A blank message form appears (see **Figure 6-11**).

2. Enter a recipient's address in the To: field either by typing or by tapping the Dictation key on the onscreen keyboard and speaking the address. If you have saved addresses in Contacts, tap the plus sign (+) in the Address field to choose an addressee from the Contacts list that appears.

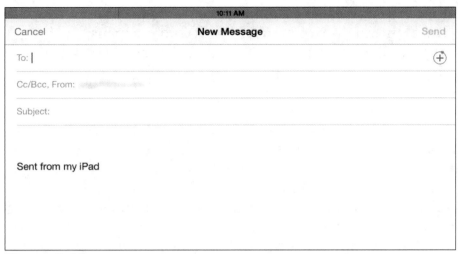

Figure 6-11

3. If you want to send a copy of the message to other people, tap the Cc/Bcc field; the Cc and Bcc fields open; enter addresses in either or both. Use the Bcc field to specify recipients of blind carbon copies, which means that no other recipients are aware that that person received this reply.

4. Enter the subject of the message in the Subject field.

5. Tap in the message body and type your message.

6. If you want to check a fact or copy and paste some part of another message into your draft message, swipe down the email's title bar to display your Inbox and other folders. Locate the message; when you're ready to return to your draft, tap the Subject of the draft email that is displayed near the bottom of the screen to open it.

7. When you've finished creating your message, tap Send.

 Mail keeps a copy of all deleted messages in the Trash folder for each email account for a time. To view deleted messages, tap Mailboxes (or the name of the mailbox that is displayed); then, in the settings that appear, tap the account name in the Accounts list of the Mailboxes pane. A list of folders opens. Tap the Trash folder and all deleted messages display.

Format Email

1. You can apply some basic formatting to email text. You can use character formats (bold, underline, and italic) and indent text by using the Quote Level feature, though available formatting features may vary by the type of email account. To use formatting, press and hold text in a new message that you're creating and choose Select or Select All in the pop-up menu to select a single word or all the words in the email (see **Figure 6-12**). Note that if you select a single word, handles appear; you can drag the handles to add adjacent words to your selection.

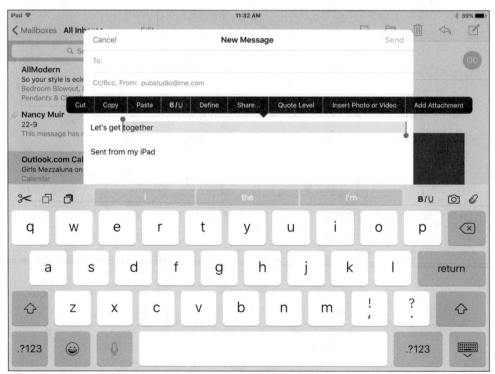

Figure 6-12

2. To apply bold, italic, or underline formatting, tap the B*I*U button.

3. In the pop-up menu that appears (see **Figure 6-13**), tap Bold, Italic, or Underline to apply the respective formatting.

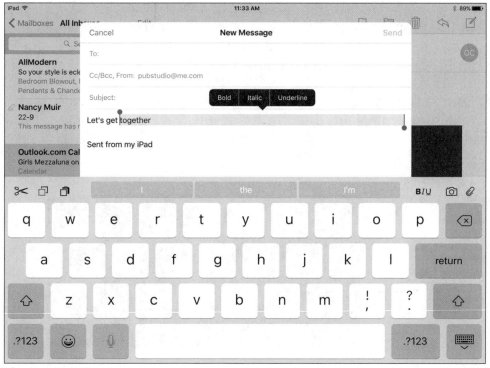

Figure 6-13

4. To change the indent level, tap and hold at the beginning of a line and then tap Quote Level.

5. Tap Increase to indent the text or Decrease to move indented text farther toward the left margin.

 To use the Quote Level feature, make sure that it's on. Tap Settings ⇨ Mail, Contacts, Calendars, and then tap Increase Quote Level and then tap the Increase Quote Level On/Off switch to turn it on.

Search Email

1. What if you want to find all messages that are from a certain person or that contain a certain word in the Subject field? You can use Mail's handy Search feature to find these emails. With Mail open, tap an account to display its Inbox.

2. In the Inbox, tap and drag down near the top of your Inbox to display the Search field; tap in the Search field and the onscreen keyboard appears.

3. Enter a search term or name, as shown in **Figure 6-14**. Matching emails are listed in the results.

Enter a search term...

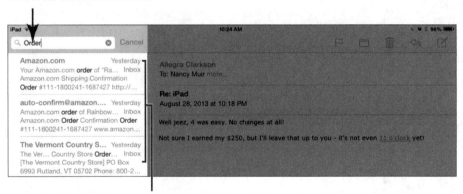

Matching emails appear

Figure 6-14

 You can also use the Spotlight Search feature covered in Chapter 2 to search for terms in the To, From, or Subject lines of mail messages from this search feature that searches several apps.

 To start a new search, tap the Delete key in the top-right corner of the onscreen keyboard to delete the term, or just tap the Cancel button next to the Search field.

Note that you can reply to an email directly from the lock screen or Notification Center.

Mark Email as Unread or Flag for Follow-Up

1. You can use a simple swipe to access tools that either mark an email as unread after you've read it (which places a blue dot before the message), or to flag an email that places an orange circle before it. These methods help you to remember to reread an email you've already read or to follow up on a message later. With Mail open and an Inbox displayed, swipe to the left a short distance to display three options: More, Flag, and Trash (see **Figure 6-15**).

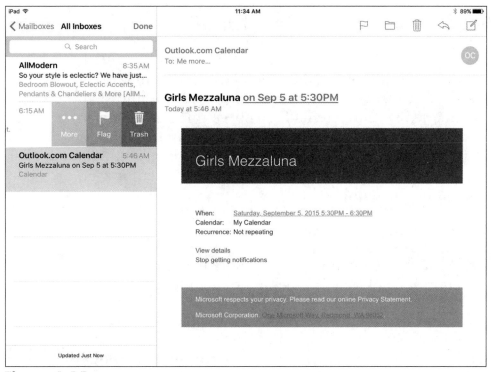

Figure 6-15

2. Tap More. On the menu that appears, you're given several options, including the Mark command; tap this and you see the Flag, Mark as Unread, and Move to Junk commands. Tapping any command applies it and returns you to your Inbox.

 You can either mark an email as unread or flag it; you can't do both. Either action provides a unique visual clue that you need to revisit this message before deleting it.

 In the menu of commands that displays when you tap More, you can also select Notify Me. This option causes Mail to notify you whenever somebody replies to this email thread.

Create an Event from Email Contents

1. Invitations sent to you in email that you accept have always been placed in the Calendar app automatically. You can create a Calendar event from certain information contained within an email. To check this out, create an email to yourself mentioning a reservation on a specific airline on a specific date and time; you can also mention another type of reservation, such as for dinner, or even just a phone number.

2. Send the message to yourself.

3. In your Inbox, open the email. Note that pertinent information is displayed in blue, underlined text.

4. Tap on underlined text, as shown in **Figure 6-16,** and in the menu, choose Create Event. A New Event form from Calendar appears. Enter additional information about the event and then tap Done.

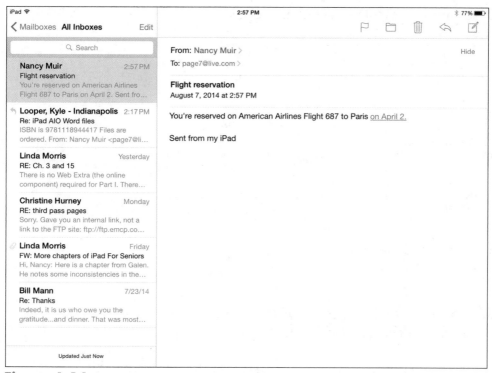

Figure 6-16

Delete Email

1. When you no longer want an email cluttering your Inbox, you can delete it. With the Inbox displayed, tap the Edit button. A circular check box displays to the left of each message (see **Figure 6-17**).

2. Tap the circle next to the message you want to delete. (You can tap multiple items if you have several emails to delete.) A message marked for deletion has a check mark in its circular check box (refer to Figure 6-17).

Check marks indicate selected messages

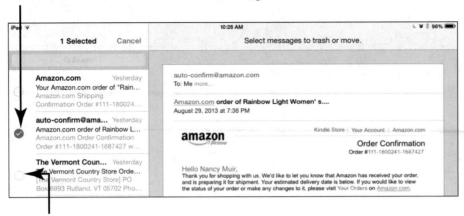

Tap to select a message

Figure 6-17

3. Tap Trash at the bottom of the Inbox. The message is moved to the Trash folder.

You can also delete an open email by tapping the Trash icon on the toolbar that runs across the top of Mail or by swiping left over a message displayed in the Inbox and then tapping Trash.

Organize Email

1. You can move messages into any of several predefined folders in Mail. (These folders will vary, depending on your email provider and the folders you've created on its server.) After displaying the folder containing the message you want to move (for example, Archive or Inbox), tap the Edit button. A circular check box is displayed to the left of each message (refer to Figure 6-17).

2. Tap the circle next to the message you want to move. A check mark appears in its circular check box.

3. Tap the Move button.

4. In the Mailboxes list that appears on the left side of the screen (see **Figure 6-18**), tap the folder where you want to store the message. The message is moved.

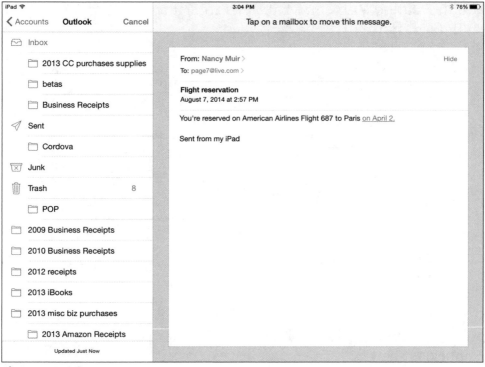

Figure 6-18

 If you receive a junk email, you may want to move it to the Spam or Junk folder, if your email account provides one.

 If you have an email open, you can move it to a folder by tapping the Folder icon on the toolbar at the top of the screen. The Mailboxes list appears (refer to Figure 6-18). Tap a folder to move the message.

Create a VIP List

1. VIP List is a way to create a list of special senders. When any of these senders sends you an email, you're notified through the iPad's Notifications feature. Any VIPs you set up in iPad sync to your Mac computer, if you have one. In the Mailboxes list in Mail (refer to Figure 6-16), tap VIP (see **Figure 6-19**).

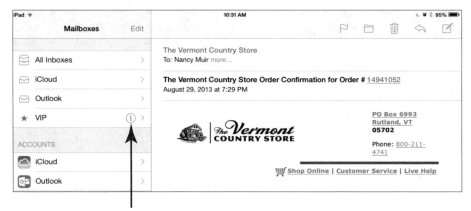

Information button

Figure 6-19

2. Tap Add VIP (see **Figure 6-20**). Your Contacts list appears.

3. Tap a contact to add that person to your VIP list.

4. Press the Home button.

5. Tap Settings ➪ Notifications ➪ Mail.

6. In the screen that appears, tap VIP.

7. In the screen shown in **Figure 6-21,** tap the Show in Notification Center On/Off switch to turn on notifications for VIP mail.

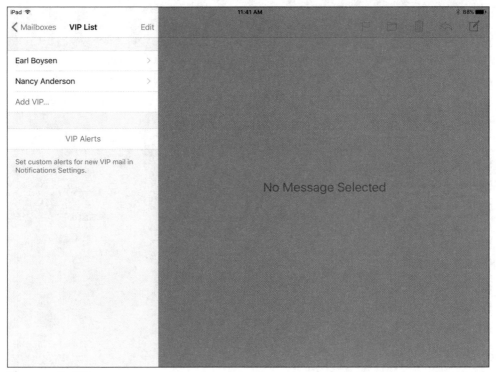

Figure 6-20

8. Tap an alert style, and specify whether the iPad should use a badge icon or sound to alert you. You can also choose to display VIP alerts on your lock screen (refer to Figure 6-21).

9. Press the Home button to close Settings. New mail from your VIPs should now appear in Notification Center when you swipe down from the top of the screen. Depending on the settings that you chose in Step 8, the iPad may play a sound, display a badge icon on your lock screen, and add a blue star icon to the left of these messages in your Mail Inbox.

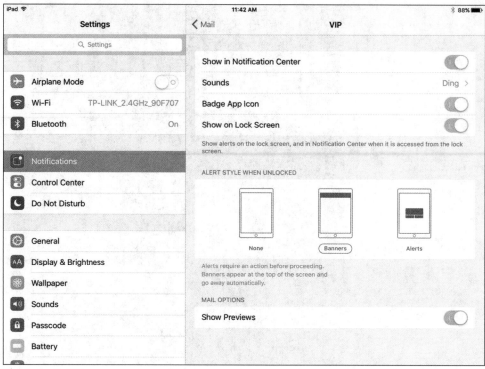

Figure 6-21

Getting Social with FaceTime, Twitter, and iMessage

FaceTime is an excellent video-calling app that's preinstalled in your iPad. The app lets you use either a phone number or an email address to call people who have FaceTime on their devices. You and your friend, colleague, or family member can see each other as you talk, which makes for a much more personal calling experience.

Twitter is a social networking service referred to as a *microblog* because it involves posting short messages. You can set up Twitter credentials in Settings and use them to post tweets whenever you like.

Twitter is incorporated into iOS 9 and integrated in a way that allows you to "tweet" people from within Safari, Photos, Camera, YouTube, Maps, and many other apps. You can also download the free Twitter app and use it to post tweets whenever you like. Facebook, a social networking service where you post text, images, and more, works in a way similar to Twitter on your iPad.

Finally, iMessage is an instant messaging (IM) feature available through the preinstalled Messages app. IM involves sending a text message to somebody's iPhone (using his phone number) or iPod touch or iPad (using his email address) to carry on an instant conversation. You can even send audio and video messages.

In this chapter, I introduce you to FaceTime, Twitter, and the Messages apps, and review their simple controls. In no time, you'll be socializing with all and sundry.

Understand Who Can Use FaceTime

Here's a boring but quick rundown of what device and what information you need to use FaceTime's various features:

⟶ FaceTime is available on all iPads except the original iPad.

⟶ You can use FaceTime to call people who have the iPhone 4 or later, the iPad 2 or later, the iPad mini, a fourth-generation or later iPod touch, or a Mac running Mac OS X 10.6.6 or later.

⟶ You can use a phone number to connect with an iPhone 4 or later.

⟶ You can connect via an email address or phone number with a Mac, iPod touch, or iPad 2 or later.

 In your iCloud settings, you can choose any email accounts or phone numbers you want to associate with your iCloud account. That setting controls how people can contact you on your iPad.

Get an Overview of FaceTime

The FaceTime app works with the cameras built into your iPad and lets you call other folks who have a device that supports FaceTime (see the previous task for compatibility). You can use FaceTime to chat while sharing video images with another person. This app is useful for seniors who want to keep up with distant family members and friends and to see (as well as hear) the latest-and-greatest news.

You can make and receive calls with FaceTime and show the person on the other end what's going on around you. Just remember that you can't adjust audio volume from within the app or record a video call. Nevertheless, on the positive side, even though its features are limited, this app is straightforward to use.

You can use your Apple ID and email address or phone number to access FaceTime, so it works pretty much right away. See Chapter 3 for more about getting an Apple ID.

If FaceTime has been turned off, to turn FaceTime on, follow these steps:

1. Tap Settings on the Home screen.

2. Tap FaceTime.

3. Enter your Apple ID and password if requested and then tap Sign In.

4. Tap the On/Off switch to turn the FaceTime feature on, if it's not already on. On this settings pane, you can also select the email account that others can use to call you.

Make a FaceTime Call with Wi-Fi or 3G/4G

1. If you know that the person you're calling has FaceTime available on a device, it's a good idea to add that person to your iPad Contacts. (See Chapter 18 for details on how to do this.)

2. Tap the FaceTime app icon on the Home screen. The first time you use the app, you may be asked to select the phone number and email accounts you want to use for FaceTime calls and then to tap Next. On the screen that appears, tap to choose a Video or Audio call at the top of the screen. Video includes your voice and image; Audio only includes your voice.

3. Tap the Enter Name, Email, or Number field and begin to enter a contact's name; a list of matching contacts appears.

4. Tap the correct contact's name to display his information (see **Figure 7-1**). (Note that if you haven't saved this person in your contacts and you know his email address, you can just enter that information in the Enter Name, Email, or Number field.)

Figure 7-1

5. In the contact's information, tap a stored phone number that's FaceTime-capable or an email address that the contact has associated with FaceTime, and then tap the FaceTime button (shaped like a video camera). You've just placed a FaceTime call!

 When you use an email address to call somebody, that person must be signed in to her Apple ID account and must have verified that the address can be used for FaceTime calls. iPad and iPod touch (fourth-generation and later) users can make this setting by tapping Settings⇨FaceTime and signing in with an Apple ID.

6. When the person accepts the call, you see the recipient's image and a small draggable box containing your image, referred to as a Picture in Picture (PiP) (see **Figure 7-2**).

Figure 7-2

 You can also simply go to the Contacts app, find a contact, tap the FaceTime icon in that person's record, and then tap the phone number or email address in the pop-up menu that appears to make a FaceTime call.

You can make audio-only FaceTime calls, which cuts down on the data streaming that can cost you when you share video. In the preceding Step 4, simply tap the Call button (shaped like a phone handset) instead of the FaceTime video button to initiate your audio-only call.

Accept and End a FaceTime Call

1. If you're on the receiving end of a FaceTime call, accepting the call is about as easy as it gets. When the call comes in, tap the Accept button to take the call, or tap the Decline button to reject it (see **Figure 7-3**).

Figure 7-3

2. Chat away with your friend, tapping the FaceTime button if you want to view video images.

3. To end the call, tap the End button, which is shaped like a phone receiver (see **Figure 7-4**).

Figure 7-4

 To mute sound during a call, tap the Mute button, which looks like a microphone with a line through it (refer to Figure 7-4). Tap the button again to unmute your iPad.

 If you'd rather not be available for calls, tap Settings ⇨ Do Not Disturb. This feature stops any incoming calls or notifications. After you turn on Do Not Disturb, you can use the feature's settings to schedule when it's active, allow calls from certain people, or accept a second call from the same person after a three-minute interval by using the Do Not Disturb Repeated Calls setting.

Switch Views

1. When you're on a FaceTime call, you may want to use the iPad's built-in camera to show the person you're talking to what's going on around you. Tap the Switch Camera button to switch from the front-facing camera that's displaying your image to the back-facing camera that captures whatever you're looking at.

2. Tap the Switch Camera button again to switch back to the front camera, which displays your image.

Experience Twitter on the iPad

Twitter is a social networking service for *microblogging*, which involves posting very short messages called *tweets*, so that your friends can see what you're up to. The capability to tweet is integrated into several apps. For example, you can post tweets by tapping the Share icon within Safari, Photos, Camera, YouTube, Maps, and other apps. First, download the Twitter app (tap Settings➪Twitter➪Install and get the app from the iTunes Store). Then tap Settings➪Twitter and add your account information. After you have an account, you can post tweets, have people follow your tweets, and follow the tweets that other people post.

When you're using an app, you can choose Twitter in the screen that appears when you tap the Share button. A form like the one shown in **Figure 7-5** appears. Just write your brief message in the form and then tap Post.

See Chapters 5, 12, and 13 for more about tweeting from the Safari, Photos, and YouTube apps, respectively.

You can also access Facebook from the Share menu and post via a Facebook form just as you can with Twitter. See Chapter 12 for instructions on using the Share feature and Chapter 18 for information about adding Facebook account information for contacts.

Figure 7-5

Set Up an iMessage Account

1. iMessage is a feature that is available through the prein-stalled Messages app that allows you to send and receive instant messages (IMs) to others using an Apple iOS device or suitably configured Mac. Instant messaging differs from email or tweeting in an important way. Whereas you might email somebody and wait days or weeks before that person responds, or you might post a tweet that could sit there a while before anybody views it, with instant messaging, the message is sent immediately. You send an IM and it appears on the recipient's Apple device right away. Assuming that the person wants to participate, a live conversation begins, allowing a back-and-forth dialogue in real time. To set up Messages, tap Settings on the Home screen.

2. Tap Messages. The settings shown in **Figure** 7-6 appear.

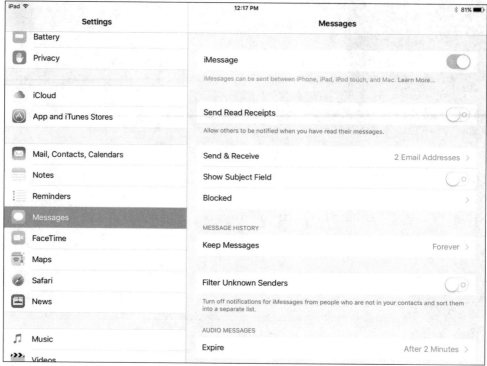

Figure 7-6

3. If iMessage isn't set to On (refer to Figure 7-6), tap the On/Off switch to turn it on.

4. Check the Send & Receive setting to be sure the email accounts associated with your iPad are correct (these should be set up automatically based on your Apple ID).

5. To allow a notice to be sent to the sender when you've read a message, tap the On/Off switch for Send Read Receipts. You can also choose to show a Subject field in your messages.

6. Tap Blocked to add people that you want to block from sending you messages.

To change the email account that iMessage uses, tap Send & Receive, tap Add Another Email, and then follow the directions to add another email account. To delete an account, tap the Information button to the right of it and then tap Remove This Email and then confirm the deletion. Then, follow the preceding steps to add another account, if you like.

Use Messages to Address, Create, and Send Messages

1. You can use either a mobile phone number or email address to send a message. First, tap the Messages button in the Dock on the Home screen. In the screen that appears (see **Figure** 7-7), tap the New Message button in the top-right corner of the left pane to begin a conversation.

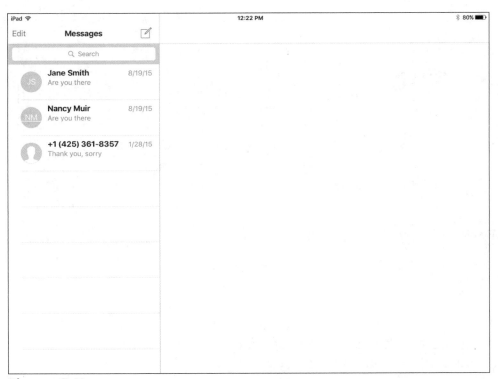

Figure 7-7

2. You can address a message in a couple of ways:

- Begin to type a name in the To: field, as shown in **Figure 7-8,** and tap the recipient in the list of matching contacts that appears. Or tap the Dictation key on the onscreen keyboard and speak the email address or number.

- Tap the plus (+) icon to the right of the To field, and the All Contacts list appears. Tap the contact to whom you want to send the message.

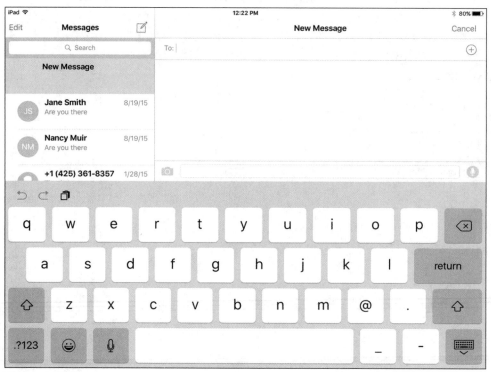

Figure 7-8

3. If the contact has both an email address and phone number stored, the Info dialog appears, allowing you to tap the method you want to use for sending the message.

4. To create a message, simply tap the message field and then type or dictate your message.

5. To send the message, tap the Send button. When your recipient responds, you see the conversation displayed on the right side of the screen, as shown in **Figure** 7-9.

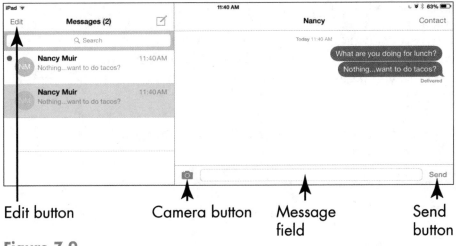

Edit button   Camera button   Message   Send
field   button

Figure 7-9

6. Tap the message field at the bottom of the screen to respond to the last comment.

 You can address a message to more than one person simply by choosing more recipients in Step 2.

Read Messages

1. Tap Messages on the Home screen.

2. When the app opens, you see a list of all text messages and all attachments that have appeared in your Messages app.

3. Tap a message to see the message string, including all attachments, as shown in Figure 7-9.

4. To view all attachments of a message, tap Details and scroll down.

Clear a Conversation

1. When you're done chatting, you may want to clear a conversation to remove the clutter before you start a new one. With Messages open, swipe to the left on the message you want to delete.

2. Tap the Delete button next to any item you want to clear (see **Figure 7-10**).

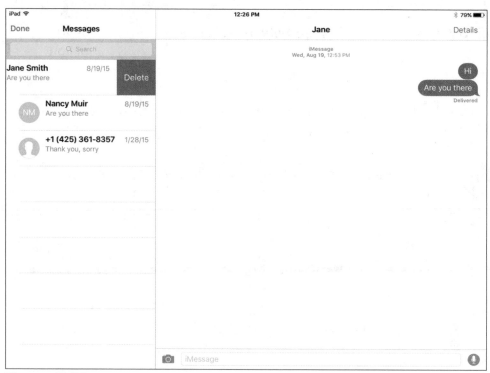

Figure 7-10

Send and Receive Audio

1. When you're creating a message, you can also create an audio message. With Messages open, tap the New Message button in the top-right corner of the left pane.

2. Enter an addressee's name in the To: field.

3. Tap and hold the Audio button (the microphone symbol to the right of the message entry field; see **Figure 7-11**).

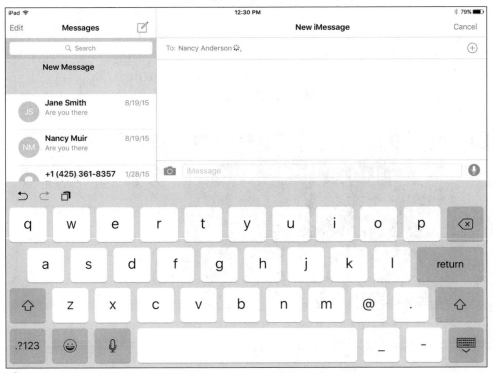

Figure 7-11

4. Speak your message or record a sound or music near you and release the Audio button to stop the recording.

5. Tap the Send button (an upward pointing arrow at the top of the recording panel). The message appears as an audio track in the recipient's Messages inbox. To play the track, she just holds the phone up to her ear or taps the play button.

Send a Photo or Video Message

1. When you're creating a message, you can also create a short video message. With Messages open, tap the New Message button in the top-right corner.

2. Press and hold the camera icon on the left of the message entry field. In the tool pop-up menu that appears (see **Figure 7-12**), tap the Photo button to take a picture; then you return to the message.

Figure 7-12

3. If you prefer to capture a video, with the choices in Figure 7-12 displayed, tap the Video button, and then tap the Record button to record your video. Tap the red Stop button when you've recorded what you want to record. Your video is attached to your message. Tap Send to send it.

 To send multiple photos or videos, repeat these steps and then tap Send to send your message and attachments.

Send a Map of Your Location

1. When sending a message you can also send a map showing your current location. Tap a message you've received and then tap Details.

2. Tap Send My Current Location (see **Figure 7-13**); a map will be inserted into the conversation as a message attachment. On the following screen, tap Allow to allow Messages to access your location.

 You can also share your location in the middle of a conversation rather than sending a map attachment with your message. In the screen shown in Figure 7-13, tap Share My Location, and then tap Share for One Hour, Share Until End of Day, or Share Indefinitely. A map showing your location will appear above your conversation until you stop sharing.

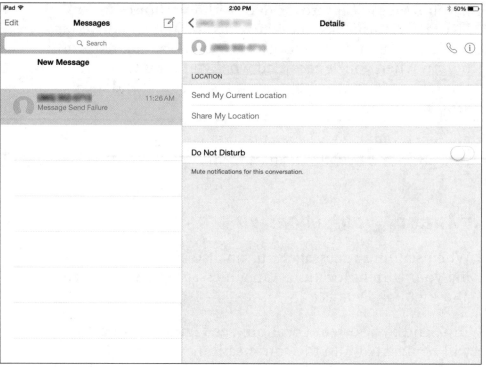

Figure 7-13

Understanding Group Messaging

If you want to start a conversation with a group of people, you can use group messaging. Group messaging is great for keeping several people in the conversational loop.

You can explore group messaging functionality, including

➡ Creating a group message simply by addressing a message to more than one person and sending it. With Group Messaging enabled under Settings, Messages on your iPad and on recipients' iOS devices, the message and replies to it are delivered to everybody in the group.

➡ When you participate in a group message, you see all participants in the Details for the message. You can drop people you don't want to include any longer and leave the conversation yourself when you want to.

➡ Turning on Do Not Disturb by tapping Details in a message so you won't get notifications of messages from this group, but you can still read the group's messages later.

Taking you through the ins and outs of group messages is beyond the scope of this book, but if you're intrigued, go to www.apple.com/ios/messages/ for more information.

Activate Do Not Disturb

1. If you don't want to get notifications of new messages from an individual or group for a while, you can use the Messages Do Not Disturb feature. With a message open, tap Details.

2. Tap Do Not Disturb to turn the feature on.

3. If you want to at another time, return to Details and tap Do Not Disturb again to turn the feature off.

 You can turn on the Do Not Disturb feature for everyone by opening the Control Center (drag up from the bottom edge of the screen to display it) and tapping the half-moon shaped button. You can also allow selected callers to get through in Settings ⇨ Do Not Disturb by choosing everyone, no one, people you've tagged as favorites, or people in one or more groups.

Shopping the iTunes Store

*T*he iTunes Store app that comes preinstalled on iPad lets you easily shop for music, movies, and TV shows.

In this chapter, you discover how to find content in the iTunes Store. The content can be downloaded directly to your iPad or to another device and then synced to your iPad. With the new Family Sharing feature, which I cover in this chapter, up to six people in a family can share purchases and make purchases using the same credit card. Finally, I cover a few options for buying content from other online stores.

Note that I cover opening an iTunes account and downloading iTunes software to your computer in Chapter 3. If you need to, refer to Chapter 3 to see how to handle these two tasks before digging into this chapter.

Explore the iTunes Store

1. Visiting the iTunes Store from your iPad is easy with the built-in iTunes Store app. Tap the iTunes Store icon on the Home screen.

2. If you're not already signed in to iTunes, the dialog shown in

Figure 8-1 appears, asking for your iTunes password. Enter your password and tap OK. You may also be prompted to set up Family Sharing, a feature that allows family members to use the same purchase method on their devices, covered later in this chapter.

Tap here and enter your password

Figure 8-1

3. Tap the Music button in the row of buttons at the bottom of the screen, if it's not already selected, to view selections, as shown in **Figure 8-2**.

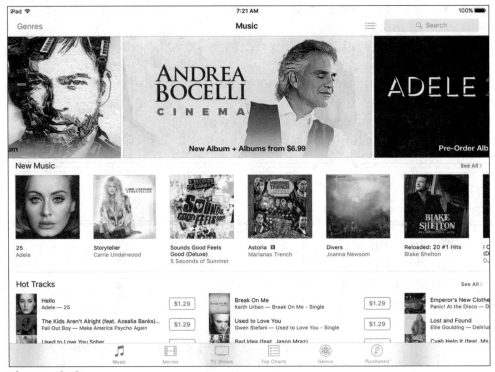

Figure 8-2

4. Tap the See All link (refer to Figure 8-2) in any category of music to display more music selections.

5. Tap the button in the top-left corner labeled Music to go back to the featured Music selections; tap the Genres button at the top left of the screen. This step displays a list of music categories you can choose among. Tap one genre. Items that are displayed are organized by criteria such as New Music and Greatest Hits.

6. Tap any listed item to see more details about it, as shown in **Figure 8-3**.

Figure 8-3

 The navigation techniques in these steps work essentially the same way in any of the content categories (the buttons at the bottom of the screen), which include Music, Movies, and TV Shows.

If you want to use the Genius playlist feature, which recommends additional purchases based on the contents of your library, in the iTunes app on your iPad, tap the Genius button at the bottom of the screen. If you've made enough purchases in iTunes, song and album recommendations appear based on those purchases as well as on the content in your iTunes Match library (a fee-based music service), if you have one.

 If you're in search of other kinds of content, the Podcast app and iTunes U app allow you to find and download podcasts and online courses to your phone.

Find a Selection

You can look for a selection in the iTunes Store in several ways. You can use the Search feature, search by genre or category, or view artists' pages. Here's how these methods work:

⟶ Tap the Search field shown in **Figure 8-4**, and enter a search term with the onscreen keyboard, which could be a genre of music, the name of an album or song, or an artist's name, for example. If a suggestion in the list of search results appeals to you, just tap it, or tap Search on the keyboard.

⟶ Tap a result; on the description page that appears when you tap a selection, you can find more offerings by the people involved, such as a singer or actor, by tapping the Related tab, as shown in **Figure 8-5**.

 If you find a selection that you like, tap the Share button at the top of its description page to share your discovery with a friend via AirDrop (fourth-generation iPad and later), Mail, Twitter, or Facebook. For all but AirDrop, a message form appears with a link that your friend can click or tap to view the selection. Enter an address in the To: field, and tap Send or Post. Now your friend is in the know.

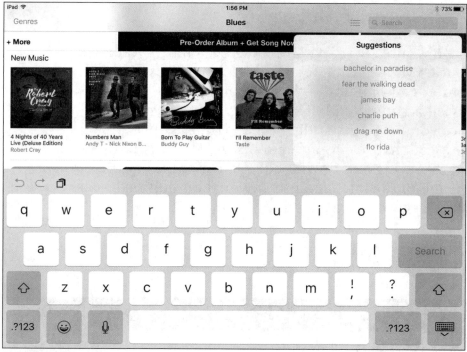

Figure 8-4

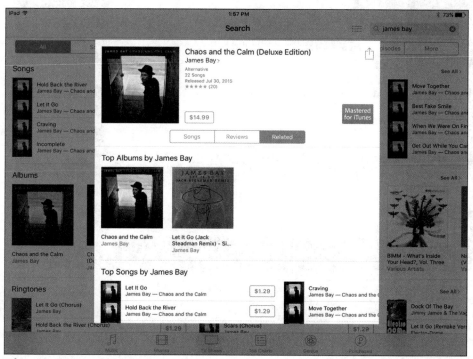

Figure 8-5

Preview Music or a Movie

1. If you've already set up an iTunes account (if you haven't done so yet, see Chapter 3), when you choose to buy an item, it's automatically charged to the credit card or PayPal account you have on record or against any allowance you have outstanding on an iTunes gift card. You may want to preview an item before you buy it. If you like it, buying and downloading are easy and quick. Open iTunes Store, and use any method outlined in earlier tasks to locate a selection you may want to buy.

2. Tap the item to see detailed information about it, as shown in **Figure 8-6**.

Figure 8-6

3. For a movie selection, tap the Play button on a Trailer (refer to Figure 8-6) to view the theatrical trailer if one's available. For a TV show, tap an episode to get further information. If you want to listen to a sample of a music selection, tap the track number (see **Figure 8-7**); a small square appears and the track plays. Tap the square to stop the preview.

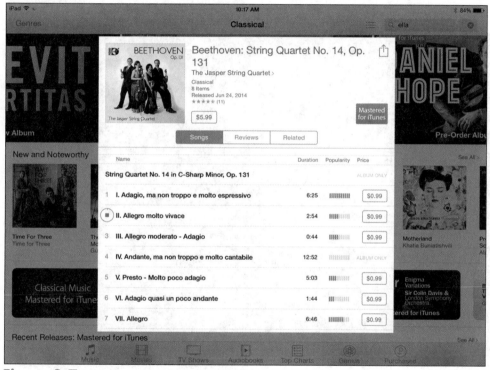

Figure 8-7

Buy a Selection

1. When you find an item that you want to buy, tap the button that shows the price (if the selection is available for purchase) or the button with the word *Get* on it (if the selection is available free). The button label changes to Buy *X*, where *X* is the type of content you're buying, such as a song or album. If the item is free, the label changes to Get Song (or whatever type of item you're purchasing).

2. Tap the Buy *X* button (see **Figure 8-8**). The iTunes Password dialog appears (refer to Figure 8-1). You may or may not be prompted to enter your Apple ID at this point, depending on what you're purchasing.

Figure 8-8

3. Enter your password and tap OK. The item begins downloading and the cost is automatically charged against your account. When the download finishes, you can view the content in the Music or Videos app, depending on the type of content.

If you want to buy music, you can open the description page for an album and tap the album price, or buy individual songs rather than the entire album. Tap the price for a song and then proceed to purchase it.

 Notice the Redeem button on many iTunes Store screens. Tap this button to redeem any iTunes gift certificates you may have received from your generous friends (or from yourself).

 If you don't want to allow purchases from within apps (such as Music or Videos) and want to allow purchases only through the iTunes Store, tap Settings ➪ General ➪ Restrictions ➪ Enable Restrictions, and enter a passcode. After you've set a passcode, you can tap individual apps to turn on restrictions for them, as well as for actions such as installing apps, sharing via AirDrop, or using Siri.

Rent a Movie

1. In the case of some movies, you can either rent or buy content. If you rent, which is less expensive than buying but makes the content yours for only a short time, you have 30 days from the time you rent the item to begin watching it. After you've begun to watch it, you have 24 hours remaining to watch it on the same device as many times as you like. With the iTunes Store open, tap the Movies button.

2. Locate the movie you want to rent, and tap either the HD or SD choice, if available. Tap the Rent button, shown in **Figure 8-9**. The Rent button changes to a Rent Movie or Rent HD Movie button.

3. Tap Rent HD Movie (see **Figure 8-10**) to confirm the rental. The movie begins to download to your iPad immediately and the rental fee is charged to your account.

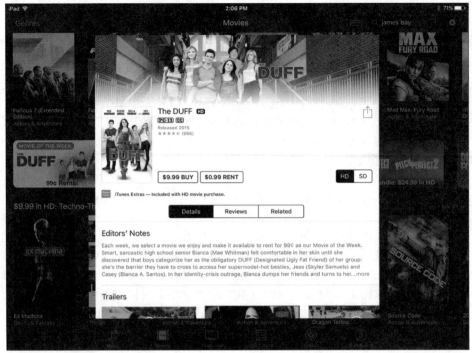

Figure 8-9

Figure 8-10

4. When the download is complete, use either the Music or Videos app to watch it. (See Chapters 11 and 13, respectively, to read about how these apps work.)

 Some movies are offered in high-definition (HD) versions as well as standard definition (SD). These HD movies look great on that crisp, colorful iPad screen, especially if you have an iPad with Retina display.

Shop Anywhere Else

Though iPads don't work with every video format, many online stores that sell content such as movies and music have added iPad-friendly videos to their collections, so you do have alternatives to iTunes for movies and TV shows. You can also shop for music from sources other than iTunes, such as Amazon.com.

You can open accounts at one of these stores by using your computer's web browser or your iPad's Safari browser and then following the store's instructions to purchase and download content.

 For non–iPad-friendly formats, you can download the content on your computer and stream it to your iPad by using Air Video ($2.99) on the iPad or Air Video Server (which is free) on your Mac or Windows computer. For more information, go to www.inmethod. com/air-video/index.html. Another free utility for Mac and Windows that converts most video to an iPad-friendly format is HandBrake. Go to http:// handbrake.fr for more information.

Enable Autodownloads of Purchases from Other Devices

1. With iCloud, you can make a purchase or download free content on any of your Apple devices and have those purchases automatically copied to all your Apple devices. To enable this autodownload feature on iPad, start by tapping Settings on the Home screen.

To use iCloud, first set up an iCloud account. See Chapter 3 for detailed coverage of iCloud, including setting up your account.

2. Tap iTunes & App Store.

3. In the options that appear, tap on or slide the On/Off switch to turn on any category of purchases you want to autodownload to your iPad from other Apple devices (see **Figure 8-11**).

 At this point, Apple doesn't offer an option to autodownload video content by using these settings because video is such a memory and bandwidth hog.

Figure 8-11

Set Up Family Sharing

1. Family Sharing is a feature in that allows up to six people in your family to share whatever anybody in the group has purchased from the iTunes, iBooks, and App Stores even if you don't share Apple accounts. Your family must all use one credit card to purchase items, but you can approve purchases by younger children. You can also share calendars, photos, and a family calendar (see Chapter 16 for information about Family Sharing and Calendar and Chapter 12 for information on sharing Photos in a Family album). Start by turning on Family Sharing. Tap Settings.

2. Tap iCloud and then tap Set Up Family Sharing.

3. Tap Get Started and on the next screen, you can add a photo for your family. Tap Continue. Your current payment method associated with your Apple account displays. Tap Continue.

4. Tap Share Your Location and then tap Add Family Member to add people to your family group.

5. Enter the person's name (assuming she is listed in your contacts) or email address (see **Figure 8-12**) and tap Next. An invitation is sent to that person's email. When the invitation is accepted, the person is added to your family.

6. Check the payment method you want to use. If it's not the payment method you want to use, you have to change it in iTunes.

 If you want to add a child aged under 13, note the separate link, Create an Apple ID for a Child, at the bottom of the pane shown in Figure 8-12. This method is provided here because kids younger than 13 can't set up their own Apple IDs.

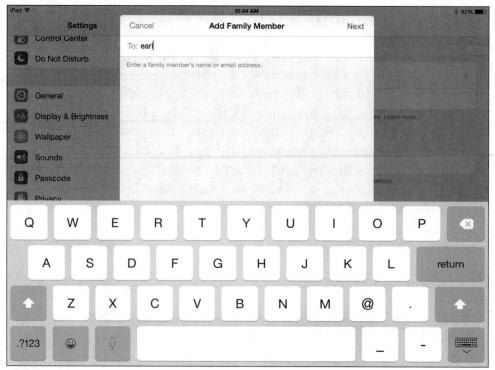

Figure 8-12

 Note that the payment method for this family is displayed under Shared Payment Method in this screen. All those involved in a family have to use a single payment method for family purchases.

Expanding Your iPad Horizons with Apps

Some *apps* (short for *applications*) come pre-installed on your iPad, such as Contacts and Videos. But there's a world of other apps out there that you can get for your iPad, some for free and some for a price (typically, from $0.99 to about $10, though some can top out at $90 or more).

Apps range from games and travel planners to financial tools such as loan calculators and productivity applications, including the iPad version of Pages, the Apple software for word processing and page layout.

In this chapter, I suggest some apps you may want to check out and explain how to use the iPad's App Store to find, purchase, and download apps.

Explore Senior-Recommended Apps

As I write this book, apps are being created for the iPad at a furious pace, so many more apps that could fit your needs will be available by the time you have this book in your hands.

Still, to get you exploring what's possible, I provide a quick list of apps that may whet your appetite.

Access the App Store by tapping the App Store icon on the Home screen. You can start by exploring the Featured or Top Charts categories (see the buttons along the bottom of the screen). Or, you can tap Explore and find apps divided into categories. Search for an app by typing its name in the Search box in the top-right corner of the screen and tapping the Search key on the onscreen keyboard. Here are some interesting apps to explore:

➥ **Sudoku 2 (free):** If you like this mental logic puzzle in print, try it out on your iPad (see **Figure 9-1**). It has three lessons and several levels ranging from easiest to nightmare, making it a great way to make time fly by in the doctor's or dentist's waiting room.

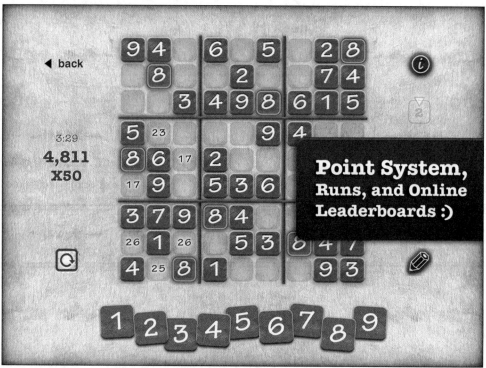

Figure 9-1

➥ **StockWatch Portfolio Tracking and Stock Market Quotes ($1.99):** This app helps you keep track of your investments in a portfolio format. You can use the app to create a watch list and record your stock performance.

➥ **DealCatcher Coupons & Deals (free):** Use this app to find low prices on just about everything local to your area. Read product reviews and compare list prices.

➥ **SpaceEffect FX HD (free):** If you need a photo-sharing service with some cool features, try SpaceEffect. You can not only upload and share photos, but apply awesome effects to them.

➥ **Paint Studio ($3.99):** Get creative! You can use this powerful app to draw, add color, and even create special effects.

➥ **Mediquations Medical Calculator ($4.99):** Use this handy utility to help calculate medications with built-in formulas and read scores for various medications. Check with your physician before using!

➥ **Nike Training Club (free):** Use this handy utility to help design personalized workouts, see step-by-step instructions to help you learn new exercises, and watch video demonstrations. The reward system in this app may just keep you going toward your workout goals.

 Most iPhone apps work on your iPad, so if you own the mobile phone and have favorite apps on it, sync them to your iPad!

Note that you can work on documents using apps in the cloud from other devices, such as your Mac laptop. Use Keynote, Number, Pages, and more apps to get your work done from any device. See Chapter 3 for more about iCloud Drive.

Search the App Store

1. Tap the App Store icon on the Home screen. The site shown in **Figure 9-2** appears.

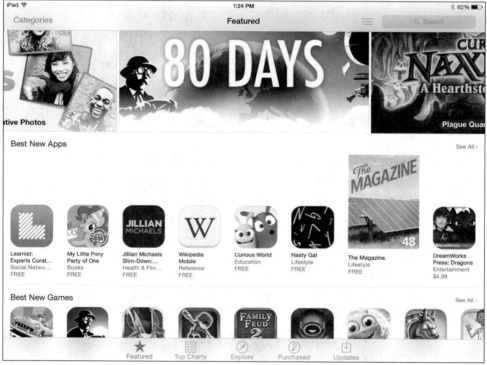

Figure 9-2

2. At this point, you have several options for finding apps:

- Tap the Search field, enter a search term, and then tap the Search button on the onscreen keyboard to see results.

- Swipe the screen downward to scroll down, or swipe to the right to see more selections.

- Tap the Categories button at the top of the screen to see different categories of apps.

- Tap the Top Charts button at the bottom of the screen to see which free and paid apps other people are downloading most.

- Tap the Explore option to display apps in categories such as Great Free Games, Get Stuff Done, and Interactive Kids Stories. Tap a category to display apps that fit within it.

- The Popular Near Me option at the top of the Explore view displays apps that are popular among people in or near your location. (This may or may not produce useful results, depending on where you are!)

- Tap the Purchased button at the bottom of the screen to view apps you've already purchased, as shown in **Figure 9-3.** An item with a cloud symbol to the right of it means you need to download it to use it; note that it might be an app you installed on another Apple device such as an iPhone, but that hasn't yet been installed on your iPad.

- Tap the See All button in any category shown in the Featured view to view all the items in that category.

- In the Top Charts view, use the Paid, Free, and Top Grossing tabs to narrow your search.

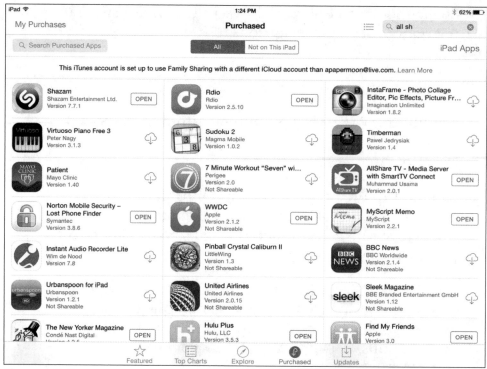

Figure 9-3

Get Applications from the App Store

1. Getting free apps or buying apps requires an iTunes account, which I cover in Chapter 3. After you have an account, you can use your saved payment information to buy apps or download free apps in a few simple steps. With the App Store open, tap the Search field, enter an app name (a free app you might like to have is Netflix, for example), and then tap Search on the onscreen keyboard.

2. Tap Netflix in the suggested search results that appear and then tap the Get button for Netflix. (To get a *paid* app, you'd tap the same button, which would be labeled with a price.) The Get button changes to Install (or, in the case of a paid app, to Buy), as shown in **Figure 9-4**.

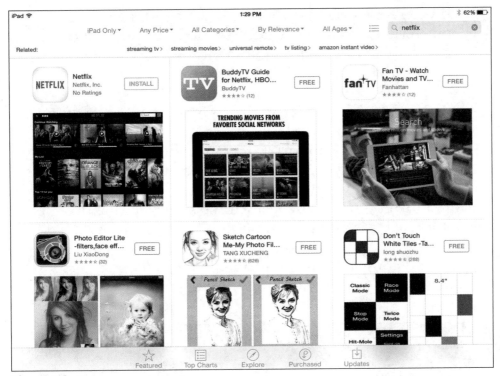

Figure 9-4

3. Tap the Install button.

4. You may be asked to enter your iTunes password. If so, enter it, and then tap the OK button to proceed. The app downloads and appears on a Home screen (probably your second Home screen, if you haven't downloaded many apps yet). If you purchase an app that isn't free, at this point, your credit card or iTunes gift card (if you're using iTunes to buy apps) is charged for the purchase price.

 Out of the box, only preinstalled apps are located on the first iPad Home screen. Apps that you download are placed on additional Home screens, and you have to scroll to view and use them. See the next task for help in finding your newly downloaded apps on multiple Home screens.

If you've opened an iCloud account, anything you purchase on your iPad can be set up to be pushed to other Apple iOS devices automatically. See Chapter 3 for more about iCloud.

Organize Your Applications on Home Screens

1. The iPad can display up to 11 Home screens. By default, the first contains preinstalled apps; other screens are created to contain any apps you download or sync to your iPad. At the bottom of any iPad Home screen (just above the Dock), dots indicate the number of Home screens, and a solid dot specifies the Home screen you're on, as shown in **Figure 9-5**. Press the Home button to open the last-displayed Home screen.

Figure 9-5

2. Flick your finger from right to left to move to the next Home screen. To move back, flick from left to right.

3. To reorganize apps on a Home screen, press and hold any app on that screen. The app icons begin to jiggle (see **Figure 9-6**), and any apps you've installed sport a Delete button (a gray circle with a black *X* on it). Some preinstalled apps cannot be deleted and so have no Delete button on them.

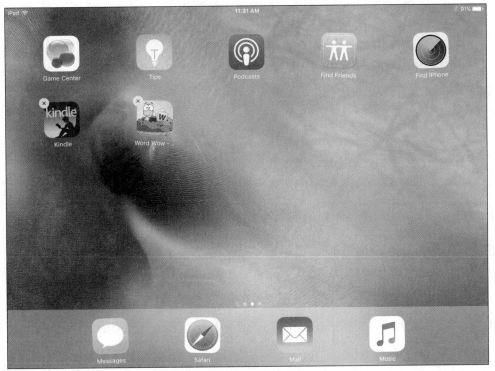

Figure 9-6

4. Press, hold, and drag an app icon to another location on the screen to move it.

5. Press the Home button to stop all those icons from jiggling!

To move an app from one page to another while the apps are jiggling, you can press, hold, and drag an app to the left or right to move it to the next Home screen. You can also use iTunes to manage what app resides on what Home screen and in which folder when you've connected the iPad to iTunes via a cable or wireless sync. This process may be easier for some people and allows you to rearrange Home screens, which you can't do from the iPad.

 Press the Home button twice, and you get a view of open apps in the App Switcher. Scroll among the apps and tap the one you want to go to. Swipe an app upward from this preview list to close it.

Organize Apps in Folders

iPad lets you organize apps in folders so that you can find them more easily. There is no limit on the number of apps you can store in a folder. The process is simple:

1. Tap and hold an app until all apps do their jiggle dance.

2. Drag one app on top of another app. The two apps appear in a box with a placeholder name in a strip above them (see **Figure 9-7**).

3. To change the folder name, tap the bar above the box. The keyboard appears.

4. Tap the Delete key to delete the placeholder name, and type one of your own.

5. Tap Done and then tap anywhere outside the bar to save the name.

6. Press the Home button to stop the icons from dancing around. Your folder appears on the Home screen where you began this process.

Figure 9-7

Delete Apps You No Longer Need

1. When you no longer need an app that you installed, it's time to get rid of it. (You can't delete apps that are prein-stalled on the iPad, such as Notes, Calendar, and Photos, however.) If you use iCloud to push content across all Apple iOS devices, note that deleting an app on your iPad won't affect that app on other devices. Display the Home screen that contains the app that you want to delete.

2. Press and hold the app until all apps begin to jiggle.

3. Tap the Delete button for the app you want to delete (see Figure 9-6). A confirmation message like the one shown in **Figure 9-8** appears.

Figure 9-8

4. Tap Delete to proceed with the deletion.

 Don't worry about wiping out several apps at once by deleting a folder. When you delete a folder, the apps that were contained within the folder are placed back on Home screens.

 If you have several apps to delete, you can delete them by using iTunes connected to your iPad, making the process a bit more streamlined.

Update Apps

1. App developers update their apps all the time to fix problems or add new features. You can use the Automatic Downloads on/off switches to set up automatic downloads of apps (this is under the iTunes & App Store settings).

If you'd rather not have updates happen automatically, or want to get the latest update in case the automatic download hasn't occurred yet, you may want to check for those updates. The App Store icon on the Home screen displays the number of available updates in a red circle. Tap the App Store icon.

2. Tap the Updates button to access the Updates screen and then tap any item you want to update. Note that if you have Family Sharing turned on, there will be a folder titled Family Purchases you can tap to display apps that are shared across your family's devices. To update all, tap the Update All button.

3. On the screen that appears, tap Update. You may be asked to confirm that you want to update or to enter your Apple ID Password; after you do, tap OK to proceed. You may also be asked to confirm that you're over a certain age or agree to terms and conditions; if so, scroll down the terms dialog (reading the terms as you go, of course), and at the bottom, tap Agree.

 You can download multiple apps simultaneously. If you choose more than one app to update, instead of downloading them sequentially, all items will download in parallel. You can keep working in the iTunes Store while you're downloading an item.

 If you have an iCloud account that you've made active on various devices, when you update an app on your iPad, it also updates automatically on any other Apple iOS devices you have (and vice versa).

Part III
Having Fun and Consuming Media

Visit www.dummies.com/extras/ipadforseniors for information about Apple Music.

Using Your iPad as an E-Reader

A traditional *e-reader* is a device that's used primarily to read the electronic versions of books, magazines, and newspapers. Apple has touted the iPad as a great e-reader, and although it isn't a traditional e-reader device like the Kindle Paperwhite, you don't want to miss this cool functionality.

Apple's free, preinstalled app that turns your iPad into an e-reader is *iBooks*, which enables you to buy and download books from Apple's iBooks Store. You can also use one of several other free e-reader apps — for example, Kindle, or Bluefire Reader. Then, you can download books to your iPad from a variety of online sources, such as Amazon and Google, so you can read to your heart's content.

Another preinstalled reading app covered later in this chapter is News. It has a similar look and feel to iBooks, but its focus is on subscribing to and reading magazines, newspapers, and other periodicals.

In this chapter, you discover the options available for reading material and how to buy books and subscribe to publications. You also learn how to navigate an e-book, interactive book, or periodical; adjust brightness and type; search books; and organize your iBooks and News libraries.

Get ready to . . .

Discover How the iPad Differs from Other E-Readers

An e-reader is any electronic device that enables you to download and read books, magazines, PDF files, or newspapers. These devices typically are portable and dedicated only to reading the electronic version of published materials.

The iPad is a bit different: It isn't only for reading books, and it allows you to use iBooks or download other e-reader apps such as Kindle (these e-reader apps are typically free). Also, the iPad doesn't offer a paperlike reading experience; you read from a computer screen (though you can adjust the brightness and background color of the screen).

When you buy a book or magazine online (or get one of many free publications), it downloads to your iPad in a few seconds over a Wi-Fi or 3G/4G connection. The iPad offers several navigation tools that let you move around an electronic book, which you explore in this chapter.

 iBooks contains tools for reading and interacting with book content. You can even create and publish your own interactive books by using a free app called iBooks Author on a Macintosh.

Find Books with iBooks

1. To shop with iBooks, tap the iBooks app on the Home screen to open it.

2. In the iBooks library that opens (see **Figure 10-1**), you see a bookshelf; yours probably has only one free book already downloaded to it. (If you don't see the bookshelf, tap the Library button in the top-left corner to go there.)

3. Tap the Featured tab on the bottom of the screen. In the iBooks Store, shown in **Figure 10-2**, you see several rows of books in categories such as Hot This Week and

Popular on iBooks. Try any of the following methods to find a book:

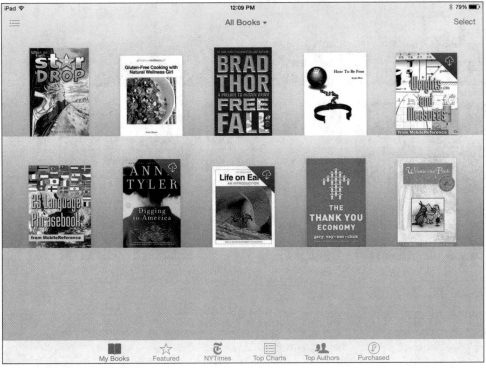

Figure 10-1

- Tap Featured at the bottom of the screen and then tap Search at the top right of the screen. Use the onscreen keyboard to type a search word or phrase.

- Tap the Categories button at the top of the screen and scroll down to browse links to popular categories of books, as shown in **Figure 10-3**.

- Tap Purchased at the bottom of the screen to see any books you've bought on devices signed in with the same Apple ID. You can tap the All tab to show content from all devices or tap the Not on This iPad tab to see only content purchased on your other devices.

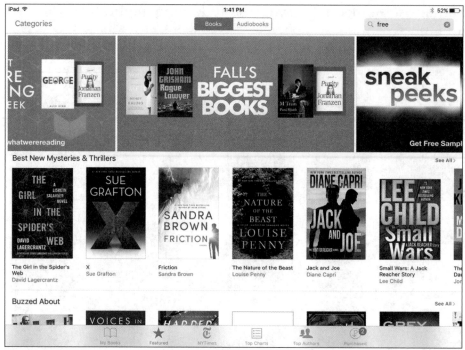

Figure 10-2

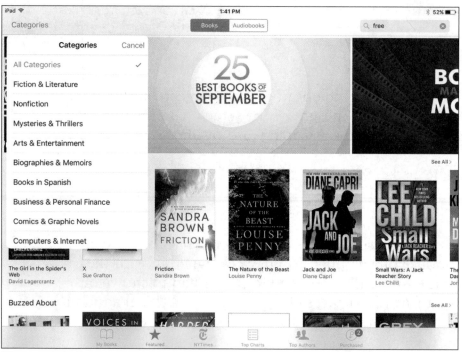

Figure 10-3

- Tap the appropriate button at the bottom of the screen to view particular categories: NYTimes to display *The New York Times* best-seller list, Top Charts for books listed on top charts, and Top Authors.

- Tap a suggested selection or featured book to open more information about it.

 Download free samples before you buy. You get to read several pages of the book to see whether it appeals to you, and it doesn't cost you a dime! Look for the Sample button when you view details about a book. If you like the book, you can buy it from within the iBooks app by tapping the sample and then tapping Buy.

Explore Other E-Book Sources

The iPad is capable of using other e-reader apps to read book content from other bookstores. To do so, first download another e-reader application, such as the Kindle from Amazon, from the App Store. (See Chapter 9 for details on how to download apps.) You can also download a non-vendor-specific app, such as Bluefire Reader, that handles ePub and PDF format, as well as the format that most public libraries use. Then use the app's features to search for, purchase, and download content.

The Kindle e-reader application is shown in **Figure 10-4.** After downloading the free app from the App Store, you just open the app and enter the email address and password associated with your Amazon account. Any content you've already bought from Amazon is archived online (display All Books in your library to see these titles) and can be downloaded to your iPad for you to read any time you like. Use features to enhance your reading experience, such as changing the background to a sepia tone or changing font. Tap the Device tab to see titles stored on the iPad. To delete a book from this reader, press the title with your finger; the Remove from Device button appears.

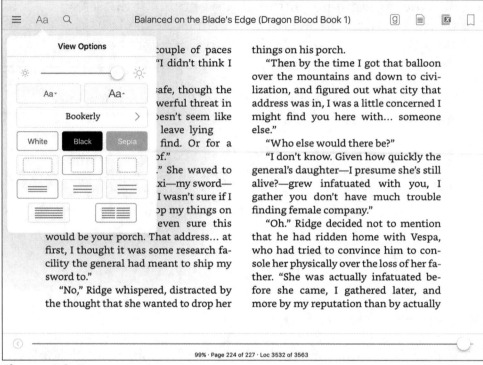

Figure 10-4

 Electronic books are everywhere! You can also get content from a variety of other sources: Project Gutenberg (www.gutenberg.org), Google, publishers such as Baen (www.baen.com), and so on. Download the content on your computer, add it to Books in iTunes, and sync with your iPad or you can register your iPad as a device with services such as Amazon and choose to download a book to that device when you buy it. Many public libraries' systems allow you to "borrow" e-book versions of books and sync them to your iPad. Certain formats may need to be associated with the apps for those formats, such as the Mobi and AZW formats for the Kindle. You can also make settings to iCloud so that books are pushed across your Apple devices, or you can place them in an online storage service such as Dropbox and access them from there.

Buy Books at the iBooks Store

1. If you've set up an account in the iTunes Store, you can use the iBooks app to buy books at the iBooks Store. (See Chapter 3 for more about iTunes.) Open iBooks and, if your bookshelf is displayed, tap Featured at the bottom of the screen and begin exploring. When you find a book you want to buy in the iBooks Store, tap it and then tap the price button (see **Figure 10-5**). The button changes to the Buy Book button (see **Figure 10-6**). (If the book is free, these buttons are labeled Get and Get Book, respectively.)

2. Tap the Buy Book or Get Book button. If you haven't already signed in, the iTunes Password dialog appears.

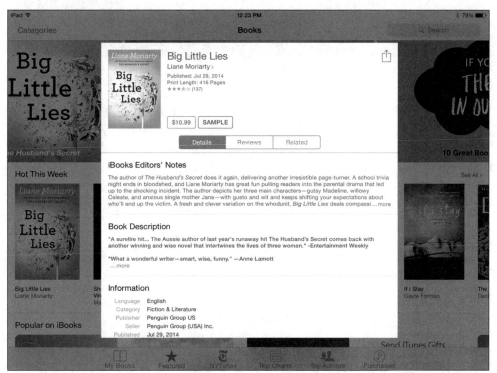

Figure 10-5

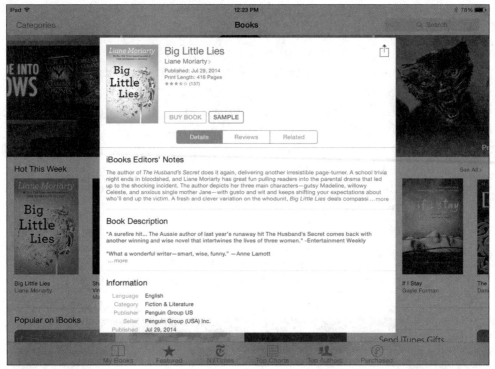

Figure 10-6

If you have signed in, your purchase is accepted immediately. No returns are allowed, so tap carefully!

3. Enter your password, and tap OK. The book appears on your bookshelf, and the cost is charged to whichever credit card you specified when you opened your iTunes account.

You can also sync books you've downloaded to your computer to your iPad from any Apple device through iCloud. Content can also be synced by connecting the USB connector to your computer and using iTunes, or by setting up iCloud and choosing to automatically download books by tapping Settings ➪ App & iTunes Store. See Chapter 3 for more about syncing content.

Navigate a Book

1. Tap iBooks, and if your library (the bookshelf) isn't already displayed, tap the Library button.

2. Tap a book to open it. If it's stored online, it may take a few moments to download. The book opens, as shown in **Figure 10-7.** (If you hold your iPad in portrait orientation, it shows one page; in landscape orientation, it shows two.)

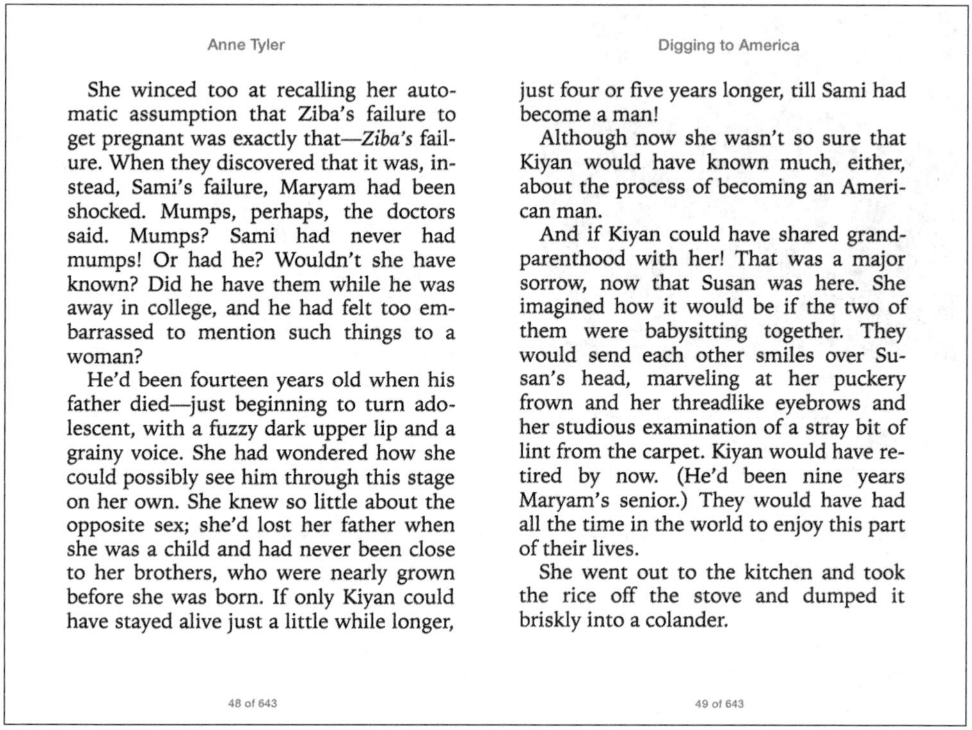

Anne Tyler

She winced too at recalling her automatic assumption that Ziba's failure to get pregnant was exactly that—*Ziba's* failure. When they discovered that it was, instead, Sami's failure, Maryam had been shocked. Mumps, perhaps, the doctors said. Mumps? Sami had never had mumps! Or had he? Wouldn't she have known? Did he have them while he was away in college, and he had felt too embarrassed to mention such things to a woman?

He'd been fourteen years old when his father died—just beginning to turn adolescent, with a fuzzy dark upper lip and a grainy voice. She had wondered how she could possibly see him through this stage on her own. She knew so little about the opposite sex; she'd lost her father when she was a child and had never been close to her brothers, who were nearly grown before she was born. If only Kiyan could have stayed alive just a little while longer,

Digging to America

just four or five years longer, till Sami had become a man!

Although now she wasn't so sure that Kiyan would have known much, either, about the process of becoming an American man.

And if Kiyan could have shared grand-parenthood with her! That was a major sorrow, now that Susan was here. She imagined how it would be if the two of them were babysitting together. They would send each other smiles over Susan's head, marveling at her puckery frown and her threadlike eyebrows and her studious examination of a stray bit of lint from the carpet. Kiyan would have retired by now. (He'd been nine years Maryam's senior.) They would have had all the time in the world to enjoy this part of their lives.

She went out to the kitchen and took the rice off the stove and dumped it briskly into a colander.

48 of 643

49 of 643

Figure 10-7

3. Take any of these actions to navigate the book:

- **To go to the book's table of contents:** Tap the screen to display various tools and then tap the Table of Contents button at the top of the page (it looks like a little bulleted list) and then tap the name of a chapter to go to it (see **Figure 10-8**).

Figure 10-8

- **To move to another page in the book:** Tap and drag the slider at the side of the page up or down.

- **To turn to the next page:** Place your finger anywhere on the right edge of a page and tap or flick to the left.

- **To turn to the preceding page:** Place your finger anywhere on the left edge of a page and tap or flick.

 To return to the Library to view another book at any time, tap the Library button. If the button isn't visible, tap anywhere on the page, and the tools appear.

Adjust Brightness

1. iBooks offers an adjustable brightness setting that you can use to make your book pages more comfortable to read. With a book open, tap the Font button, shown in **Figure 10-9**.

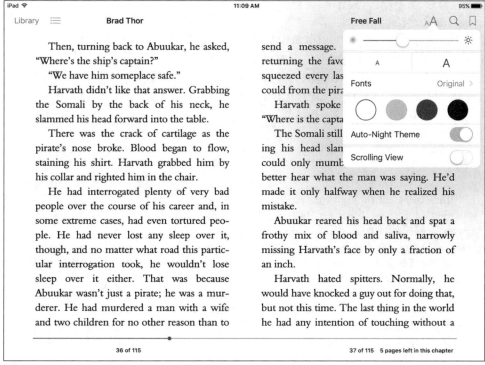

Figure 10-9

2. In the Font dialog that appears at the top (refer to Figure 10-9), tap and drag the Brightness slider to the right to make the screen brighter, or tap and drag the slider to the left to dim the screen.

3. Tap anywhere on the book page to close the dialog.

 Try tapping a Themes circle in the Font dialog to choose a different background color, which is covered in the next task.

Bright-white screens are commonly thought to be hard on the eyes, so setting the brightness halfway relative to its default setting or less is probably a good idea (and saves battery life). Sepia mutes the background to a soft beige that may work better for some people.

Change the Font Size and Type

1. If the type on your screen is a bit small for you to make out, you can change to a larger font size or choose a different font for readability. With a book open, tap the Font button (it sports a small letter *A* and a large *A*, as shown in **Figure 10-10**).

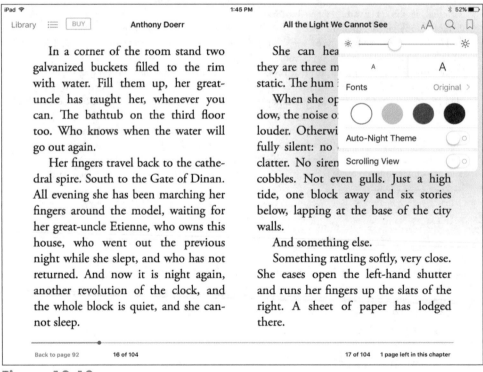

Figure 10-10

2. In the Font dialog that appears (refer to Figure 10-10), tap the button with a small *A* on the left to use smaller text, or tap the button with the large *A* on the right to use larger text.

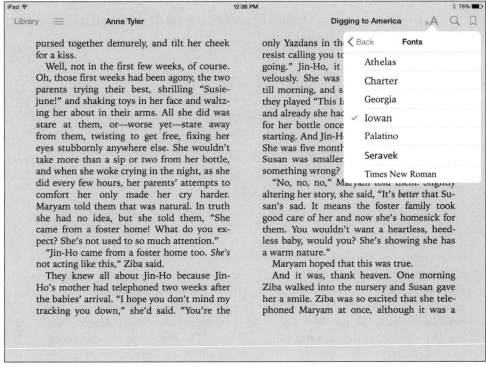

Figure 10-11

3. Tap Fonts. The list of fonts shown in **Figure 10-11** appears.

4. Tap a font name to select it. The font changes on the book page.

5. If you want to add a sepia tint to the pages or to reverse black and white, which can be easier on the eyes, in the Font dialog, tap White, Sepia, or Gray or Black to choose the theme you want to display. Black causes the iPad to detect a dark environment and automatically display the page in Night mode, even if another theme is set.

6. Tap outside the Font dialog to return to your book.

Some fonts appear a bit larger on your screen than others because of their design. If you want the largest font, use Iowan.

 If you're reading a PDF file, you're reading a picture of a document rather than an electronic book, so be aware that you can't modify the page's appearance using the Font dialog.

Search in Your Book

1. You may want to find a certain sentence or reference in your book. To do so, with a book displayed, tap the Search button, shown in **Figure 10-12**. The onscreen keyboard appears.

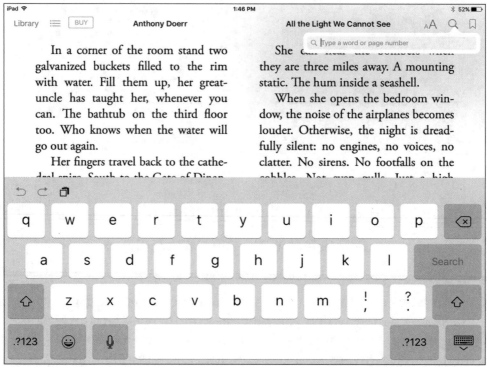

Figure 10-12

2. Type a search term (or tap the Dictation key on the onscreen keyboard and speak the term) and then tap the Search key on the keyboard. iBooks searches for any matching entries.

3. Use your finger to scroll down the entries (see **Figure 10-13**).

4. You can tap either the Search Web or Search Wikipedia button at the bottom of the Search dialog if you want to search for information about the search term online.

 You can also search for other instances of a particular word by pressing your finger on the word and tapping Search on the toolbar that appears. If what you're looking for is a definition of the word, consider tapping Define rather than Search on this toolbar.

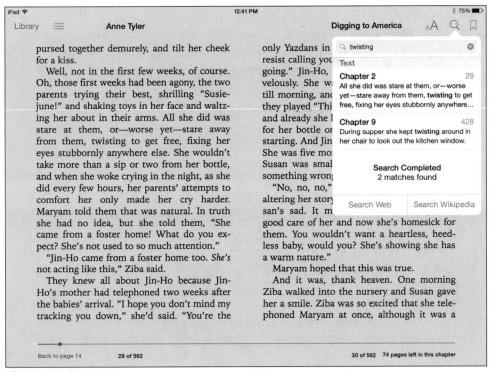

Figure 10-13

Use Bookmarks and Highlights

1. Bookmarks and highlights in your e-books are like favorite sites you save in your web browser: They enable you to revisit a favorite passage or refresh your memory about a character or plot point. To bookmark a page, display the page and tap the Bookmark button in the top-right corner (see **Figure 10-14**). A red ribbon appears in the top-right corner of the page.

iPad 🔋		3:22 PM			⚡ 20% 🔋⚡
Library ☰	**Brad Thor**		**Free Fall**	ₐA 🔍 🔖	

Bookmark button

Figure 10-14

2. To highlight a word or phrase, press a word until the toolbar shown in **Figure 10-15** appears.

3. Tap the Highlight button and then tap the button with 3 colored circles. A colored highlight is placed on the word and the color palette shown in **Figure 10-16** appears.

4. Tap one of these options:

- *The Colors buttons:* Tap any colored circle to change the highlight color.

- *The Remove Highlight button:* Tapping the white circle with an A in it removes the current highlight color, allowing you to apply a different color.

- *The Trash button:* Removes the highlight and hides the Highlight menu.

- *The Note button:* Tap the Note button to add a note to the item.

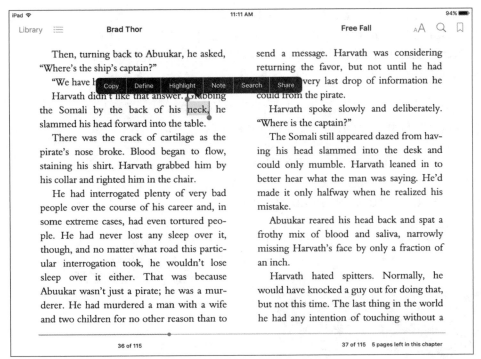

Figure 10-15

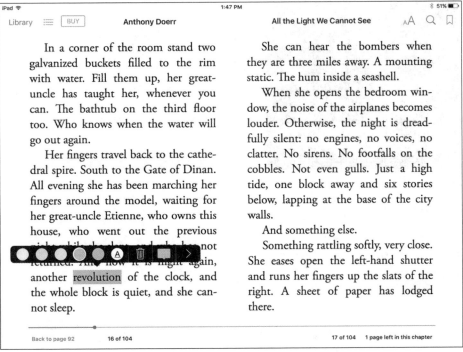

Figure 10-16

5. You can also tap the arrow button at the right end of the toolbar to return to the Copy, Define, Highlight, and Note tools. Tap outside the highlighted text to close the toolbar.

6. To go to a list of bookmarks and notes, tap the Table of Contents button on a book page.

7. In the table of contents, tap the Bookmarks or Notes tab. As shown in **Figure 10-17,** all bookmarks or notes are displayed on their respective tabs.

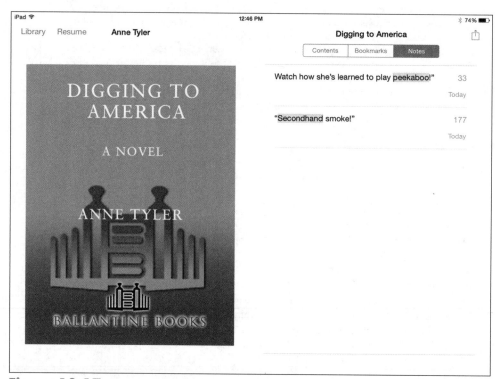

Figure 10-17

8. Tap a bookmark or note in one of these lists to go to that location in the book.

The iPad automatically bookmarks the place where you left off reading in a book so you don't have to do it manually. Because that information is stored in the iTunes Store, you can even pick up where you left off on your iPhone, Mac, iPod touch, or another iPad.

Check Words in the Dictionary

1. As you read a book, you may come across unfamiliar words. Don't skip them; take the opportunity to learn new words! With a book open, press a word and hold it until the toolbar shown in **Figure 10-18** appears.

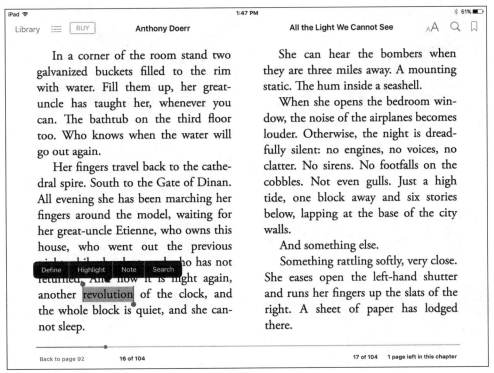

Figure 10-18

2. Tap the Define button. A definition pop-up menu appears, as shown in **Figure 10-19**.

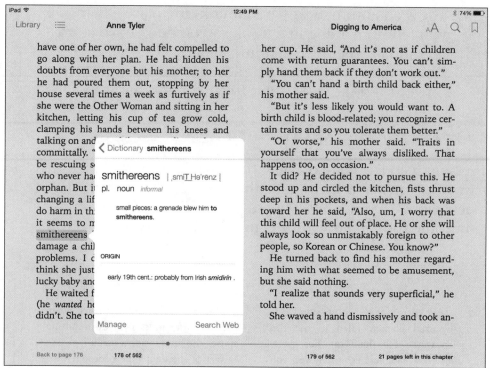

Figure 10-19

3. Tap the definition, and scroll down, if necessary, to view more.

4. When you finish reviewing the definition, tap anywhere on the page, and the definition disappears.

 If a definition doesn't appear, you can tap the Manage button to choose the dictionary from which your definitions will come.

Organize Your Library

 1. iBooks lets you create collections of books to help you organize them by your own logic, such as Tear Jerkers, Work-Related, and Great Recipes. You can place a book in only one collection, however. To create a collection from the Library bookshelf, tap Select.

2. On the screen that appears, tap a book and then tap Move. In the Collections dialog shown in **Figure 10-20**, tap New Collection. On the blank line that appears, type a name.

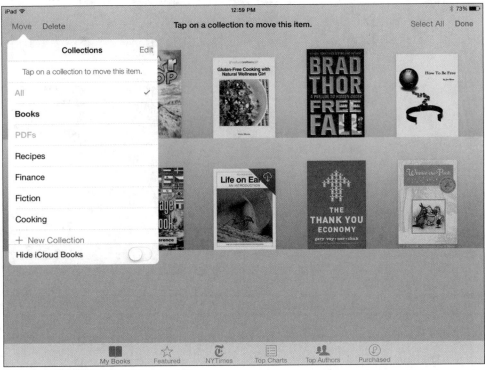

Figure 10-20

3. Tap Done, which closes the dialog and returns you to your library. To add a book to a collection from the library, tap Select.

4. Tap a book and then tap the Move button that appears in the top of the screen (see **Figure 10-21**). In the dialog that appears, tap the collection to which you'd like to move the book and the book appears on the bookshelf in that collection. To change which collection you're viewing, tap the button with the current collection's name (or tap All Books if you're not displaying a category) to display other collections, and tap the one you want.

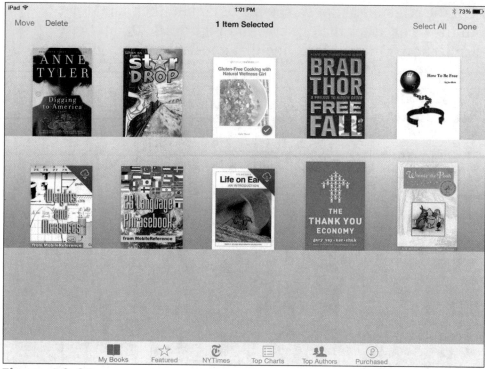

Figure 10-21

5. To delete a book from a collection, tap the button in the top middle of the Library to display a list of collections. Tap the collection and it displays; tap Select, tap the book, and then tap Delete.

 Tap the My Books tab at the bottom to remove categories and list the most recently downloaded book first.

Delete Books in Collections

1. To delete a book, tap the List view button in the top-left corner. Swipe to the left on a title in the list, and then tap Delete.

2. To delete a collection, tap Select and then Select All and then tap Move. Swipe to the left on any collection, and then tap Delete to get rid of it (see **Figure 10-22**).

A message appears, asking you to tap Remove (to remove the contents of the collection from your iPad) or Don't Remove.

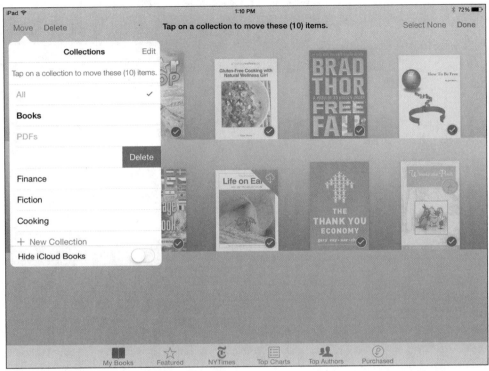

Figure 10-22

 Note that if you choose Remove, all titles within a deleted collection are returned to their original collections in your library, the default one being Books.

Playing Music on the iPad

*i*Pad includes an app called Music that allows you to take advantage of the iPad's amazing little sound system to play your favorite music.

In this chapter, you get acquainted with the Music app and its features that allow you to sort and find music and control playback. You also get an overview of AirPlay, which you can use to access and play your music over a home network or any connected device. Finally, I introduce you to iTunes Radio for your listening pleasure.

View the Library Contents

1. Tap the Music app icon, located on the Dock on the Home screen. The Music library appears. **Figure 11-1** shows the library in Albums view.

2. Tap the Categories drop-down list at the top of the library (refer to Figure 11-1) to view your music according to criteria such as Songs or Genres.

Categories drop-down list

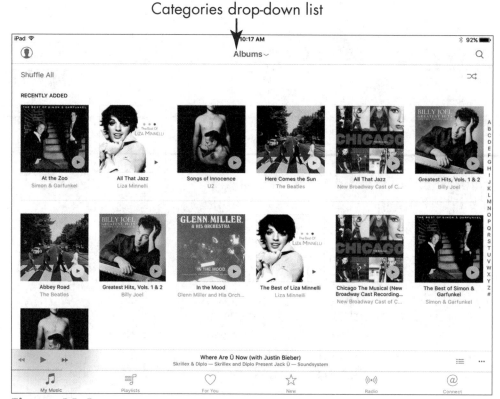

Figure 11-1

You can tap the New button at the bottom of the page to go to the iTunes Store to buy additional music.

3. Tap a category (see **Figure 11-2**) to view music by album, genre, or computer.

iTunes has several free items you can download and use to play around with the features in Music. You can also sync content stored on your computer or other Apple devices to your iPad and play that content using the Music app. (See Chapter 3 for more about syncing and Chapter 8 for more about getting content from iTunes.)

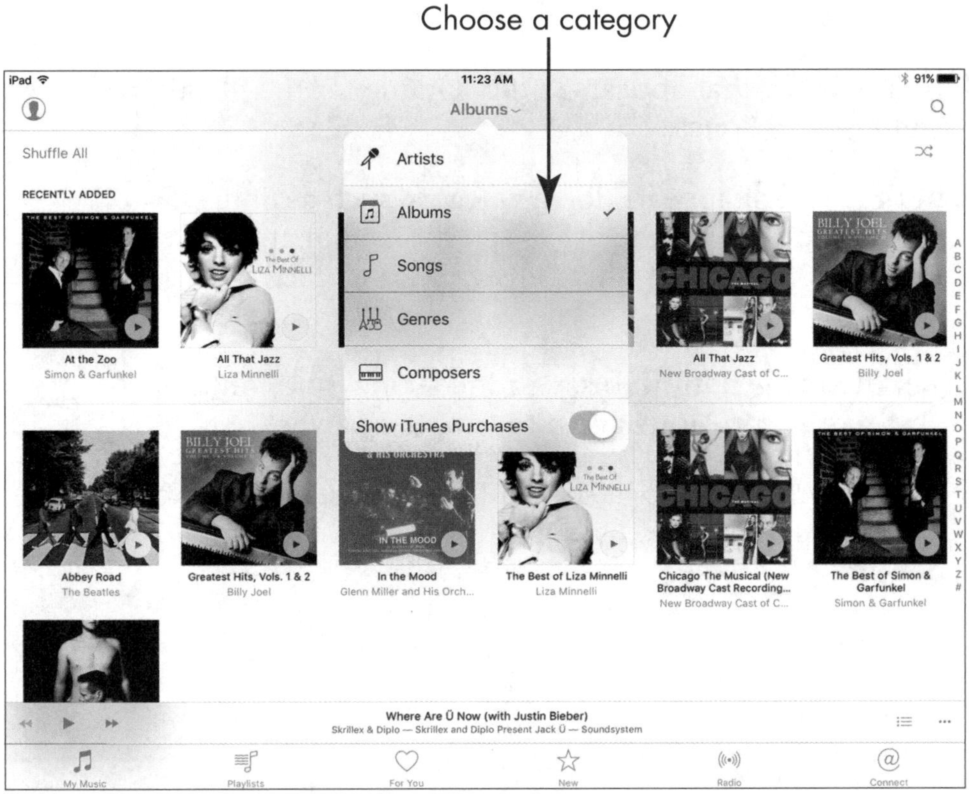

Choose a category

Figure 11-2

 Apple offers a service called iTunes Match (www.apple.com/itunes/itunes-match). You pay $24.99 per year for the capability to match the music you've bought from other providers or recorded yourself (and stored on your computer) with what's in the iTunes catalog. If iTunes Match finds a match (and it usually does), that content is added to your iTunes library (up to 25,000 tracks). Then, using iCloud, you can sync the content among all your Apple devices.

Create Playlists

1. You can create your own playlists to put tracks from various sources in collections of your choosing. In the Music app, tap the Playlists button at the bottom of the screen.

2. Tap New.

3. In the dialog that appears, enter a name for the playlist and tap Add Songs.

4. In the list that appears, tap a category such as Songs or Artists and then, in the list of selections that appears (see **Figure 11-3**), tap the plus (+) sign next to each item you want to include.

5. Tap the Done button to save added songs and, on the next screen, tap Done again to save the playlist.

6. Your playlist appears in the All Playlists list, and you can play it by tapping the list's name and then the Play button.

Figure 11-3

Search for Audio

1. You can search for an item in your Music library by using the Search feature. With Music open, tap the Search button (see **Figure 11-4**) to open the onscreen keyboard.

Tap the Search button

Figure 11-4

2. Enter a search term in the Search field, or tap the Dictation key on the onscreen keyboard (see **Figure 11-5**) and speak the search term. Then tap the Search button on the onscreen keyboard. Results display, narrowing as you type.

3. Tap an item to play it.

 You can enter (or speak) an artist's name, an author's or a composer's name, or a word from the item's title in the Search field to find what you're looking for.

Enter a search term

Figure 11-5

Play Music

1. Locate the song you want to play, using the methods described in previous tasks in this chapter.

2. Tap the item, such as an album that contains the song you want to hear. *Note:* If you're displaying the Songs tab, you don't have to tap an album to open a song; you need only tap a song to play it. If you're using any other category, you have to tap items such as albums or multiple songs from one artist to find the song you want to hear.

3. Tap the item you want to play in the list that appears and then tap the Play button (see **Figure 11-6**). If the item is stored on iCloud, you may have to tap the iCloud symbol next to it to download it. The item begins to play. Tap the bar with the playback controls at the bottom of the screen to display the album cover full-screen (see **Figure 11-7**).

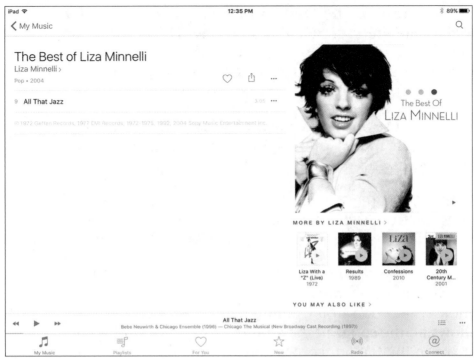

Figure 11-6

Figure 11-7

4. Use the Previous and Next buttons shown in Figure 11-7 to navigate the audio file that's playing. The Previous button takes you back to the beginning of the item that's playing or the previous track if you're at the beginning; the Next button takes you to the next item.

5. Tap the Pause button to pause playback. Note that you can also use music controls for music that's playing from the lock screen.

6. Tap and drag the line just below the album cover that indicates the current playback location on the Progress bar to the left or right to "scrub" to another location in the song.

7. If you don't like what's playing, here's how to find another selection in the album: From the screen that shows all the songs in the album, tap the Back to Library arrow in the top-left corner to return to Library view, or tap the Up Next button near the bottom-right corner to show other songs in this album (it looks like a bulleted list). Tap another song to play it.

You can use Siri to play music hands-free. Just press and hold the Home button, and when Siri appears, say something like "Play 'Take the A Train'" or "Play the *White Album.*"

The Home Sharing feature of iTunes allows you to share music among devices that have Home Sharing turned on. To use the feature, each device has to have the same Apple ID on your network. After you set up the feature via iTunes, you can retrieve music and videos from your iTunes shared library to any of the devices. For more about Home Sharing, visit www.apple.com/support/homesharing.

Using Family Sharing, up to six members of your family can share purchased content even if they don't share the same iTunes account. You can set up Family Sharing under Settings ⇨ iCloud ⇨ Family. See Chapter 8 for more about Family Sharing.

Shuffle Music

1. If you want to play a random selection of the music that you've purchased or synced to your iPad, you can use the Shuffle feature. With Music open, tap the Categories button at the top of the screen, tap Albums, and then tap an album. (This also works with Playlists.)

2. With a song in an album playing, tap the Shuffle button (see **Figure 11-8**). Your content plays in random order.

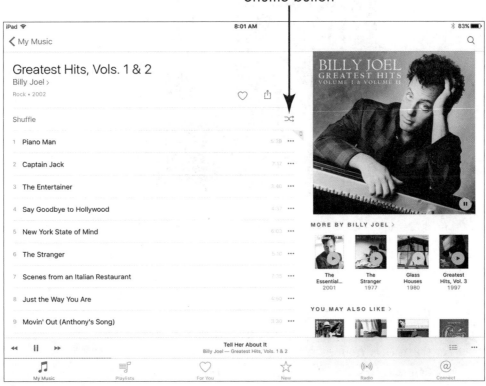

Figure 11-8

Adjust the Volume

1. Music offers its own volume control that you can adjust during playback. This volume is set relative to the system volume you control using iPad's Settings. If you set it to 50%, it plays at 50 percent of the system's volume setting. With Music open, tap a piece of music to play it.

2. In the controls that appear onscreen (see **Figure 11-9**), press and drag the button on the Volume slider to the right for more volume or to the left for less volume.

Figure 11-9

 If the volume is set high, but you're still having trouble hearing, consider getting a headset. It cuts out extraneous noises and may improve the sound quality of what you're listening to, as well as adding stereo to the iPad's mono speaker. I recommend that you use a 3.5mm stereo headphone; insert its plug into the headphone jack at the top of your iPad.

Use AirPlay

The AirPlay streaming technology is built into the iPhone, iPod touch, and iPad, as well as into the iTunes app on Macs and PCs. *Streaming* technology allows you to send media files from one device to play on another. You can send, say, a movie you've purchased on your iPad or a slide show of your photos to be played on your TV — and control the TV playback from your iPad. You can also send music to play over speakers.

You can take advantage of AirPlay in a few ways: Purchase Apple TV and stream video, photos, and music to the TV, or purchase AirPort Express and attach your speakers to it to play music. Finally, if you buy AirPort-enabled wireless speakers, you can stream audio directly to them.

Because this combination of equipment varies, my advice — if you're interested in using AirPlay — is to visit your nearest Apple Store or certified Apple Reseller and find out which hardware combination will work best for you.

 iOS 9 supports peer-to-peer AirPlay support, which means that if you can make a direct connection to another device, you can share content such as music and photos without being on the same network.

 If you get a bit antsy watching a long movie, one of the beauties of AirPlay is that you can still use your iPad to check email, browse photos or the Internet, or check your calendar while the media file is playing on the other device.

Play Music with iTunes Radio

1. You can access iTunes Radio with any Apple device that has iOS 7 or later, or a computer running iTunes 11 or later. Begin by tapping the Music icon on the Home screen.

2. Tap the Radio button at the bottom of the screen that appears.

3. Tap a Featured Station (see **Figure 11-10**). A featured radio station begins to play.

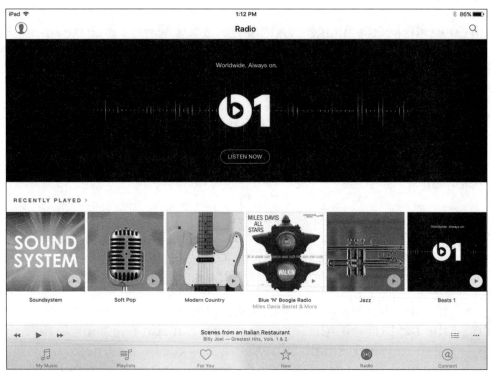

Figure 11-10

4. Use the tools at the bottom of the screen, shown in **Figure 11-11,** to control playback.

 The more you use iTunes Radio, the better it gets at building stations that fit your taste.

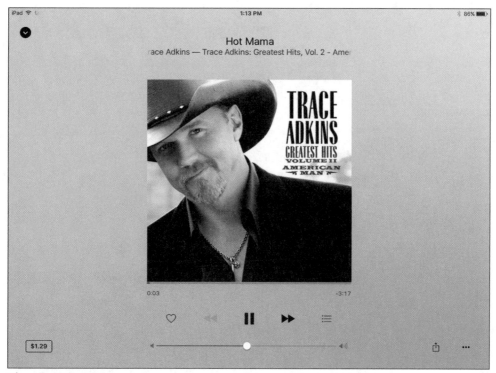

Figure 11-11

Explore Categories of Radio Stations

1. You can find stations by category. To do so, first tap the Music button on the Dock.

2. Tap Radio.

3. On the iTunes Radio home page, scroll down to view stations organized by category and tap a station (see **Figure 11-12**). The station begins to play.

 Shazam is a music recognition app that is integrated into Siri. Essentially, Siri can now "recognize" and identify music playing around you. Find out more about this feature in Chapter 19.

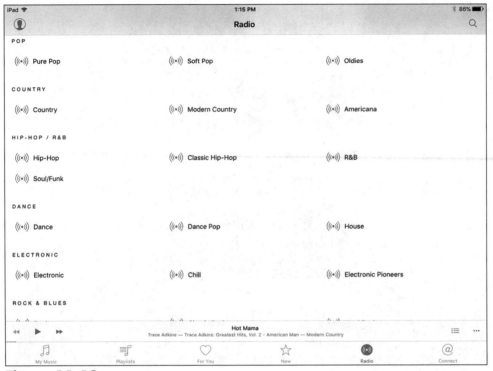

Figure 11-12

Playing with Photos

Chapter

12

With its gorgeous screen, the iPad is a natural for taking and viewing photos. It supports most common photo formats, such as JPEG, TIFF, and PNG. You can shoot your photos by using the iPad's built-in cameras with built-in square or panorama modes, and you can edit your images using smart adjustment filters. You can also sync photos from your computer, iPhone, or digital camera. You can save images you find online or receive by email or Messages to your iPad. You can then share photos with groups of people using Photo Stream and your iCloud Photo Library, which makes storing and sharing easier.

The rear-facing camera is a built-in 8 megapixel iSight camera on all three iPad models. The camera comes with an illumination sensor that adjusts for whatever lighting is available. Face detection balances focus across as many as ten faces in your pictures. The video camera option offers 1080p high-definition (HD) video recording with video stabilization that makes up for some shaking as you hold the device to take videos. Newer video recording features you'll want to check out are time-lapse and Slo-mo videos.

When you have photos to play with, the Photos app lets you organize photos and view photos in albums, individually, or in a slideshow. You can also view photos by the years they were taken, with images divided into collections based on where or when you took them. You can also AirDrop, email, message, or post photos to Facebook; tweet photos to friends; print photos; or use your expensive gadget as an electronic picture frame. Finally, you can create time-lapse videos with the Camera app, allowing you to record a sequence in time, such as a flower opening up as the sun warms it. You can read about all these features in this chapter.

Take Pictures with the iPad Cameras

1. The cameras in the iPad are just begging to be used. Tap the Camera app on the Home screen to open it.

2. The orange highlighted word below the Capture button (see **Figure 12-1**) is the active setting. Slide it to Photo if it's not already set there.

Figure 12-1

3. You can set the Square option by sliding down. This setting lets you create square images like those you see on the popular Instagram site. Sliding one setting further down sets the camera to take a panoramic view; you begin to capture an image, move the camera across the view, and then tap Done to capture a pano image.

4. With the active setting at Photo, move the camera around until you find a pleasing image.

5. You can do a couple of things at this point to help you take your photo:

- Tap the area of the grid where you want the camera to autofocus.

- If you want a time delay before the camera snaps the picture, tap the Time Delay button near the top right of the screen and then tap 3s or 10s for a 3- or 10-second delay.

- Pinch the screen to display a zoom control and then drag the circle in the zoom bar to the right or left to zoom in or out on the image.

6. Press the Capture button on the right-center side of the screen and release it when you have the image in view. You've just taken a picture (refer to Figure 12-1), and that picture has been stored in the Photos app's gallery automatically.

 You can also use the up switch on the volume buttons on the right side of your iPad to capture a picture or start or stop video camera recording.

7. Tap the icon in the top-right corner to switch between the front camera and rear camera. Now you can take selfies (pictures of yourself, as the camera is now facing you); so go ahead and press the Capture button to take another picture.

8. To view the last photo taken, tap the thumbnail of the latest image in the bottom-right corner of the screen. The Photos app opens and displays the photo (see **Figure 12-2**).

Figure 12-2

9. Tap the Done button to return to the Camera app.

10. Press the Home button to close the Camera app and return to the Home screen.

 If you want to capture a series of photos in rapid succession, which can help you get the right shot, especially when your subject is in motion, use the Burst feature in your iPad (this feature wasn't available on iPad mini 2 but is with iPad mini 4). Simply press and hold the Capture button while aiming at your subject, and iPad continuously snaps photos. This feature is called Burst mode.

You can use the iCloud Photo Library feature to automatically sync your photos with your iCloud account and share them among your various Apple devices. Turn on iCloud Photo Library by tapping Settings on the Home screen; then tap Photos & Camera and tap to turn the iCloud Photo Library on.

Import Photos from a Digital Camera

1. Your computer isn't the only photo source available to you. You can also import photos from a digital camera if you buy the iPad Camera Connection Kit from Apple. The kit contains two adapters (see **Figure 12-3**): a USB Camera Connector to import photos from a digital camera or an iPhone/iPod touch, and an SD Card Reader to import image files from an SD card.

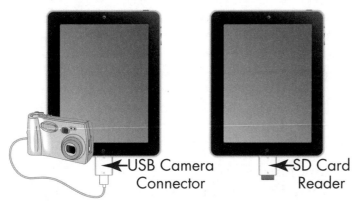

Figure 12-3

2. Insert the USB Camera Connector into the Lightning Connector slot of your iPad.

3. Connect the USB end of the cord that came with your digital camera into the USB Camera Connector.

4. Connect the other end of the cord that came with your iPad into that device.

5. Wake your iPad. The Photos app opens and displays the photos on the digital camera.

6. Tap Import All on your iPad or — if you want to import only selected photos — tap those photos and then tap Import. A prompt asks if you want to delete or keep the images on the media. Make your choice at the prompt and the photos are saved to the Last Import album.

7. Disconnect the cord and the adapter. You're done!

 You can also import photos stored on a *secure digital (SD)* memory card that you purchase, often used by digital cameras as a storage medium. Simply put the iPad to sleep, insert the SD Card Reader into the iPad, insert the SD card containing the photos, and then follow Steps 5 through 7 in the preceding list.

 Remember that with AirDrop on a recent iPad model, you can quickly send photos directly from your iPad to your recent model iPhone, another iPad, or a Mac as long as the devices are within about 12 feet of each other.

Save Photos from the Web

1. The web offers a wealth of images you can download to your Photo Library. Open Safari, and navigate to the web page containing the image you want.

2. Press and hold the image. A menu appears, as shown in **Figure 12-4.**

3. Tap Save Image. The image is saved to your Recently Added album in the Photos app.

 For more about how to use Safari to navigate to or search for web content, see Chapter 5.

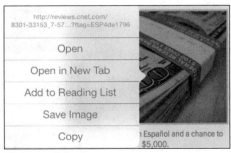

Figure 12-4

 Many sites protect their photos from being copied by applying an invisible overlay. This blank overlay image ensures that you don't actually get the image you're tapping. Even if a site doesn't take these precautions, be sure that you don't save images from the web and use them in ways that violate the rights of the person or entity that owns them.

View an Album

1. The Photos app organizes your pictures into albums, using such criteria as the folder on your computer from which you synced the photos or photos captured with the iPad's camera. You may also have albums for images you synced from devices such as your iPhone or digital camera. To view your albums, start by tapping the Photos app icon on the Home screen.

2. Tap the Albums button to display your albums, as shown in **Figure 12-5**.

3. Tap an album. The photos in it are displayed.

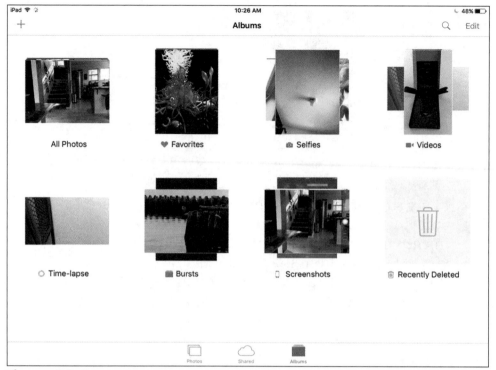

Figure 12-5

View Individual Photos

1. Tap the Photos app icon on the Home screen. The Photos app opens.

2. Tap the Photos button at the bottom of the screen. Your photos are displayed by criteria, such as a time taken or location (see **Figure 12-6**).

3. To view a photo, from the Photos view, tap the photo to view it (see **Figure 12-7**). Place your fingers on the photo and then spread your fingers apart. The picture expands.

4. Flick your finger to the left or right to scroll through the album and look at the individual photos in it.

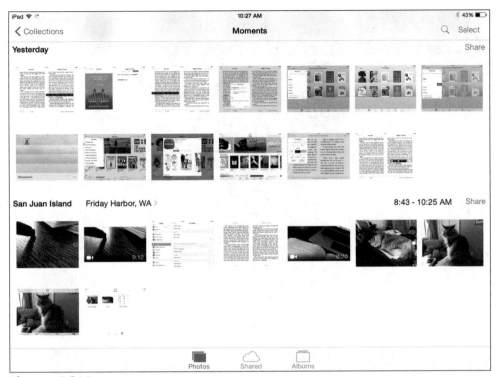

Figure 12-6

5. To reduce the individual photo and return to the multi-picture view, place two fingers on the photo and then pinch them together. You can also tap the arrow button in the top-left corner (which may display different words depending on where you are in a collection of photos) to view the next-highest level of your photo collection.

 A new feature called Live Photos lets you take photos on an iPhone and the 1.5 second of action on either side of the moment of capture is recorded. When you tap one of these photos in the Photos app on your iPad, it plays back like a very short video.

 You can place a photo from the Photos app on a person's information page in the Contacts app. For more about how to do it, see Chapter 18.

Figure 12-7

Edit Photos

1. The Photos app also lets you edit photos, and with iOS 8, several new editing tools appeared for you to work with, including smart adjustment filters and smart composition tools. Tap the Photos app on the Home screen to open it.

2. Using methods previously described in this chapter, locate and display a photo you want to edit.

3. Tap the Edit button. The Edit Photo screen shown in **Figure 12-8** appears.

Figure 12-8

4. At this point, you can take a few possible actions:

- *Enhance:* Tap Enhance to turn it on or off. Enhance improves the overall "crispness" of the figure with one tap.

- *Crop:* To crop the photo to a portion of its original area, tap the Crop button. You can then tap any corner of the image and drag inward or outward to remove areas of the photo. Tap Crop and then Save to apply your changes.

- *Filters:* Apply any of nine filters such as Fade, Mono, or Noir to change the feel of your image. These effects adjust the brightness of your image or apply a black-and-white tone to your color photos. Tap the Filters button in the middle of the tools at the bottom of the screen and scroll to view available filters. Tap one and then tap Apply to apply the effect to your image.

- *Adjustments:* Tap Light, Color, or B&W to access a slew of tools that you can use to tweak contrast, color intensity, shadows, and more.

5. If you're pleased with your edits, tap the Done button, and the edited photo is saved.

 Each of the editing features has a Cancel, an Undo, and a Revert to Original button. If you don't like the changes you made, tap these buttons to stop making changes or undo the changes you've already made.

Organize Photos

1. If you want to create your own album, display an existing album.

2. Tap the Select button in the top-right corner and then tap individual photos to select them. Small check marks appear on the selected photos (see **Figure 12-9**).

3. Tap the Add To button; then tap Add to Album (which appears only if you've previously created albums) or New Album.

4. Tap an existing album or enter a name for a new album (depending on your previous selection) and tap Save. When you create a new album, it appears in the Album screen with the other albums.

 You can also tap the Share or Delete button after you select photos in Step 2 of this task. Doing this allows you to share or delete multiple photos at the same time.

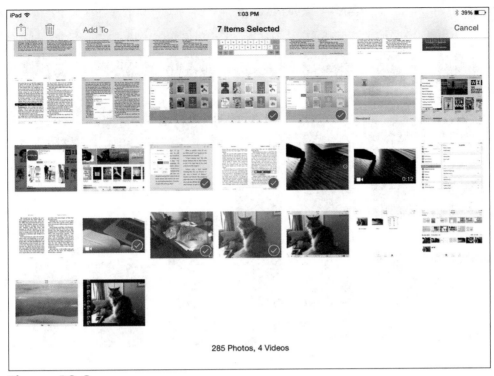

Figure 12-9

View Photos by Year and Location

1. You can view your photos in logical categories such as Years and Moments. These so-called smart groupings let you, for example, view all photos taken by date or by a location where they were taken. Tap Photos on the Home screen to open the Photos app.

2. Tap Photos at the bottom of the screen. The display of photos by date appears (see **Figure 12-10**).

3. Tap the Collections button in the top-left corner, and you see collections of photos arranged by date range or location (see **Figure 12-11**).

Figure 12-10

4. Tap Years in the top-left corner and you see all your photos grouped by year taken.

> To go back to larger groupings, such as from a moment in a collection to the larger collection to the entire past year, just keep tapping the Back button in the top-left corner of the screen (which will be named after the next collection up in the hierarchy, such as Collections or Years).

> With all these photos available to you, you'll need to be able to search a library for the one you want. From the Photos tab, tap the Search button at the top of the screen. A list of so-called "smart" suggestions appears. Tap on one of these suggestions, or enter the date or time of the photo, a location, or an album name such as "Vacation" in the Search field to locate the photo.

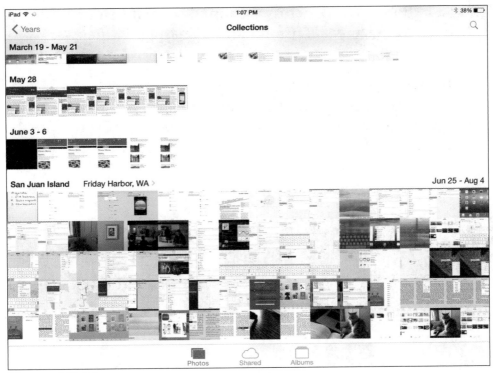

Figure 12-11

Share Photos with Mail, Twitter, and Facebook

1. You can easily share photos stored on your iPad by sending them as email attachments, posting them to Facebook, sharing them via iCloud Photo Sharing, via Flickr, or by tweeting them via Twitter. You have to go to Facebook or Twitter in a web browser and set up an account before you can use this feature. Next, tap the Photos app icon on the Home screen.

2. Tap the Photos or Albums button and locate the photo you want to share.

3. Tap the photo to select it and then tap the Share icon. (It looks like a box with an arrow jumping out of it.) The menu shown in **Figure 12-12** appears.

4. Tap additional photos across the top to share if you wish, then tap Message, Mail, iCloud Photo Sharing, Twitter, Facebook, or Flickr.

5. In the message form that appears, make any modifications that apply in the To, Cc/Bcc, or Subject field; then type a message for email or enter your Facebook post or tweet text.

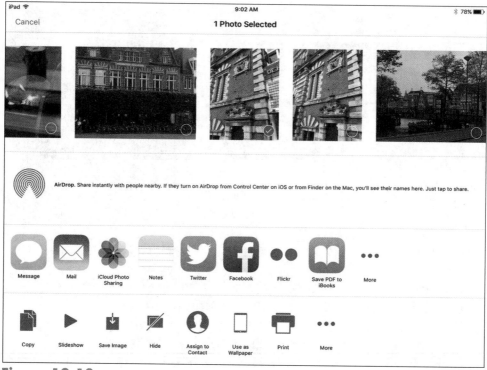

Figure 12-12

6. Tap the Send or Post button, depending on which sharing method you chose. The message and photo are sent or posted.

 Using the options shown in Figure 12-12, you can also save a photo to a Notes document. Just tap Notes in that pop-up menu, add note text, and then choose New Note or an existing note to add the photo to.

Share Photos with AirDrop

1. AirDrop provides a way to share content such as photos with others who are nearby and who have AirDrop-enabled devices. Follow the steps in the previous task to locate a photo you want to share, and then tap the Share button.

2. If an AirDrop-enabled device is in your immediate vicinity (say, within 12 or so feet), you see the device listed at the top of the Share dialog. Tap the device name, and your photo is shared with the other device. The recipient has the option of accepting or declining the share.

 Note that the other iOS device has to have AirDrop enabled (if an iPhone, it has to be an iPhone 5 or later) and has to be an Apple device running iOS 7 or later. To enable a device, open Control Center by swiping up from the bottom of any screen and then tap the AirDrop button in the bottom center of the screen to turn the feature on. Tap the AirDrop button at the bottom of the screen and choose Contacts Only or Everyone from the menu that appears to specify with whom you can use AirDrop.

See Chapter 2 for more about using Control Center. On a recent-model Mac running OS X Yosemite or later, open a Finder window and click AirDrop from the Sidebar. Set the sharing permissions at the bottom of the screen.

Share Photos with iCloud Photo Sharing

1. iCloud Photo Sharing allows you to share photo streams with others when you're connected to a Wi-Fi network. You can also subscribe to another person's photo stream if she shares it with you. To set up Photo Stream, tap Settings ⇨ Photos & Camera; then tap the On/Off button for iCloud Photo Sharing to share among your devices, and tap My Photo Streaming to share with others who don't have iCloud accounts.

2. To share photos with somebody else who has an iCloud account, return to the Home screen, and tap Photos.

3. Tap the Share button and then tap to select the photos you want to share (see Figure 12-12). Tap iCloud Photo Sharing. Enter a Shared Album name (see **Figure 12-13**), and then tap Next.

4. Enter a comment and then tap Post. The selected photos are posted to your iCloud Photo Library.

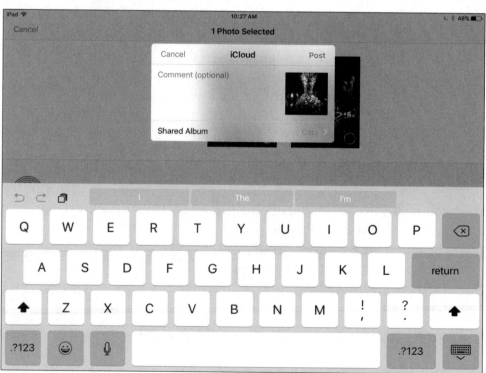

Figure 12-13

Print Photos

1. If you have a wireless printer that's compatible with Apple AirPrint technology or you use a device such as Lantronix xPrintServer plugged into your network, you can print photos from your iPad. With Photos open, locate the photo you want to print, and tap it to maximize it.

2. Tap the Share button and then tap Print (see **Figure 12-14**).

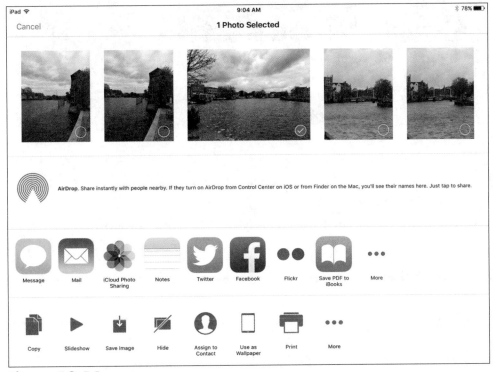

Figure 12-14

3. In the Printer Options dialog that appears (see **Figure 12-15**), tap Select Printer. The iPad searches for any compatible printers on your local network. Tap to select the one you want to use.

Figure 12-15

4. Tap the plus or minus symbol in the Copy field to set the number of copies to print. If your printer supports double-sided or color printing, you'll see that option here.

5. Tap the Print button. Your photo goes on its way to the printer.

Run a Slideshow

1. You can run a slideshow of your images in Photos and even play music and choose transition effects for the show. Tap the Photos app on the Home screen.

2. Tap the Photos button (refer to Figure 12-5) and then tap photo in a collection.

3. Tap the Share button, and then tap Slideshow to begin the slideshow. To make changes, tap to pause the show and then click the Options button in the bottom-right corner to see the Slideshow Options dialog, shown in **Figure 12-16.**

Figure 12-16

4. If you don't want to play music along with the slideshow, tap the Music and then tap None.

5. To choose music to play along with the slideshow, tap Music, and in the list that appears, tap any selection in your Music library.

6. In the Slideshow Options dialog, tap Themes and then tap the transition effect you want to use for your slideshow.

7. Tap Music and select the music you want to play or choose None if you don't want music.

8. Adjust the volume slider if you wish.

9. Tap outside the Options dialog to close it.

10. To stop the show, tap Done.

 To run a slideshow that includes only the photos contained in a particular album, tap the Albums button instead of the Photos button in Step 2, tap an album to open it, and then tap the Slideshow button in the top-right corner to run a slideshow.

Delete Photos

1. You may find that it's time to get rid of some of those old photos of the family reunion or the last community-center project. If the photos weren't transferred from your computer but were downloaded or captured as screen shots on the iPad, you can delete them. Tap the Photos app's icon on the Home screen.

2. Tap the Albums or Photos button; then, if you've opened Albums, tap an album to open it.

3. Tap the Trash icon.

4. Tap Delete Photo (see **Figure 12-17**).

5. Tap the Delete Photo/Selected Photos button that appears to finish the deletion.

 To delete more than one photo, with a collection or album displayed, tap Select; then tap all the photos you want to delete before tapping the Trash icon.

Figure 12-17

Shoot Videos

Shooting a video is as simple as setting the selection slider near the bottom right of the Camera app's screen to Video, pressing the red Record button, scanning around with your iPad, and then pressing the Record button again.

1. Capturing photos with the Time Lapse feature allows you to create a time-lapse photo show. iPhone captures photos at select intervals, making the capture of a dynamic scene such as a sunset possible. Tap Camera on the Home screen.

2. Swipe the listing at the bottom right of the screen until Time Lapse is active (see **Figure 12-18**).

3. Tap the Capture button. Leave the camera recording as long as you like, and then tap the End button. Your new time-lapse image appears in the bottom-right corner. Tap the image and then tap Play.

Time Lapse setting

Figure 12-18

4. Finally, try the Slo-mo video setting. Move the setting in the bottom right to Slo-mo, and then press the Record button. Your video is recorded in slow motion, allowing you to view every detail of faster activities such as a car race or an archery tournament during playback.

Getting the Most Out of Video Features

*U*sing the Videos app, you can watch downloaded movies or TV shows, as well as media you've synced from iCloud or your Mac or PC.

In addition, all iPads (except the original iPad) sport two video cameras you can use to capture your own videos. You can take advantage of the rear-facing iSight camera, which can record video in 1080p high definition (HD), with video stabilization to prevent those wobbly video moments. You can also benefit from the Retina display on fourth-generation and later iPads to watch videos with super-high resolution, which simply means that those videos will look very, very good.

By downloading the iMovie app (a more limited version of the longtime mainstay on Mac computers), you add the capability to edit those videos.

In this chapter, I explain all about shooting and watching video content from a variety of sources. For practice, you may want to refer to Chapter 8 first to purchase or download one of many available free TV shows or movies, and see Chapter 9 for help with downloading the iMovie app.

Capture Your Own Videos with the Built-in Cameras

1. To capture a video, tap the Camera app on the Home screen. The Camera app opens.

 On all iPads except the original iPad, two video cameras can capture video from either the front or back of the device and make it possible for you to edit the videos with third-party video apps or share them with others. (See more about this topic in the next task.)

2. Tap the row of words below the Capture button on the right side and slide up to switch from the still camera to the video camera (see **Figure 13-1**).

3. If you want to switch between the front and back cameras, tap the icon near the top-right corner of the screen (refer to Figure 13-1).

4. Tap the red Record button shown in Figure 13-1 to begin recording the video. (This button turns into a red square when the camera is recording, as shown in **Figure 13-2**).

5. When you're finished, tap the Record button again. Your new video is listed in the bottom-left corner of the screen.

6. Tap the video to play it, share it, or delete it. In the future, you can find and play the video in your Camera Roll when you open the Photos app.

Figure 13-1

Figure 13-2

Before you start recording, remember that when you're holding the iPad in portrait orientation, the camera lens is in the top-right corner of the back. You could easily put your fingers directly over the lens!

 At the announcement of the latest version of iPad Air and iPad mini, Apple called attention to two great apps that help you edit your videos. Replay (a free app) and Pixelmator are both designed to take full advantage of the new A9 processor chip and offer a stunning array of video editing features. Check them out in the App Store.

Play Movies, Podcasts, or TV Shows with Videos

1. When you first open the Videos app by tapping its button on the Home screen, you may see a relatively blank screen with a note that reads you don't have any videos on your iPad and a link to the iTunes Store. After you've purchased TV shows and movies or rented movies from the iTunes Store (see Chapter 8 to find out how) or other sources, you'll see tabs listing the different kinds of content you own. Tap the Videos app icon on the Home screen to open the application.

2. On a screen like the one shown in **Figure 13-3,** tap the appropriate category at the top of the screen (TV Shows or Movies, depending on the content you've downloaded).

Figure 13-3

3. Tap an item to open it. A description appears, as shown in **Figure 13-4**. Details about TV Shows include Episodes, Details, and Related tabs; Movies contain Details, Chapters, and Related tabs.

Figure 13-4

4. For a TV show, tap the Episodes tab to display episodes, each of which has a Play button; for a movie, the Play button appears no matter which tab is selected. When you tap the Play button for the content you want to watch, the movie, TV show, or podcast begins playing. (If you see a small cloud-shaped icon instead of a Play button, tap it if you want to download the content from iCloud rather than stream it.) The progress of the playback is displayed on the Progress bar (see **Figure 13-5**), showing how many minutes you've viewed and how many remain. If you don't see the bar, tap the screen once to display it briefly, along with a set of playback tools at the bottom of the screen.

Figure 13-5

5. With the playback tools displayed, take any of these
   actions:

   • Tap the Pause button to pause playback.

   • Tap either Go to Previous Chapter or Go to Next
     Chapter to move to a different location in the video
     playback.

   • Tap the circular button on the Volume slider and drag
     the button left or right to decrease or increase the vol-
     ume, respectively.

6. To stop the video and return to the information screen, tap the Done button to the left of the Progress bar.

 If you've watched a video and stopped it partway, it opens by default to the last location that you viewed. To start a video from the beginning, tap and drag the circular button on the Progress bar all the way to the left.

 If your controls disappear during playback, just tap the screen to make them reappear.

 If you like to view things on a bigger screen, you can use the iPad's AirPlay feature to send your iPad movies and photos to your TV via the Apple Digital AV Connector (a $39.95 accessory) or Apple TV (a device that costs $99). Depending on your TV model, you may need the Composite connector (for virtually any analog set rather than the Digital AV Connector, which is used only for HD TV).

Turn on Closed Captioning

1. iTunes and the iPad offer support for closed captioning and subtitles. If a movie you purchased or rented has either closed captioning or subtitles, you can turn on this feature in iPad. Look for the "CC" logo on media you download to use this feature; be aware that video you record won't have this capability. Begin by tapping the Settings icon on the Home screen.

2. Tap General ⇨ Accessibility. On the screen that appears, tap Subtitles & Captioning (see **Figure 13-6**).

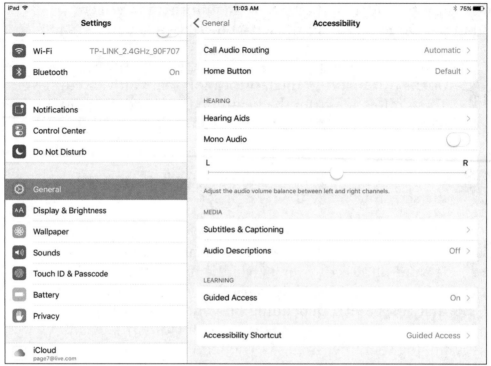

Figure 13-6

3. On the menu that appears on the right side of the screen, tap the Closed Captions + SDH On/Off button to turn on the feature. Now when you play a movie that supports closed captioning, you can tap the Audio and Subtitles button to the right of the playback controls to manage this feature.

Go to a Movie Chapter

1. Tap the Videos app icon on the Home screen.

2. Tap the Movies tab, if it isn't already displayed.

3. Tap the title of the movie you want to watch. Information about the movie is displayed (refer to Figure 13-4).

4. Tap the Chapters tab. A list of chapters is displayed, as shown in **Figure 13-7**.

5. Tap a chapter to play it.

 You can also use the playback tools to go back one chapter or forward one chapter. See the "Play Movies, Podcasts, or TV Shows with Videos" task earlier in this chapter for more information.

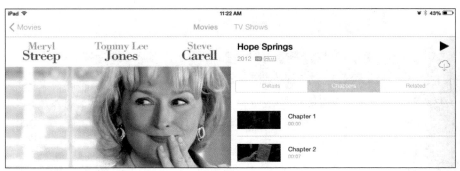

Figure 13-7

 If you buy a video using iTunes, sync to download it to your iPad and then delete it from your iPad, it's still saved in your iTunes library. You can sync your computer and iPad again to download the video once more at no additional charge. Remember, however, that rented movies are gone with the wind when you delete them.

 The iPad has much smaller storage capacity than your typical computer, so downloading lots of TV shows or movies can fill its storage area quickly. If you don't want to view an item you've downloaded again, delete it to free up space. With your TV Shows or Movies displayed, tap Edit. Tap the Delete button on an item and then tap Delete in the confirmation that appears.

Share Your Favorite Videos

1. You can share your opinion about a video by using Mail, Twitter, or Facebook. Tap the Videos app to open it and then tap the Store button.

2. Find and tap a video that you want to share.

3. In the information screen shown in **Figure 13-8,** tap the Share icon (a box with an arrow at the top of it at the top of the screen).

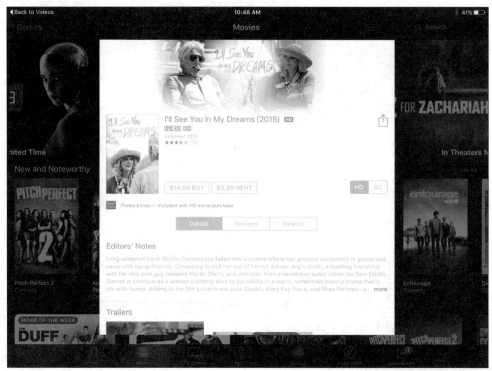

Figure 13-8

4. In the resulting menu, tap Mail, Twitter, or Facebook to use one of these methods of sharing your enthusiasm for the item (see **Figure 13-9**). Note that you can also share the item as a reminder or note to yourself.

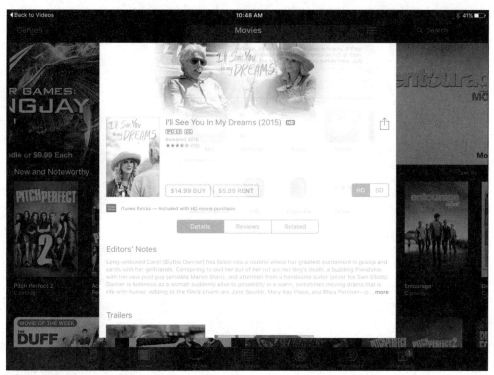

Figure 13-9

5. In the form that appears, enter a recipient in the To: field and add to the message, if you like. If you chose to post to your Facebook page, enter your message in the Facebook form.

6. Tap the appropriate Send button to send your recommendation by your preferred method.

 When you're viewing information about a video in the iTunes Store, you can tap the Related tab to find information about other movies or TV shows watched by those who watched this one.

Playing Games

Chapter

14

*T*he iPad is super for playing games, with its bright screen (especially bright if you're using the Retina display on a third-generation or later iPad) and great sound system, as well as its capability to rotate the screen as you play and track your motions. You can download game apps from the App Store and play them on your device. You can also use the preinstalled Game Center app to find and buy games, add friends to play against, and track and share scores.

In this chapter, you get an overview of game-playing on your iPad, including opening a Game Center account, adding a friend, purchasing and downloading games, and playing basic games solo or against friends.

Get ready to . . .

You can also download games from the App Store and play them on your iPad without having to use Game Center. What Game Center provides is a place where you can create a gaming profile, add a list of gaming friends, keep track of and share your scores and perks, and shop for games (and only games) in the App Store, along with listings of top-rated games and game categories to choose among.

Open an Account in Game Center

1. On the Home screen, tap the Game Center icon. If you've never used Game Center, you're asked whether to allow *push* notifications. If you want to receive these notices alerting you that your friends want to play a game with you, tap OK. You should be aware, however, that push notifications can drain your iPad's battery more quickly.

2. Sign in on the Game Center opening screen (see **Figure 14-1**) by tapping in the ID and Password fields and enter your current account information using the onscreen keyboard that appears, and then tap the Go key on the keyboard. The screen that appears shows games you've downloaded, requests from other players, friends, and so on.

3. Tap any of the floating balloons to get to any of the displayed categories, or tap a button along the bottom of the screen (see **Figure 14-2**).

When you first register for Game Center, if you use an email address other than the one associated with your Apple ID, you may have to create a new Apple ID and verify it by responding to an email message that's sent to your email address. See Chapter 3 for more about creating an Apple ID when opening an iTunes account.

Figure 14-1

Figure 14-2

Create a Profile

1. When you have an account with which you can sign in to Game Center, you're ready to specify some account settings. On the Home screen, tap Settings.

2. Tap Game Center.

3. In the pane that appears (see **Figure 14-3**), specify whether you want other players to be able to invite you to play games when Game Center is open. Tap the Allow Invites Off/On switch to turn off this feature.

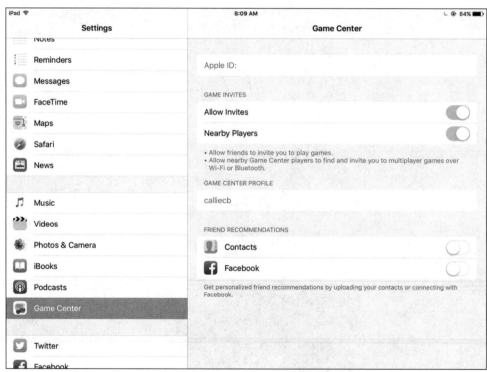

Figure 14-3

4. If you want your friends to be able to send you requests for playing games via email, check to see whether the primary email address listed in this dialog is the one you want them to use. If not, tap the current Apple ID, and in the dialog that appears, tap Sign Out. On the screen that appears, tap the Apple ID field and enter another account, or tap Create a New Apple ID.

5. Tap the Nearby Players On/Off button (refer to Figure 14-3) if you want others to be able to find you and invite you to games.

6. If you want others to see your profile, including your real name, scroll down to tap the current profile; tap the Public Profile On/Off switch to turn on your public profile.

7. Tap Done and then press the Home button when you're finished making the settings. You return to the Home screen.

8. Tap Game Center. You return to Game Center, already signed in to your account, with information displayed about your friends, games, and gaming achievements (all set to zero initially).

 After you create an account and a profile, whenever you go to Game Center, you are signed in automatically to your Apple account.

Add Friends

1. If you want to play Game Center games with others who have an Apple ID and an iPhone, iPod touch, or iPad, add them as friends so that you can invite them to play. (Game Center is also available on Macs with 2012's Mountain Lion OS and later, but few cross-platform games are available for it at this time.) On the Game Center home screen, tap the Friends button at the bottom of the screen.

2. On the Friends page, tap the Add Friends button in the top-left corner (shaped like a plus sign).

3. Enter an email address in the To: field and then enter an invitation, if you like (see **Figure 14-4**).

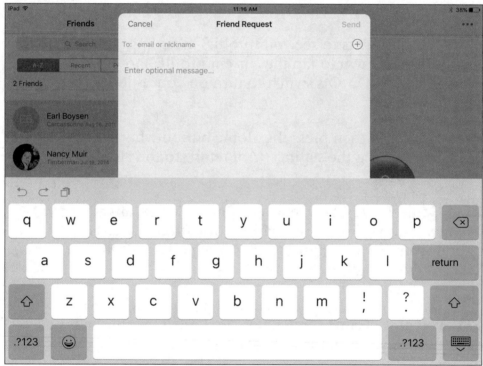

Figure 14-4

4. Tap the Send button. After your friend accepts your invitation, her name is listed on the Friends screen.

 Game Center contains a Friend Recommendations feature. Tap the Friends tab and then tap the A-Z button in the top-left corner. A Recommendations section appears below the list of your current friends. These people play the same games as you, or similar ones, so if you like, try adding one or two as friends. You can tap the Points tab to view the points these folks have accumulated so you can stay in your league.

 You'll probably receive requests from friends who know that you're on Game Center. When you get such an email invitation, be sure that you know the person sending it before you accept it — especially if you've allowed email access in your account settings. If you don't double-check, you could be allowing a stranger into your gaming world.

Purchase and Download Games

Time to get some games to play! Remember that you can buy any game app from the App Store or other sources and simply play it by tapping to open it on your iPad. But if you want to use Game Center to buy games, here are the steps involved.

1. Open Game Center.

2. Tap the Games button at the bottom of the screen, and in the Recommended category, tap Show More.

3. Scroll through the list of featured games that appears and tap one that appeals to you. Tap the price/free button (see **Figure 14-5**) to display details about the game. Note that you can tap the Store button from here to go to the App Store to view more games.

4. To buy a game, tap the button labeled with either the text *Get* or the price (such as $1.99).

5. In the detailed app page that appears, tap the button again and then tap the Buy or Install button. An alert may appear, asking you to enter your Apple ID password. Enter it and then tap OK.

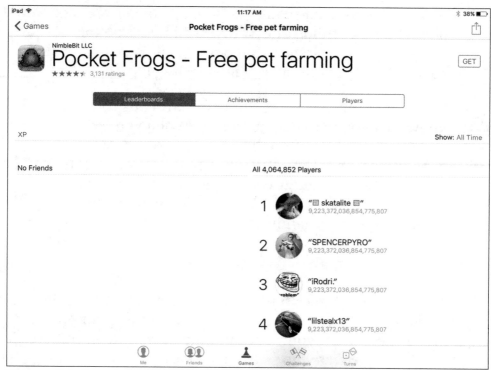

Figure 14-5

6. Follow the instructions on the next couple of screens to enter your password and verify your payment information if this is the first time you've signed in to your account from this device.

7. When the verification dialog appears, tap Buy or Install. The game downloads.

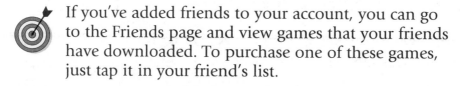 If you've added friends to your account, you can go to the Friends page and view games that your friends have downloaded. To purchase one of these games, just tap it in your friend's list.

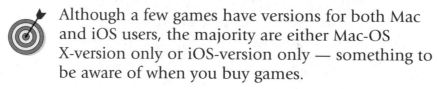 Although a few games have versions for both Mac and iOS users, the majority are either Mac-OS X-version only or iOS-version only — something to be aware of when you buy games.

Master iPad Game-Playing Basics

It's almost time to start playing games, but first, let me give you an idea of the iPad's gaming strengths. For many reasons, such as the following, the iPad may be the ultimate gaming device:

➡ **Fantastic-looking screen:** The high-resolution, 9.7-inch iPad Air screen (7.9 inch for iPad mini) has a backlit LED display that Apple describes as "remarkably crisp and vivid." The third-, fourth-, and fifth-generation iPad with Retina display takes this crisp screen to the max. In-plane switching (IPS) technology lets you hold your iPad at almost any angle (it has a 178-degree viewing angle) and still see good color and contrast. In addition, iPad Air 2 has a new antireflective coating to reduce reflections by about 56 percent.

➡ **Faster processor:** The dual-core A9X chip in the iPad Air 2 and iPad mini 4 are super-fast processors, making the iPad ideal for gaming. In iPad Pro, the A9X is a whiz at displaying graphics that are so central to gaming.

➡ **Game play in full-screen mode:** Rather than play on a small iPhone screen, you can play most games designed for the iPad in full-screen mode. Seeing the full screen brings the gaming experience to you in an even more engaging way than a small screen ever could.

➡ **Ability to drag elements onscreen:** Though the iPad's Multi-Touch screen is based on the same technology that's in the iPhone, it has been redone from the ground up for the iPad. The newer screen is responsive — and when you're about to be zapped by virtual aliens in a fight to the death, responsiveness counts.

➡ **Ten-hour battery life:** A device's long battery life means that you can tap energy from it for many hours of gaming fun. Even with the extra power required for the Retina display of third-generation and later iPads, Apple managed to maintain this excellent battery life.

➡ **Specialized game-playing features:** Some newer games have features that take full advantage of the iPad's capabilities. One example is N.O.V.A. (from Gameloft), which features Multiple Target Acquisition, letting you target multiple bad guys in a single move to blow them out of the water with one shot. In Real Racing 3 (Firemint), you can look in your rearview mirror as you're racing to see what's coming up behind you — a feature made possible by the iPad's larger screen. The 64-bit MB motion coprocessor in iPad Air 2 and iPad mini 4 is what supports games that make the most of motion.

➡ **Stellar sound:** The built-in iPad speakers are powerful little items, but if you want an experience that's even more up-close and personal, you can plug a headphone, some speaker systems, or a microphone into the built-in jack.

In addition to the M9 motion coprocessor, recent models of iPad have a built-in motion sensor — the *three-axis accelerometer* — as well as a gyroscope. These features provide lots of fun for people who develop apps for the iPad because they use the automatically rotating screen to become part of the gaming experience. A built-in compass device, for example, reorients itself automatically as you switch your iPad from landscape to portrait orientation. In some racing games, you can grab the iPad as though it were a steering wheel and rotate the device to simulate the driving experience.

Play against Yourself

Many games allow you to play a game all on your own. Each game has different rules and goals, so study a game's instructions to learn how to play it. Here's some general information about games:

➡ Often, a game can be played in two modes: with others or in a solitaire version, in which you play against yourself or the computer.

➡ Many games that you may be familiar with in the offline world, such as Carcassonne and Scrabble, have online versions. You already know the rules of play, so you simply need to figure out the execution. In the online Carcassonne game, for example, you tap to place a tile on the board, tap the placed tile to rotate it, and then tap the check mark to complete your turn and reveal another tile.

➡ Game Center records the scores of all the games you play on your own, so you can track your progress.

Challenge Friends in Game Center

1. After you've added a friend and both of you have downloaded the same games, you can challenge your friend to beat your scores. Tap the Game Center app icon on the Home screen and sign in, if necessary.

2. Tap Me and then tap the Games bubble.

3. In the My iOS Games section, tap a game.

4. In the resulting screen, tap the Achievements tab and then tap an achievement (see **Figure 14-6**).

Figure 14-6

5. At this point, some games offer you an option to challenge your friend. To do so, tap the Challenge Friends bubble.

6. On the screen that appears, tap a friend and then tap Next.

7. In the form that appears, enter a message if you like, and then tap Send (see **Figure 14-7**).

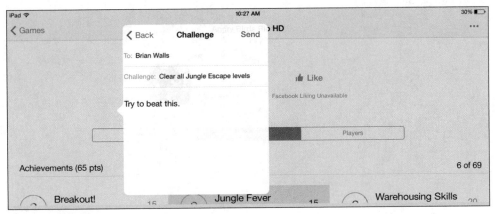

Figure 14-7

 If your friends aren't available, you can play a game by tapping its icon on the Home screen. You can then return to Game Center and compare your scores with others around the world who have also played the game.

Finding Your Way with Maps

Y̶ou may have used a maps app on a smartphone before. The big difference with the iPad is its large screen, on which you can view all the beautiful map visuals, traffic flow, and maps in standard views and even 3D as long as you have an Internet connection. You can also display the map and written directions simultaneously or have Maps speak your directions, guiding you as you drive.

If you're new to the Maps app, you'll find that it has lots of useful functions. You can find directions with suggested alternative routes from one place to another. You can bookmark locations to return to them. Also, the Maps app makes it possible to get information about locations, such as the phone numbers and web links to businesses. You can even add a location to your Contacts list or share a location with a buddy by using Mail, Messages, Twitter, or Facebook. New with iOS 9 comes the Nearby feature to help you explore local attractions and businesses and the Transit view for public transit maps for select cities around the world.

You're about to have lots of fun exploring the world of Maps in this chapter.

Chapter 15

Get ready to . . .

Go to Your Current Location

1. The iPad can figure out where you are at any time and display your current location as long as you have an Internet connection and have turned Location Services on in Privacy Settings. On the Home screen, tap the Maps icon.

2. Tap the Current Location icon (the small arrow in the bottom-left corner; see **Figure 15-1**). Your current location is displayed with a pin in it and a pulsating blue circle around it. The circle indicates how accurate the location is; it can be anywhere within the area of the circle.

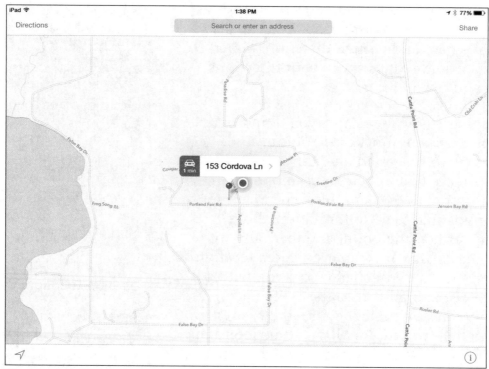

Figure 15-1

3. Double-tap the screen to zoom in on your location. (Additional methods of zooming in and out are covered in the "Zoom In and Out" task later in this chapter.)

If you don't have a 3G or 4G iPad, your current location is a rough estimate based on a triangulation method. Only 3G- and 4G-enabled iPads with the Global Positioning System (GPS) can pinpoint where you are. Still, if you type a starting location and an ending location to get directions, you can get pretty accurate results even with a Wi-Fi–only iPad.

Change Views

1. The Maps app offers three views: Map, Satellite, and Transit. iPad displays Map view (the top-left image in **Figure 15-2**) by default the first time you open Maps. To change views, with Maps open, tap the Information button in the bottom-right corner of the screen. The Information pop-up menu appears, as shown in the top-right image in Figure 15-2.

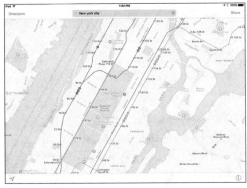

Figure 15-2

2. Tap the Satellite option. Satellite view (refer to the top-right image in Figure 15-2) appears.

3. Tap Show Labels if labels aren't currently displayed (if they are this option is titled Hide Labels). Satellite view is displayed with street names superimposed.

4. Tap Transit (refer to the bottom image in Figure 15-2).

5. Finally, you can display a 3D effect (see **Figure 15-3**) on any view by tapping 3D Map in the Information pop-up menu. Tap 2D in the pop-up menu to return to a 2D view.

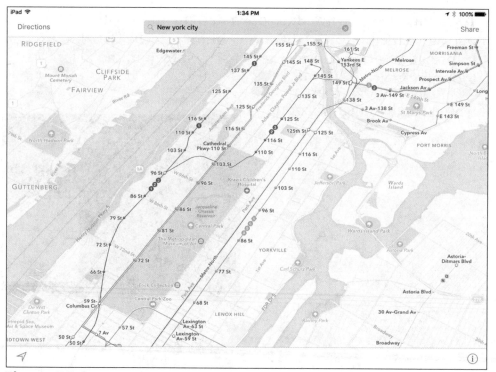

Figure 15-3

 The Information pop-up menu Show Traffic feature only provides a traffic overlay on the map in a larger metropolitan area (this feature doesn't really work in small towns or rural settings — neither does the

Transit view), the traffic overlay shows red dashes on roads indicating accidents or road closures and orange dashes to indicate traffic slowdowns to help you navigate your rush-hour commute or trip to the mall.

 You can drop a pin to mark a location on a map that you can return to. See the task "Drop a Pin," later in this chapter, for more about this topic.

 To print any displayed map to an AirPrint-compatible printer, just tap Share in the top-right corner and then tap the Print button.

Zoom In and Out

1. You'll appreciate the Zoom feature because it gives you the capability to see more or less detailed maps and move around a map. With a map displayed, double-tap with a single finger to zoom in.

2. Double-tap with two fingers to zoom out, revealing less detail.

3. Place two fingers together on the screen and move them apart to zoom in.

4. Place two fingers apart on the screen and then pinch them together to zoom out.

5. Press your finger to the screen and drag the map in any direction to move to an adjacent area.

 It can take a few moments for the map to redraw itself when you enlarge, reduce, or move around it, so have a little patience. Areas that are being redrawn look like blank grids that fill in eventually. Also, if you're in Satellite or Transit view, zooming in may take some time; wait, because the blurred image resolves itself.

Go to another Location

1. With Maps open, tap the Search field. The keyboard opens. If you've displayed directions for a route, you won't see the Search field; tap the Clear button on a directions screen to get back to the Search field.

2. Type a location, using a street address with city and state, a stored contact name, or a destination such as *Empire State Building* or *Detroit airport.* Maps first displays buttons for categories such as Food and Health that you can use to narrow your search, and then displays suggestions (see **Figure 15-4**) as you type if it finds any logical matches. Tap a suggestion or tap the Search key on the keyboard, and the location appears, with a pin inserted into it and a label with the location and an Information icon. Note that if several locations match your search term, several pins may display in a suggestions list.

Figure 15-4

3. Tap the arrow on the right side of the information box to see more about the destination (see **Figure 15-5**).

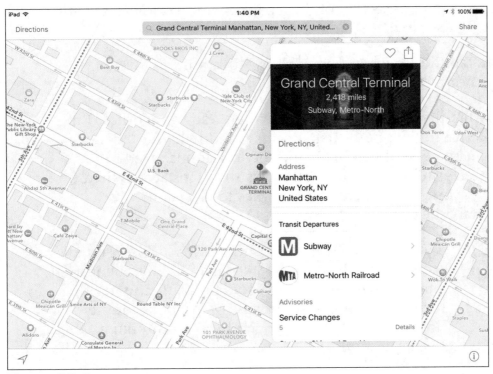

Figure 15-5

 You can tap the Dictation key on the onscreen keyboard and speak a location to the iPad if you prefer. Tap the Search field, tap the Dictation key, speak the location, and then tap the Dictation key or the Search field again. What you've spoken appears there. Next, tap the Search button on the keyboard to display the location.

 Try pressing the Home button and asking Siri for a type of business or location by zip code. If you crave something with pepperoni, for example, say, "Find pizza in 99208 zip code." Tap an item in the results to display a small map you can tap to open the Maps app to find your way there. See Chapter 19 for more about using Siri.

When you start a search, icons for categories of nearby businesses appear. This Nearby feature is new in iOS 9. Find out more about using this feature in the last section of this chapter, Find Local Places with Nearby.

4. Tap the screen and drag in any direction to move to a nearby location.

5. Tap the Share button and then tap Add to Favorites. Tap Save in the screen that appears (modifying the location name first, if you like), and the location is saved to Favorites. Now when you tap in the Maps Search field, Favorites are listed. Tap Favorites to view and go to a favorite site.

 If you enter a destination such as *Bronx Zoo*, you may want to enter its city and state as well. Entering just *Bronx Zoo* landed me in Woodland Park Zoo in Tacoma, Washington, because Maps looks for the closest match to your geographical location in a given category.

Drop a Pin

1. *Pins* are markers. A green pin marks a start location, a red pin marks a search result, and a blue pin (referred to as the *blue marker*) marks your iPad's current location. If you drop a pin yourself, it appears in a lovely purple. Display a map that contains a spot where you want to drop a pin to help you find directions to or from that site. If you need to, you can zoom in to a more detailed map to see a better view of the location you want to pin.

2. Tap and hold your finger on the screen at the location where you want to place the pin. The pin appears.

3. Tap the arrow on the right of the information box to display details about the pin's location (see **Figure 15-6**).

 If a site has associated reviews on the review site Yelp (www.yelp.com), you can display details about the location and scroll down to read those reviews.

Figure 15-6

View Favorites

1. To view your favorites, tap the Search field, and then tap Favorites on the list that appears.

2. Tap a favorite to go to that location in Maps.

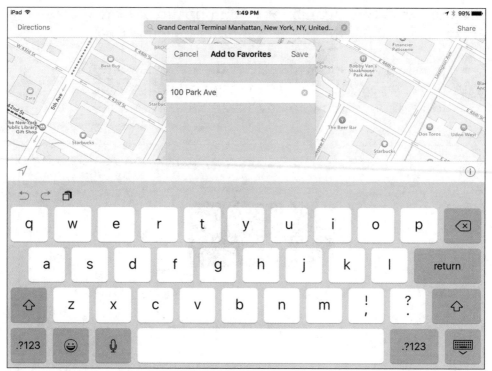

Figure 15-7

Delete a Favorite

1. Tap the Search field and then tap Favorites. In the pop-up menu that appears, tap Edit. A red minus icon appears to the left of each favorite, as shown in **Figure 15-8**.

2. Tap a red minus icon.

3. Tap Delete. The favorite is removed.

 You can also use a touchscreen shortcut after you've displayed the Favorites in Step 1. Simply swipe across a favorite and then tap the Delete button that appears.

Figure 15-8

Find Directions

1. You can get directions in a couple of ways. With at least one pin on your map in addition to your current location, tap the Directions button and then tap the End field and enter another address or destination. Tap Route. A line appears, showing the route between your current location and the specified destination (see **Figure 15-9**). Tap the Drive or Walk tab to get the kind of directions you prefer. Tap Clear to return to the Maps main screen.

2. You can also enter two locations other than your current location to get directions from one to the other. Tap the Directions button in Maps and then tap the Start field. The keyboard appears along with an End field.

3. Enter a starting location.

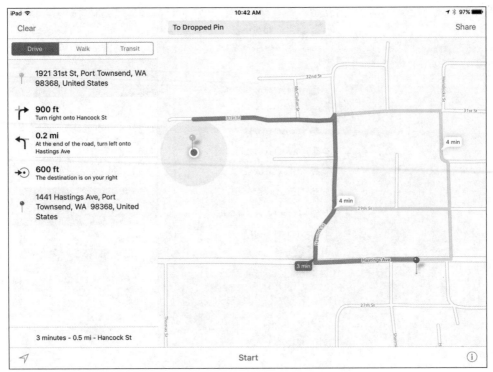

Figure 15-9

4. Tap the End field and enter a destination location.

5. Tap the Route button. The route between the two locations is displayed along with step-by step-directions (see **Figure 15-10**).

6. You can also tap the arrow on the right side of the information bar that appears when you tap any selected pin and use the Directions button to generate directions (refer to Figure 15-6).

7. When a route is displayed, an information bar appears along the bottom of the Directions pane, telling you the distance and the time it takes to travel between the two locations. Tap the menu button on the right side of this bar to display directions.

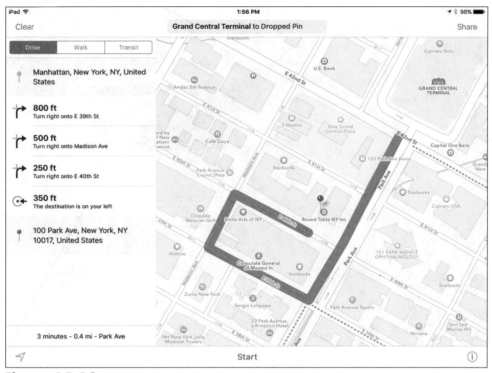

Figure 15-10

View Information about a Location

1. In earlier tasks in this chapter, you display the Information pop-up menu for locations to get directions. In this task, you focus on the useful information displayed there. Go to a location and tap the pin.

2. On the information box that appears above the pinned location, tap the arrow on the right (refer to Figure 15-1).

3. In the Information pop-up menu (see **Figure 15-11**), tap the web address listed in the Homepage field to be taken to the location's web page, if it has one associated with it.

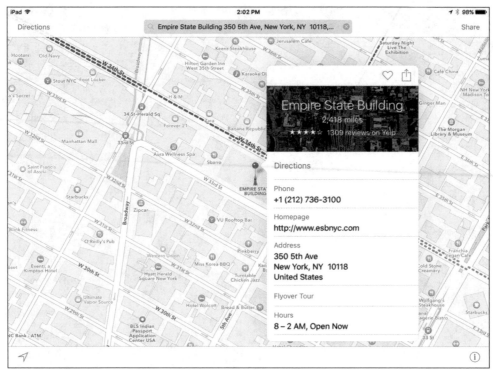

Figure 15-11

4. You can also press and hold either the Phone (refer to Figure 15-11) or Address field and use the Copy button to copy the phone number, for example, so that you can place it in a Notes document for future reference.

5. Tap the map to return to Map view.

 Rather than copy and paste information, you can easily save all information about a location in your Contacts address book. See the next task, "Add a Location to a Contact," to find out how.

 New to iOS 9 is the ability to share a map with the Notes app, which places the current map in a new note. Just tap the Share button and select Notes from the list of options.

Add a Location to a Contact

1. Tap a pin to display the information box.

2. Tap the arrow on the right side of the box.

3. In the Information popover that appears, scroll down and then tap Create New Contact (refer to Figure 15-6).

4. In the resulting dialog, whatever information was available about the location has already been entered. Enter any additional information you need, such as name, phone, or email address.

5. Tap Done. The information is stored in your Contacts address book.

 If you tap Add to Existing Contact instead in Step 3, you can choose a contact from your Contacts list to add the location information to.

 You can choose a distinct ringtone or text tone for a new contact. Just tap the Ringtone or Text Tone field in the New Contact form to see a list of options. When that person calls via FaceTime or texts you via iMessage, you'll recognize him from the tone that plays.

Share Location Information

1. Tap a pin to display the information box.

2. Tap the arrow on the right of the box.

3. In the Information pop-up menu that appears, tap the Share button.

4. In the resulting pop-up menu (see **Figure 15-12**), you can choose to share via AirDrop, Mail, Twitter, or Facebook. New with iOS 9, you also have the ability to share to Notes or Reminders. Tap Mail to see how this option works.

5. On the form that appears, use the onscreen keyboard to enter the recipient's email address. (If you chose Facebook or Twitter in Step 4, you'd enter recipient information as appropriate to the service you chose.) Then enter a message if you wish, and tap Send to share the map.

Figure 15-12

 You may have to install and set up the Twitter or Facebook app before sharing Maps content with those services. You also must have an account with these services to use them to share content.

Get Turn-by-Turn Navigation Help

1. When you've entered directions for a route and displayed that route, you can begin listening to turn-by-turn navigation instructions that can be helpful as you're driving. Tap the Start button at the bottom of the screen to start. The narration begins, and large text instructions are displayed, as shown in **Figure 15-13**.

2. Continue driving according to the route until the next instruction is spoken.

3. For an overview of your route at any time, tap the Overview button in the top-right corner. Tap Resume to go back to the step-by-step instructions.

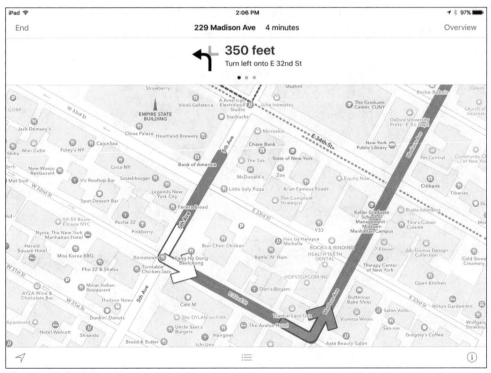

Figure 15-13

To change route information from miles to kilometers, from the Home screen tap Settings ⇨ Maps, and tap In Kilometers to change the setting.

Find Local Places with Nearby

1. When you perform a search, a row of buttons appears across the top of the results. These take you to Nearby results; that is, businesses and services that are near your current location. Begin a search and tap one of these buttons, such as Food.

2. Results for the Food category are shown in **Figure 15-14**. These offer additional buttons that help you to narrow down the type of food you're looking for, as well as a list of nearby restaurants. Tap an item in the list. A map of all results in that category, including an information bar for the item you selected, is displayed.

Figure 15-14

3. Tap the information bar for the location you selected to display more information about it (see **Figure 15-15**).

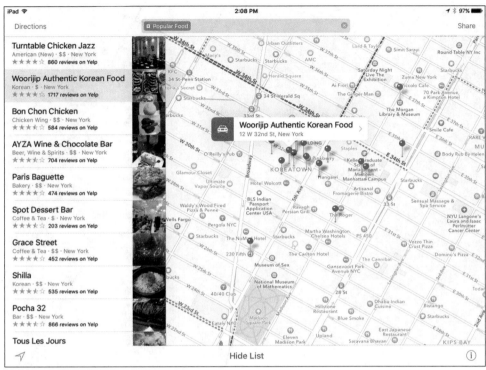

Figure 15-15

Part IV
Managing Your Life and Your iPad

Visit www.dummies.com/extras/ipadforseniors for information about working with Siri commands.

Keeping On Schedule with Calendar and Clock

Whether you're retired or still working, you have a busy life full of activities (even busier if you're retired, for some unfathomable reason). You may need a way to keep on top of all those activities and appointments. The Calendar app on your iPad is a simple, elegant, electronic daybook that helps you do just that.

In addition to being able to enter events and view them by the day, week, month, or year, you can set up Calendar to send alerts to remind you of your obligations and search for events by keywords. You can even set up repeating events, such as weekly poker games, monthly get-togethers with the girls or guys, or weekly babysitting appointments with your grandchild. To help you coordinate calendars on multiple devices, you can also sync events with other calendar accounts or use iCloud to sync calendars between supported devices. And, by taking advantage of the Family Sharing feature, you can create a Family Calendar that everybody in your family can view and add events to.

Another preinstalled app that will help you stay on time is Clock. Though simple to use, Clock helps you view the time in multiple locations, set alarms, and use a timer.

In this chapter, you master the simple procedures for getting around your calendar, creating a family calendar, entering and editing events, setting up alerts, syncing, and searching. You also learn the simple ins and outs of using Clock.

View Your Calendar

1. Calendar offers several ways to view your schedule. Start by tapping the Calendar app icon on the Home screen to open it; if it's your first time using Calendar you may be asked whether Calendar can use your Location (tap Allow or Don't Allow). When you open Calendar, depending on what you last had open, you may see the day calendar or the weekly, monthly, or yearly calendar with today's date highlighted. You might also see an open event.

2. If today's calendar page isn't already displayed, double-tap the Today button at the bottom of the screen. Tap the Search button and you see all saved appointments. The Today view with Search open, shown in **Figure 16-1**, displays your daily appointments with times listed on the left page and an hourly breakdown of the day on the right page. Tap an event on the list on the left to view more details.

3. Tap the Week button to view all events for the current week, as shown in **Figure 16-2**. In this view, appointments appear against the times listed along the left side of the screen.

4. Tap the Month button to get an overview of your busy month (see **Figure 16-3**). In this view, you see the name and timing of each event.

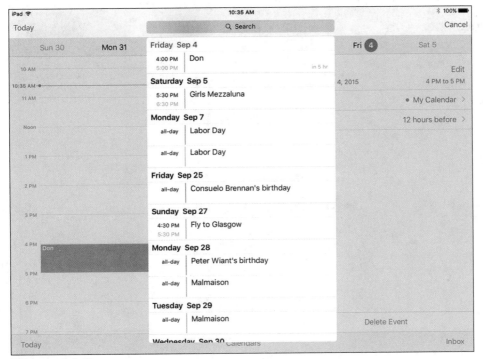

Figure 16-1

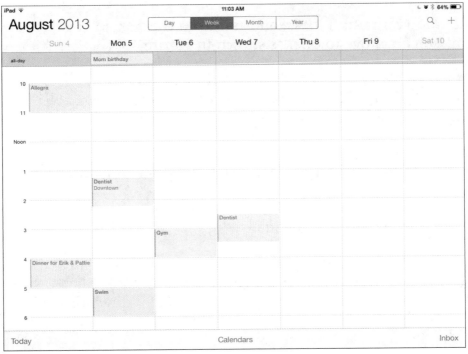

Figure 16-2

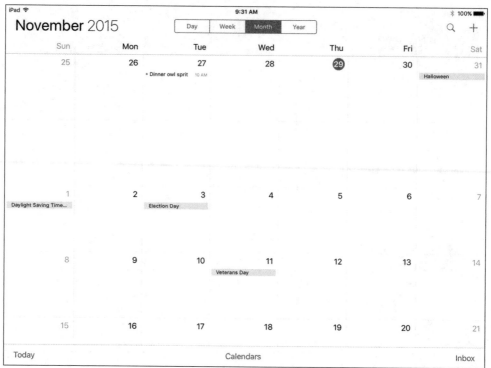

Figure 16-3

5. Tap the Year button to see all months in the year so you can quickly move to one, as shown in **Figure 16-4.**

6. In any calendar view, tap the Search button to see List view, which lists all your commitments in a drop-down list on the right side of the page, as shown in **Figure 16-5.**

7. To move from one month, or year to another, use your finger to scroll up or down the list and tap on an item.

8. To jump back to today, tap the Today button in the bottom-left corner of Calendar.

Portrait and landscape orientation of your iPad with the Calendar app gives a slightly different look. Play around with turning your iPad in different directions to see which one you prefer to work in.

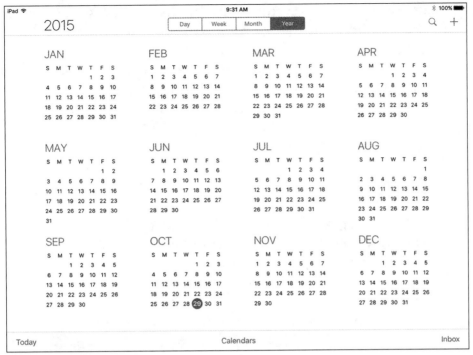

Figure 16-4

Figure 16-5

Note that you can use information within emails such as a flight number or phone number to add an event to Calendar. To turn on this feature, go to Settings ⇨ Mail, Contacts, Calendars and then turn on the Contacts Found in Mail and Events Found in Mail settings. To view any event that added an event to your calendar, tap Inbox; a list of events displays. Tap Done to return to the calendar.

Add Calendar Events

1. With any view displayed, tap the Add button to add an event. The New Event dialog, shown in **Figure 16-6,** appears.

Figure 16-6

2. Enter a title for the event and, if you want, a location.

3. Tap the All-day switch for an all-day event, or tap the Starts or Ends field. The tool for setting a date and time appears, as shown in **Figure 16-7**.

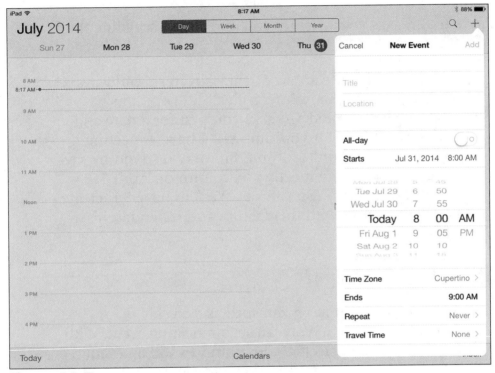

Figure 16-7

4. Place your fingertip on the date, hour, minute, or AM/PM column, and move your finger to scroll up or down.

5. If you want to add notes, use your finger to scroll down in the Add Event dialog and tap the Notes field. Type your note and then tap the Add button to save the event.

 You can edit any event at any time simply by tapping it in any view of your calendar and then tapping Edit. The Edit dialog appears, offering the same settings as the New Event dialog (refer to Figure 16-6). Tap the Add button to save your changes or Cancel to return to your calendar without saving any changes.

Add Events Using Siri

1. Press and hold the Home button.

2. Say a command, such as "Create Meeting October 3rd at 2:30 p.m."

3. When Siri asks you whether you're ready to schedule the event, say "Yes."

 You can schedule an event with Siri in several ways because the feature is pretty flexible. You can say, "Create event," and Siri asks you first for a date and then for a time. Or you can say, "I have a meeting with John on April 1st," and Siri may respond by saying "I don't find a meeting with John on April 1st; shall I create it?" You can say "Yes" to have Siri create it. Play around with this feature and Calendar; it's a lot of fun!

Create Repeating Events

1. If you want an event to repeat, such as a weekly or monthly appointment, you can set a repeating event. With any view displayed, tap the Add button to add an event. The New Event dialog appears (refer to Figure 16-6).

2. Enter a title and location for the event, and set the start and end dates and times, as shown in the earlier task "Add Calendar Events."

3. Scroll down the page, if necessary, and tap the Repeat field. The Repeat dialog, shown in **Figure 16-8**, is displayed.

4. Tap a preset time interval: Every Day, Week, 2 Weeks, Month, or Year. If you want, you can tap Custom and enter a Frequency and Day. For example, you could create an event to happen monthly, but only every three months or daily every three days.

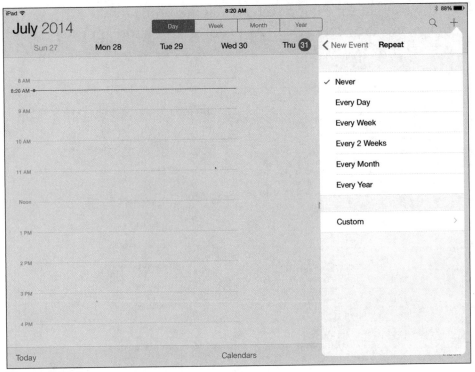

Figure 16-8

5. Tap New Event to close the Repeat dialog, and then tap Add. You return to the calendar.

Add Alerts

1. If you want your iPad to alert you when an event is coming up, you can use the Alert feature. First, tap the Settings icon on the Home screen, and choose Sounds.

2. Scroll down and tap Calendar Alerts and then tap any Alert Tone, which causes the iPad to play the tone for you.

3. Press the Home button; tap Calendar; and create an event in your calendar or open an existing one for editing, as covered in earlier tasks in this chapter.

4. In the New Event dialog (refer to Figure 16-6) or the Edit dialog, tap the Alert field. The Event Alert dialog appears, as shown in **Figure 16-9**.

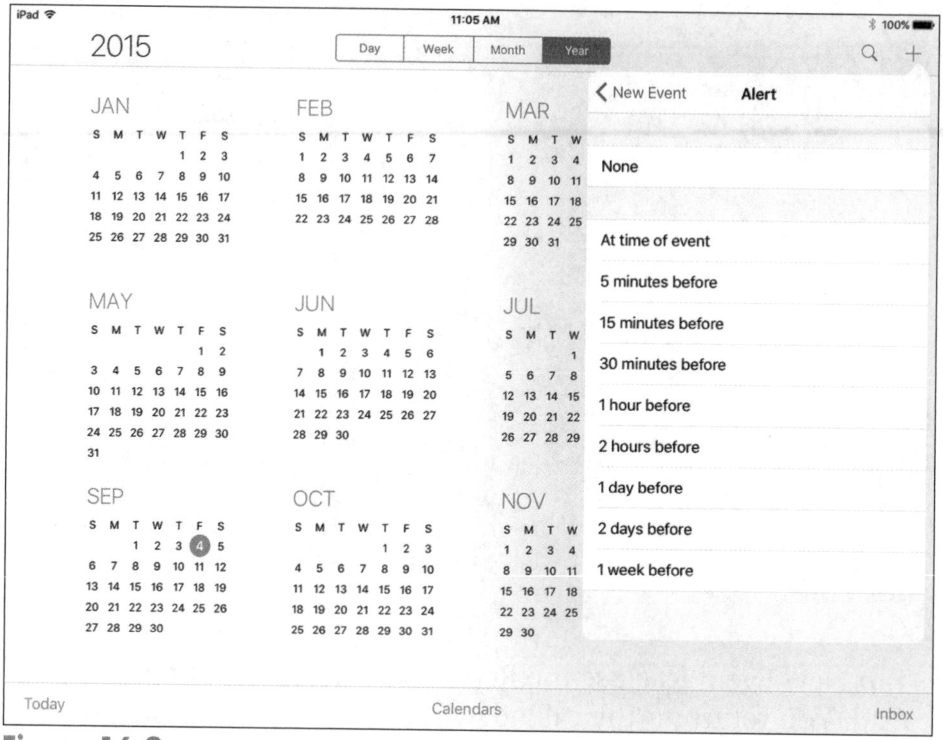

Figure 16-9

5. Tap any preset interval, from 5 Minutes to 2 Days Before or at the time of the event. Tap New Event or Edit Event to return to the New Event or Edit Event dialog.

6. Tap Add (for a new event) or Done (if you're editing an existing event) to save the alert.

7. Tap the Day button to display Day view of the date of your event and then tap the event. The alert information is included in that view, as shown in **Figure 16-10**.

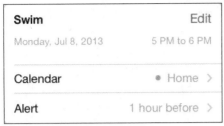

Figure 16-10

Search Calendars

1. With Calendar open in any view, tap the Search button in the top-right corner (refer to Figure 16-5).

2. Tap the Search field (the onscreen keyboard appears), type a word or words to search by, and then tap the Search key. While you type, the Results dialog appears, as shown in **Figure 16-11**.

3. Tap any result to display it in the view you were in when you started the search. The event details are displayed on the right.

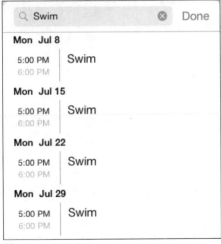

Figure 16-11

Subscribe to and Share Calendars

1. If you use a calendar from an online service such as Yahoo! or Google, you can subscribe to that calendar to read events saved there on your iPad. Note that you can only read, not edit, these events. Tap the Settings icon on the Home screen to get started.

2. Tap the Mail, Contacts, Calendars option on the left.

3. Tap Add Account. The Add Account options, shown in **Figure 16-12,** appear.

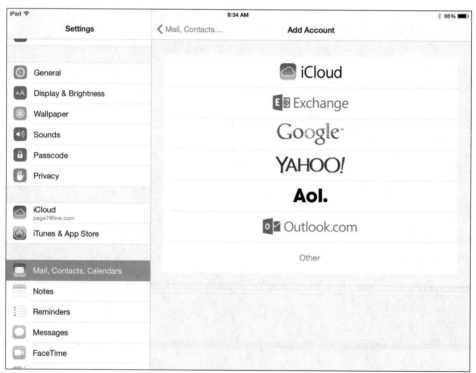

Figure 16-12

4. Tap an email choice, such as Outlook.com, Gmail, or Yahoo!.

5. In the settings that appear (see **Figure 16-13**), enter any requested information, such as name, email address, and email account password.

Cancel	**Gmail**	Next

Name	John Appleseed
Email	example@gmail.com
Password	Required
Description	My Gmail Account

Figure 16-13

6. Tap Next or Sign In, depending on the type of account. The iPad verifies your address.

7. In the following settings, tap the On/Off switch for the Calendars field. Your iPad retrieves data from your calendar at the interval you've set to fetch data. To review these settings, tap the Back arrow in the top-left corner, and then tap the Fetch New Data option in the Mail, Contacts, Calendars pane.

8. In the Fetch New Data pane that appears (see **Figure 16-14**), be sure that the Push option's On/Off switch is set to On and then choose the option you prefer for how frequently data is pushed to your iPad: every 15 or 30 minutes, hourly, or manually.

 If you store your contacts' birthdays in the Contacts app, the Calendar app displays each one when the day comes around so that you won't forget to pass on your congratulations . . . or condolences.

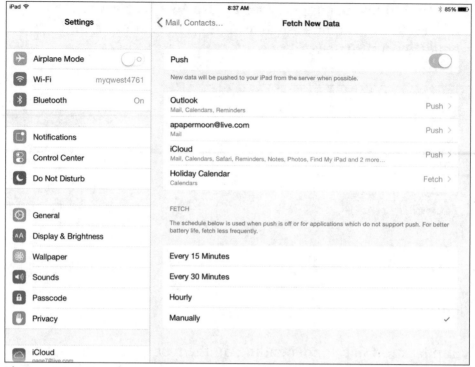

Figure 16-14

Create a Family Calendar

1. If you set up the Family Sharing feature (see Chapter 8 for how to do this), you create a group calendar that you can use to share family events with up to five other people. After you set up Family Sharing, you have to make sure the Calendar sharing feature is on. On the Home screen, tap Settings.

2. Tap iCloud and check that Family Sharing is set up on the second line (see **Figure 16-15**). (It will say Family rather than Set Up Family Sharing if it's been set up.) If it's not, go to Chapter 8 for step-by-step instructions for setting it up.

3. Tap the On/Off switch for Calendars to turn that choice on if it's not already on.

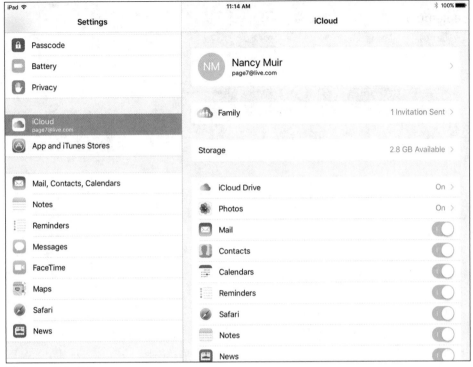

Figure 16-15

4. Tap the Home button and then tap Calendar. Tap Calendars at the bottom of the screen. Scroll down and make sure Family is selected. Tap Done.

5. Now, when you create a new event in the New Event dialog, tap Calendar and choose Family or Show All Calendars. In the details of events is a notation that an event is from the Family calendar.

Delete an Event

1. When an upcoming luncheon or meeting is canceled, you may want to delete the appointment. With Calendar open, tap an event.

2. Tap Delete Event at the bottom of the screen (see **Figure 16-16**). Confirming options appear, including a Delete Event button.

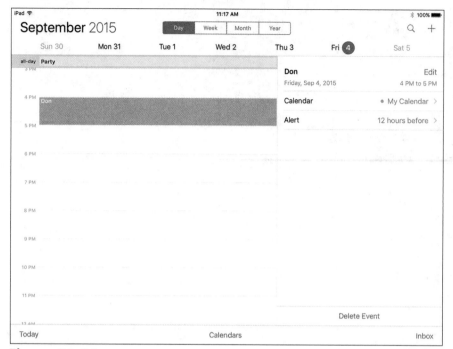

Figure 16-16

3. If this event is a repeating event, you see two buttons that offer the option to delete this instance of the event or this instance and all future instances of the event (see **Figure 16-17**). Tap the button for the option you prefer. The event is deleted, and you return to Calendar view.

Figure 16-17

If an event is moved but not canceled, you don't have to delete the old one and create a new one: Simply edit the existing event to change the day and time in the Edit dialog.

Display Clock

1. Clock is a preinstalled app. You can access it from the Home screen that contains all the other preinstalled apps, such as Notes and Camera. Tap the Clock app to open it. In World Clock view, preset location clocks are displayed along the top of the screen, and the locations of these clocks are displayed on a world map below them.

2. Tap a clock at the top of the screen to display it full-screen (see **Figure 16-18**).

Figure 16-18

3. Tap the World Clock button to return to the World Clock screen. (If the World Clock button isn't visible, tap the screen to make it appear.)

 Clocks for cities that are currently in nighttime are displayed in black. Clocks for cities that are currently in daytime are displayed in white.

Add or Delete a Clock

1. You can add a clock for many (but not all) locations around the world. With Clock open, tap Add on the clock on the far-right side.

2. Tap a city in the resulting list, or tap a letter on the right side of the screen to display locations that begin with that letter. The clock appears in the last spot on the right side of the screen, and the location is displayed on the world map.

3. To remove a location's clock, tap the Edit button in the top-left corner of the World Clock screen. Then tap the minus symbol next to a location and tap the Delete button (see **Figure 16-19**).

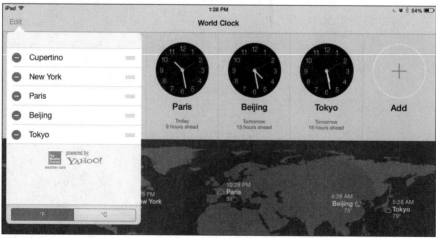

Figure 16-19

Set an Alarm

1. With the Clock app open, tap the Alarm tab at the bottom of the screen.

2. Tap the Add button (a button represented by a plus symbol in the top-right corner).

3. In the Add Alarm dialog, shown in **Figure 16-20**, take any of the following actions, tapping the Back button after you make each setting to return to the Add Alarm dialog:

- Tap Repeat if you want the alarm to repeat at a regular interval, such as every Monday or every Sunday.

- Tap Label if you want the alarm to have a name such as "Take Pill" or "Call Mom."

- Tap Sound to choose the tone the alarm will play.

- Tap the On/Off switch for Snooze if you want to use the Snooze feature.

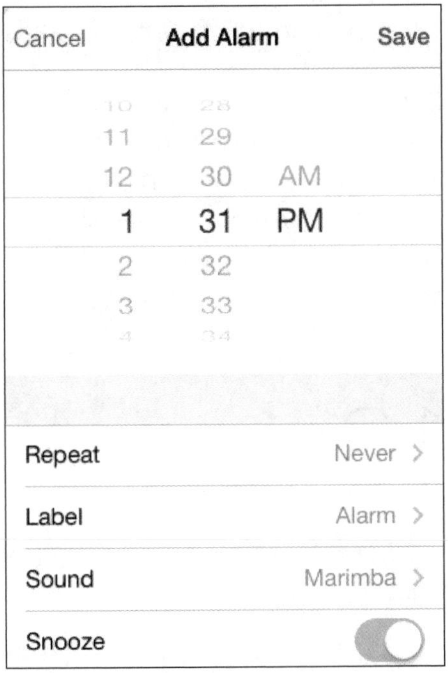

Cancel	**Add Alarm**	Save
10	28	
11	29	
12	30	AM
1	31	PM
2	32	
3	33	
4	34	

Repeat	Never >
Label	Alarm >
Sound	Marimba >
Snooze	

Figure 16-20

4. Place your finger on the three wheels at the top of the dialog, scroll to set the time when you want the alarm to occur, and tap Save. The alarm appears on the calendar's Alarm tab.

To delete an alarm, tap the Alarm tab and then tap Edit. All alarms appear. Tap the red circle with a minus in it next to the alarm and then tap the Delete button.

Use Stopwatch and Timer

Sometimes, life seems like a countdown or a ticking clock counting the minutes you've spent on a certain activity. You can use the Stopwatch and Timer tabs of the Clock app to count down to a specific time, such as the moment when your chocolate chip cookies are done, or to time a walk.

These two apps work very similarly. Tap the Stopwatch or Timer tab and tap the Start button (see **Figure 16-21**). When you set the Timer app, the iPad uses a sound to notify you when time's up. When you start the Stopwatch app, you have to tap the Stop button when the activity is done.

 If you want to time incremental events, such as a series of laps you swim in a pool, with the Stopwatch running, tap the Lap button at the end of each segment and each segment is displayed in a list beneath the main timing field.

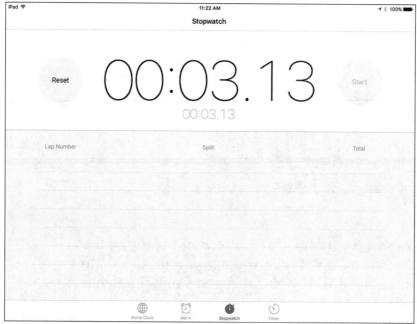

Figure 16-21

Working with Reminders and Notifications

*T*he Reminders app and Notification Center features warm the hearts of those of us who occasionally have a "senior" moment.

Reminders is a kind of to-do list that lets you create tasks and set reminders so you don't forget important commitments.

Notifications allows you to review all the things you should be aware of in one place, such as new mail messages, text messages, calendar appointments, reminders, and alerts. You can also display weather and stock reports in Notification Center.

If you occasionally need to escape all your obligations, try the Do Not Disturb feature. Turn this feature on, and you won't be bothered with alerts until you turn it off again.

In this chapter, you discover how to set up and view tasks in Reminders, and you see how Notification Center can centralize all your alerts.

Get ready to . . .

Create a Task in Reminders

1. Creating a task in Reminders is pretty darn simple. Tap Reminders on the Home screen.

2. On the screen that appears, tap any list on the left to add a task to it (see **Figure 17-1**). The onscreen keyboard appears.

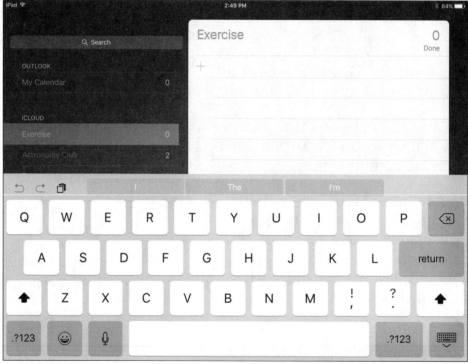

Figure 17-1

3. Enter a task name or description and tap the Done button. The new task is added to the Reminders list.

 See the next task to discover how to add more specifics about an event for which you've created a reminder.

Note that when you first use Reminders, you have only the Reminders list to add tasks to. However, you can create your own list categories. See the task "Create a List" later in this chapter to find out how to do this.

Edit Task Details

1. Tap a task and then tap the Details button (it looks like a small "i") that appears to the right of it to open the Details dialog, shown in **Figure 17-2**. (I explain reminder settings in the task that follows.)

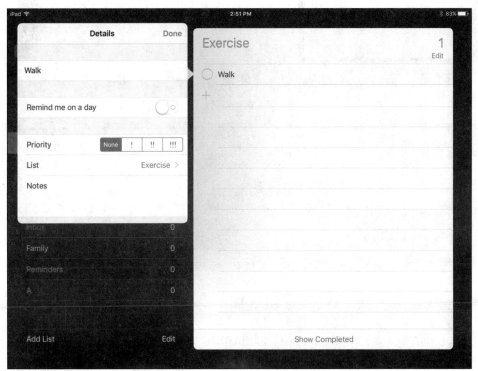

Figure 17-2

2. Tap a Priority (None, Low, Medium, or High).

3. Tap List and then choose any list name (for example, one that you may have created such as "Club" or the default Reminders categories) to access the tasks from that list.

4. Tap Notes and then, using the onscreen keyboard, enter a note about the task (see **Figure 17-3**).

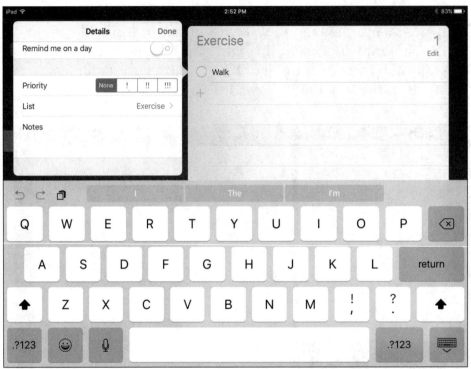

Figure 17-3

5. Tap Done to save the task details.

 Priority settings display exclamation points on a task in a list to remind you of the importance of that task.

Schedule a Reminder

1. One of the major purposes of Reminders is to remind you of upcoming tasks. To set a reminder, tap a task and then tap the Details button that appears to the right of the task.

2. In the Details dialog that appears, tap Remind Me on a Day to turn the feature on.

3. Tap the Alarm field that appears below this setting. The settings shown in **Figure 17-4** appear.

4. Tap and flick the day, hour, and minutes fields to scroll to the date and time for the reminder.

5. Tap Done to save the settings for the reminder.

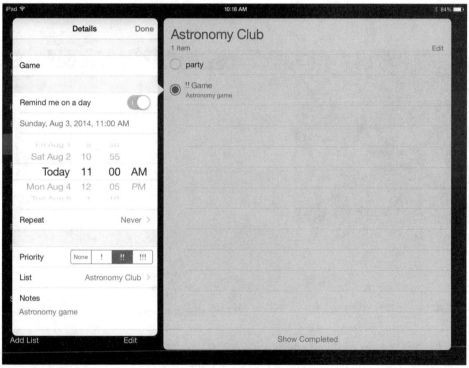

Figure 17-4

 If you want a task to repeat with associated reminders, tap the Repeat field in the Details dialog, and in the dialog that appears, tap Every Day, Week, 2 Weeks, Month, or Year (so you remember those annual meetings — or remember to buy your partner an anniversary gift). To stop the task from repeating, tap End Repeat in the Details dialog, tap End Repeat Date, and select a date from the scrolling calendar when you want to stop the event from repeating.

Create a List

1. You can create your own lists of tasks to help you keep different parts of your life organized. Tap Reminders on the Home screen.

2. Tap Add List to display the New List form, shown in **Figure 17-5**.

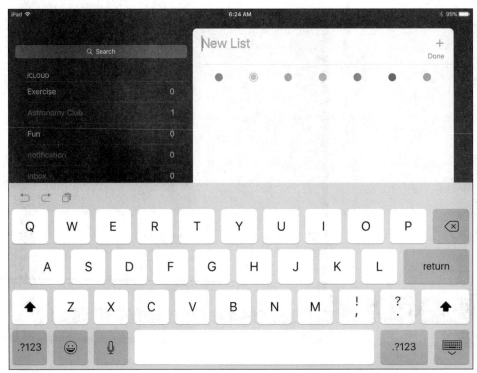

Figure 17-5

3. Enter a name for the list and tap a color. Tap Done and the list name appears in that color in List view.

4. Tap a blank line to create a task in the list.

Sync with Other Devices and Calendars

 To make all these settings work, you should set up your default Calendar and then set up your iCloud account by tapping Settings ⇨ Mail, Contacts, Calendars and then under Accounts, tap iCloud. Verify that you're set up with the account you want to use.

1. To determine which tasks are brought over from other devices or calendars such as Outlook on a PC or Mac or Reminders on the Mac, tap the Settings icon on the Home screen.

2. Tap iCloud and make sure that in the list that appears in the right pane, Reminders is set to On (see **Figure 17-6**).

Figure 17-6

3. Tap Mail, Contacts, Calendars, and scroll down to the Calendars settings.

4. Tap the Sync field and then choose how far back to sync Reminders (see **Figure 17-7**).

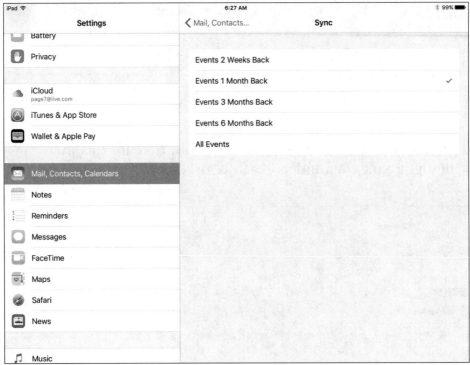

Figure 17-7

Mark as Complete or Delete a Reminder

1. You may want to mark a task as completed or just delete it entirely so you don't continue to get notifications about it. With Reminders open and a list of tasks displayed, tap the button to the left of a task to mark it as complete.

2. To delete more than one task, display a list and then tap Edit in the upper-right corner. Red circles appear to the left of the tasks, as shown in **Figure 17-8**.

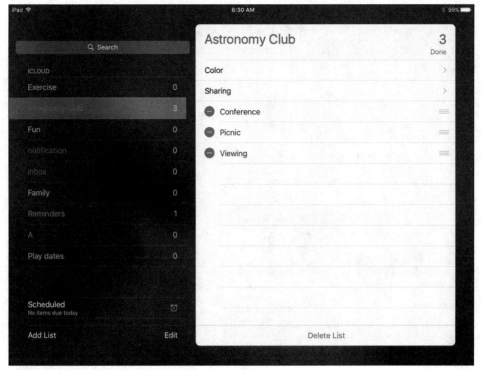

Figure 17-8

3. Tap the red circle to the left of the task and then tap the Delete button. The task is deleted. To delete all tasks, simply tap Delete List at the bottom of the screen.

4. Tap Done to return to the list.

Set Notification Types

1. Notification Center is a list of various alerts, appointments, and useful information such as stock quotes and weather that you can display by swiping down from the top of any iPad screen. Notification Center is on by default, but you can make settings to control what types of notifications are displayed. Tap Settings and then tap Notifications.

2. In the settings that appear (see **Figure 17-9**), note the list of items you can set to be included in Notification Center — or not. Messages and Reminders may be included, for example.

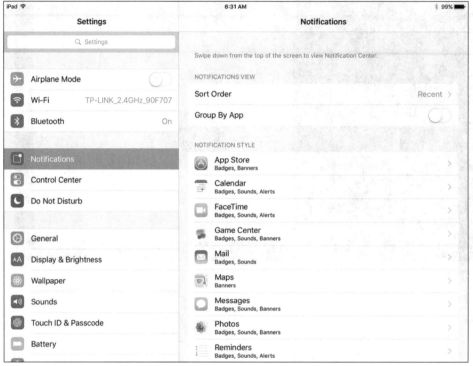

Figure 17-9

3. Tap any item, and in the settings that appear (see **Figure 17-10**), tap the Show in Notification Center On/Off switch to include that item in, or exclude it from, Notification Center.

4. Tap an Alert Style to have no alert, a banner across the top of the screen, or a boxed alert. If you choose Banner, the banner appears and then disappears automatically. If you choose Alerts, you have to take an action to dismiss the alert when it appears.

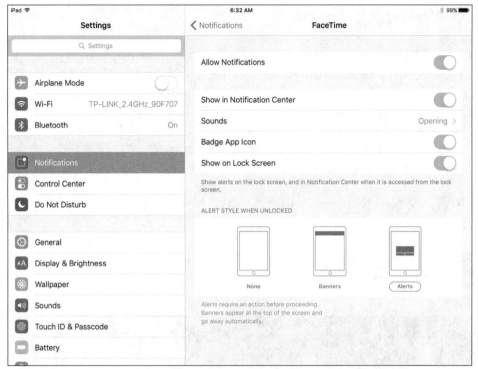

Figure 17-10

5. Badge App Icon is a feature that places a red circle and number on icons on your Home screens to represent alerts associated with those apps. When this feature is turned on, you might see an indication of how many new emails you have waiting for you, for example. To turn this feature off, tap the On/Off switch for Badge App Icon.

6. If you want to be able to view alerts such as those about new messages when the Lock screen is displayed, turn on the Show on Lock Screen setting.

7. When you finish making settings for an individual app, tap the Notifications button to go back to the Notifications settings, or press the Home button to return to the Home screen.

View Notification Center

1. After you've made settings to specify what should appear in Notification Center, you'll want to take a look at those alerts and reminders regularly. On any screen, tap at the top and drag down to display Notification Center (see **Figure 17-11**). Note that items are divided into lists by type depending on what notifications you have at the moment, such as Reminders, Mail, and Calendar.

2. To close Notification Center, tap the bold arrow at the bottom center of the notification area.

 To determine what's displayed in Notification Center, see the preceding task.

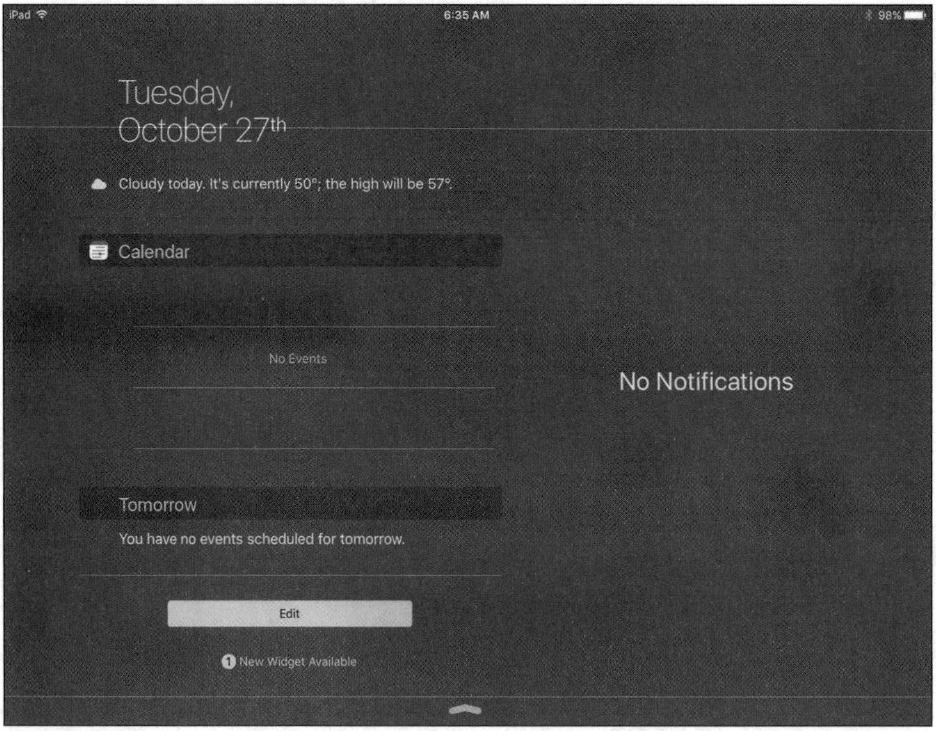

![Notification Center screenshot showing Tuesday, October 27th; Cloudy today. It's currently 50°; the high will be 57°. Calendar, No Events, No Notifications, Tomorrow — You have no events scheduled for tomorrow. Edit button. New Widget Available.]

Figure 17-11

You can also view Notification Center from the Lock screen. Just swipe down from the top of the screen to reveal it, and swipe up to hide it again.

Check Out Today and Notifications Tabs

1. If you hold your iPad in portrait orientation, you get two tabs in Notification Center to play with: Today and Notifications (see **Figure 17-12**). Tap and swipe down from the top of the screen to display Notification Center.

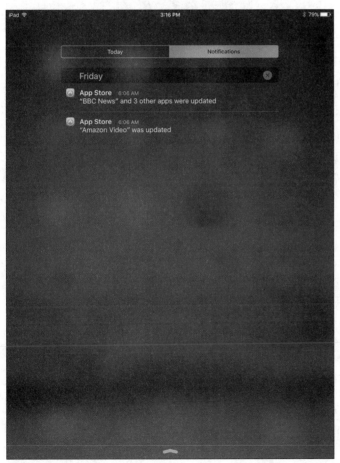

Figure 17-12

2. Tap the Today tab to show all Reminders and other items you've selected to display in Notification Center (see the previous task) that occur today.

3. Tap the Notifications tab to see items for today plus missed and future items.

 To change what's shown on the Today tab, with it displayed tap Edit. Tap a minus button to the left of any item you don't want displayed.

Go to an App from Notification Center

1. You can easily jump from Notification Center to any app that caused an alert or reminder to appear. Tap the top of the screen and drag down to display Notification Center.

2. Tap any item under a category, such as Reminders or Stocks; it opens in its originating app. If you've tapped a message such as an email, you can then reply to the message by following the procedure described in Chapter 6.

Get Some Rest with Do Not Disturb

1. Do Not Disturb is a simple but useful setting you can use to stop any alerts and FaceTime calls from appearing or making a sound. You can make settings to allow calls from certain people through or to allow several repeat calls from the same person in a short period to come through. (Apple is assuming that such repeat calls may signal an emergency or an urgent need to get through to you.) Tap Settings and then tap Do Not Disturb.

2. Tap the Manual On/Off switch to turn the feature on.

3. In the other settings shown in **Figure 17-13**, do any of the following:

- Tap the Scheduled switch to allow alerts during a specified time period to appear.

- Tap Allow Calls From, and in the next screen, select Everyone, No One, or All Contacts.

- Tap the Repeated Calls switch to allow a second call from the same person in a three-minute period to come through.

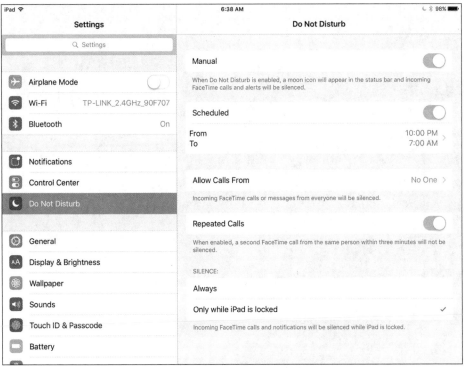

Figure 17-13

4. Press the Home button to return to the Home screen.

 Do Not Disturb can also be applied to individual threads in Messages. This can be handy when you don't want to be pinged each time someone in a Messages conversation replies. See Chapter 7 for more about working with Messages.

Managing Contacts

Contacts is the iPad equivalent of the dog-eared address book that used to sit by your home phone. The Contacts app is simple to set up and use, and it has some powerful features beyond simply storing names, addresses, and phone numbers.

You can pinpoint a contact's address in the iPad's Maps application, for example. You can use your contacts to address emails, Facebook messages, and tweets quickly. If you store a contact record that includes a website, you can use a link in Contacts to view that website instantly. And, of course, you can easily search for a contact by a variety of criteria, including people related to you by family ties and mutual friends, or by groups that you create.

In this chapter, you discover the various features of Contacts, including how you can save yourself time by syncing many email contacts lists to your iPad instantly.

Add a Contact

1. Tap the Contacts app icon on the Home screen to open
the app. If you haven't entered any contacts yet, you see a
blank address book (except for your own contact information, which may have been added when you set up
your iPad), like the one shown in **Figure 18-1**.

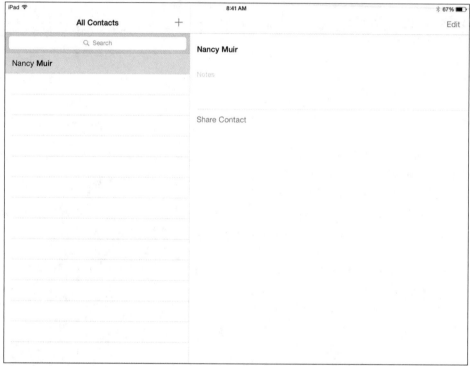

Figure 18-1

2. Tap the Add button, which has a plus sign (+) on it. A
blank New Contact page opens (see **Figure 18-2**), and
the onscreen keyboard displays.

3. Enter any contact information you want. (You only have
to enter first name, last name, or company to create a
contact.)

Figure 18-2

4. To scroll down the contact page and see more fields, flick up on the page with your finger.

5. If you want to add information such as a mailing or street address, you can tap the related Add field, which opens additional entry fields.

6. To add another information field, such as Nickname or Job Title, tap Add Field toward the bottom of the screen. In the Add Field pop-up menu that appears (see **Figure 18-3**), choose a field to add.

7. Tap the Done button when you finish making entries. The new contact appears in your address book. **Figure 18-4** shows an address book with entries added.

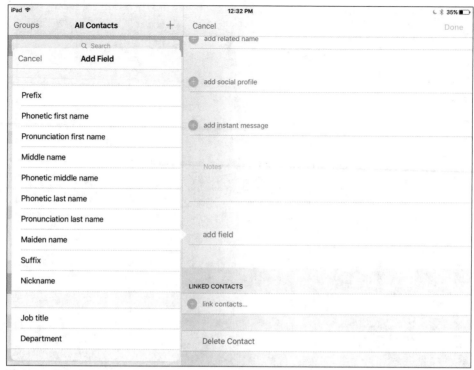

Figure 18-3

 If your contact has a name that's difficult for you to pronounce, consider adding the Phonetic First Name or Phonetic Last Name field, or both, to that person's record (refer to Step 6).

 If you want to add multiple email addresses to a contact so that you can easily send email to all of that contact's email addresses, enter a work email address in the preceding steps and then tap the Add email field, enter an appropriate title, and then enter another email address. Another Other field opens, and so on. Simply enter all email addresses you want to include for that contact and then tap Done.

Figure 18-4

Sync Contacts with iCloud

1. You can use your iCloud account to sync contacts from your iPad and various services such as an email account to back them up. These contacts also become available to your iCloud email account, if you set one up. Tap Settings on the Home screen and then tap iCloud.

2. In the iCloud settings shown in **Figure 18-5,** make sure the On/Off switch for Contacts is set to On to sync contacts.

3. In the Merge Contacts dialog that appears, tap Merge (see **Figure 18-6**) to merge your iPad Contacts with iCloud.

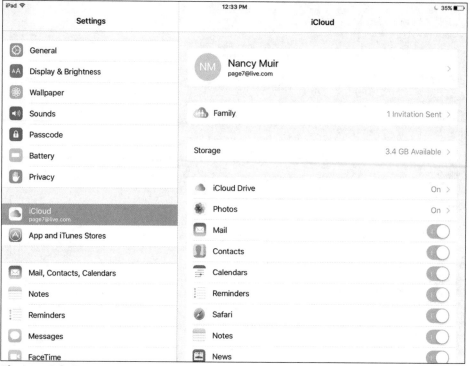

Figure 18-5

Figure 18-6

 You can use the iTunes Wi-Fi sync feature in iPad's Settings under General to sync with iTunes wirelessly from a computer connected to the same Wi-Fi network.

Assign a Photo to a Contact

1. With Contacts open, tap a contact to whose record you want to add a photo.

2. Tap the Edit button.

3. In the settings that appear, tap Add Photo.

4. In the pop-up menu that appears (see **Figure 18-7**), tap Choose Photo to choose an existing photo from the Photos Gallery. You can also choose Take Photo to take that contact's photo on the spot using iPad's camera.

Figure 18-7

5. If you select Choose Photo in Step 4, in the Photos pop-up menu that appears, choose a source for your photo (such as Recently Added or All Photos).

6. In the photo album that appears, tap a photo to select it. The screen shown in **Figure 18-8** appears.

7. Tap the Use button to use the photo for this contact. The photo appears on the contact's details (see **Figure 18-9**).

8. Tap Done to save changes to the contact.

 While you're choosing a photo in Step 6, you can modify the photo before saving it to the contact information. You can unpinch your fingers on the screen to expand the photo. You can also move the photo around the selected area with your finger to focus on a particular section and then tap the Use button to use the modified version.

Figure 18-8

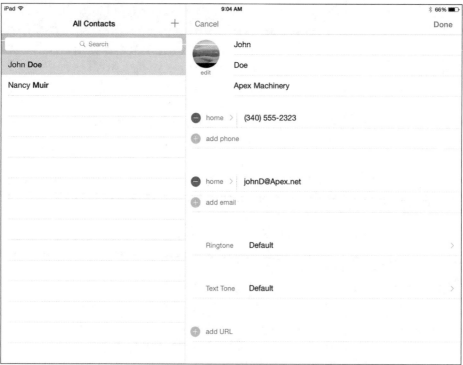

Figure 18-9

Add Twitter or Facebook Information

1. You can add Twitter information to a contact so that you can quickly follow contacts via Twitter or enter Facebook account information so that you can go to your contact's Facebook page. With Contacts open, tap a contact.

2. Tap the Edit button.

3. Scroll down and tap Add Social Profile.

4. In the Twitter field that appears (see **Figure 18-10**), enter a Twitter handle.

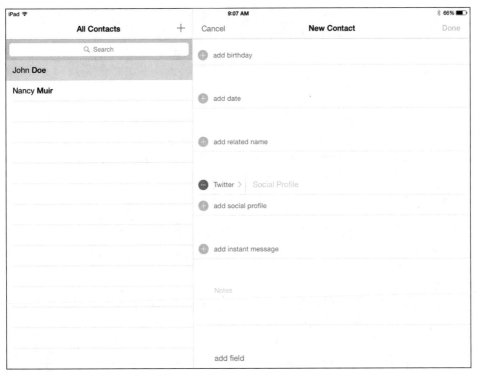

Figure 18-10

5. If you want to create a different social networking field, tap Add Social Profile or tap the word *Twitter* to display other social network options and tap one, such as

Facebook or LinkedIn. The new field appears for you to enter information.

6. Tap Done, and the information is saved. The account is now displayed when you select the contact, as shown in **Figure 18-11**, and you can send a Twitter, Facebook, or other message simply by tapping the username for a service and choosing the appropriate command (such as Tweet).

Figure 18-11

Designate Related People

1. You can quickly designate family relations in a contact record if those people are saved to Contacts. Tap a contact and then tap Edit.

2. Scroll down the record, and tap Add Related Name. A new field labeled Mother appears (see **Figure 18-12**).

3. Enter the contact name for your mother, or tap the Information icon to the right of the field to see a list of your contacts from which you can choose your mother.

4. Tap Add Related Name again, and a new blank field titled Father appears (see **Figure 18-13**). You can tap a field name such as Mother or Father and a list of other possible relationships appears. Tap the relationship you want to add.

5. Tap Done to save the edits.

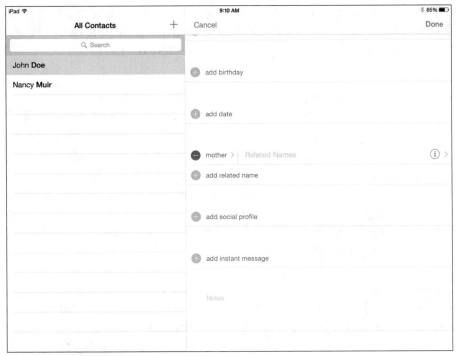

Figure 18-12

Figure 18-13

After you add relations to a contact record, when you select the person in the Contacts main screen, all the related people for that contact are listed there.

Set Ringtones for Contacts

1. If you want to hear a unique tone when you receive a text or a FaceTime call from a particular contact, you can set up this feature in Contacts. If you want to be sure that you know instantly when your spouse, sick friend, or boss is calling, set a unique tone for that person. Tap to add a new contact or select a contact in the list of contacts and then tap Edit.

2. Tap the Ringtone field, and a list of tones appears (see **Figure 18-14**). (Note that you can also tap Text Tone and perform this same procedure for incoming texts.) You can scroll to the top of the list of tones and tap Buy More Tones to buy additional ringtones from Apple.

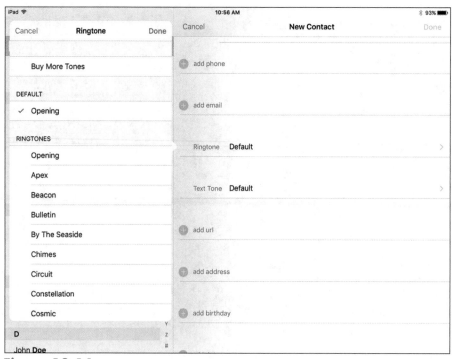

Figure 18-14

3. Tap a tone, and it previews.

4. When you hear a tone that you like, tap Done.

5. Tap Done again to close the contact form.

 You can set a custom tone for FaceTime calls by tapping Settings ⇨ Sounds.

 If your Apple devices are synced via iCloud, setting a unique ringtone for an iPad contact also sets it for your iPhone and iPod touch, as well as for FaceTime on a Mac. See Chapter 3 for more about iCloud.

Search for a Contact

1. With Contacts open, tap the Search field at the top of the left pane. The onscreen keyboard opens (see **Figure 18-15**).

Tap in the Search field

Figure 18-15

2. Type the first letter of the contact's first or last name or the contact's company. All matching results appear, as shown in **Figure 18-16**. In this example, pressing *J* displays *J*ane Arnold and *Ted and J*oan in the results, all of which have *J* as the first letter of the first or last part of the name.

3. Tap a contact in the results to display that person's information in the pane on the right (refer to Figure 18-16).

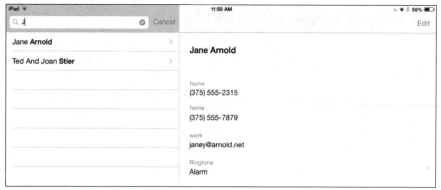

Figure 18-16

 You can search by phone number, website, or address in Contacts as well as by name.

 If you've entered many contacts, you can also use the alphabetical listing that appears along the right side of All Contacts to locate a record. Also, you can tap and drag to scroll down the list of contacts on the All Contacts pane on the left.

Go to a Contact's Website

1. If you entered website information in the Home Page field of a contact record, it automatically becomes a link in the contact's record. Open a contact record.

2. Tap a contact's name to display the person's contact information on the pane at the right and then tap the website link in the Home Page field (see **Figure 18-17**). The Safari browser opens, with the web page displayed.

 You can't go directly back to Contacts after you follow a link to a website. You have to press the Home button and then tap the Contacts app icon again to re-enter the application, or use the multitasking feature by double-pressing the Home button and choosing Contacts from the icons that appear along the bottom of the screen. However, if you have Multitasking Gestures turned on in Settings in the General category, you can do the four-finger swipe to the right to return to the app you just left and keep swiping to go to other open apps.

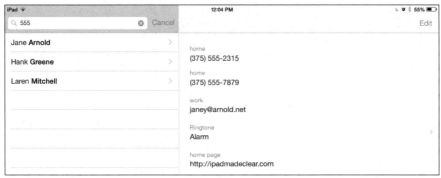

Figure 18-17

Address Email Using Contacts

1. If you entered an email address for a contact, the address automatically becomes a link in the contact's record. Tap the Contacts app icon on the Home screen to open Contacts.

2. Tap a contact's name to display the person's contact information on the pane at the right and then tap the email address link (labeled Work in the example shown in **Figure 18-18**). The New Message form appears, as shown in **Figure 18-19**. Initially, the title bar of this dialog reads New Message, but as you type a subject, New Message changes to the specific title.

3. Tap in a field and use the onscreen keyboard to enter a subject and message.

4. Tap the Send button. The message goes on its way!

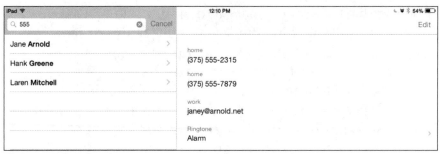

Figure 18-18

Figure 18-19

Share a Contact

1. After you've entered contact information, you can share it with others via an email message. With Contacts open, tap a contact name to display its information.

2. On the Info page, tap Share Contact (refer to Figure 18-4).

3. In the pop-up menu that appears, shown in **Figure 18-20**, tap Mail. The New Message form appears, as shown in **Figure 18-21**.

4. Use the onscreen keyboard to enter the recipient's email address. *Note:* With the person saved in Contacts, you just have to type his name here.

5. Modify the information in the Subject field, if you like.

Figure 18-20

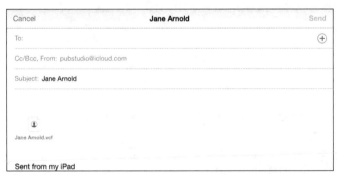

Figure 18-21

6. Enter a message and then tap the Send button. The message goes to your recipient with the contact information attached as a .vcf file. (This *vCard* format is commonly used to transmit contact information.)

When somebody receives a vCard containing contact information, she needs only to click (or tap) the attached file to open it. At this point, depending on the recipient's email or contact management program, she can perform various actions to save the content. Other Mac, iPhone, iPod touch, or iPad users can easily import .vcf records into their own Contacts apps. Even PC and Android users can do this if their contact management programs support .vcf records.

 In Step 3, you can select AirDrop and then tap the name of a device near to you to send the contact information to that device wirelessly. This works with other recent iPads, iPhones (version 5 or later), and Macs that run OS X Yosemite or later.

View a Contact's Location in Maps

1. If you've entered a person's address in Contacts, you have a shortcut for viewing that person's location in the Maps application. Tap the Contacts app icon on the Home screen to open it.

2. Tap the contact you want to view to display his information.

3. Tap the address. Maps opens and displays a map to the address (see **Figure 18-22**).

 This task works with more than just your friends' addresses. You can save information for your favorite restaurant, movie theater, or any other location and then use Contacts to jump to the associated website in the Safari browser or to the address in Maps. For more about using Safari, see Chapter 5. For more about the Maps application, see Chapter 15.

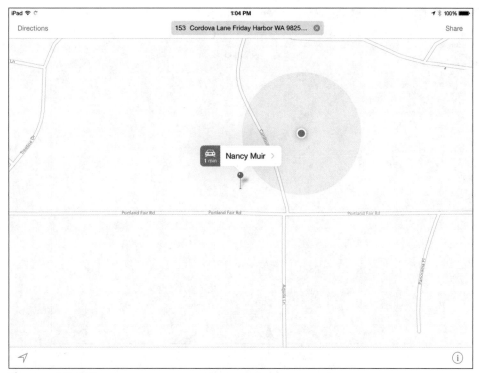

Figure 18-22

Delete a Contact

1. When you want to remove a name or two from your Contacts list, it's easy to do. With Contacts open, tap the contact you want to delete.

2. Tap the Edit button in the top-right corner of the screen (refer to Figure 18-4).

3. On the screen that appears, drag your finger upward to scroll down and then tap the Delete Contact button at the bottom (see **Figure 18-23**). The confirming dialog shown in **Figure 18-24** appears.

4. Tap the Delete Contact button to confirm the deletion.

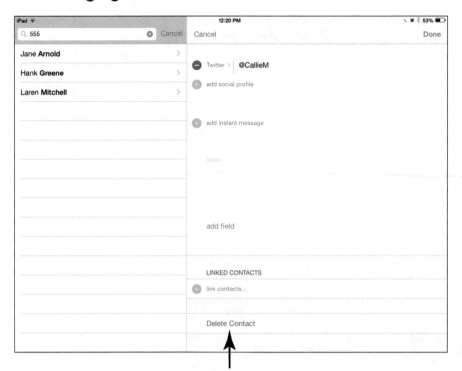

Tap to delete contact

Figure 18-23

Figure 18-24

During this process, if you change your mind before you tap Delete Contact, tap the Cancel button in Step 4. But be careful: After you tap Delete, there's no going back!

Talking to Your iPad with Siri

One of the coolest features in iPad is Siri, a personal-assistant feature that responds to spoken commands. With Siri on your iPad, you can ask for nearby restaurants, and a list appears. You can open apps with a voice command and ask Siri to open the App Store. You can dictate your email messages rather than type them. Placing a FaceTime call to your mother is as simple as saying "Call Mom." Want to know the capital of Rhode Island? Just ask. Siri checks several online sources to answer questions ranging from the result of a mathematical calculation to the size of Jupiter. With iOS 9, Siri searches more broadly, more quickly, and returns more results.

You can also have Siri perform tasks such as returning calls and controlling iTunes Radio. You can even play music and have Siri identify songs for you.

With iOS 9, Siri has gained some other improvements. For example, you can have Siri search photos and videos and locate what you need by date, location, or album name. You can also ask Siri to remind you about an app you're working in, such as Safari, Mail, or Notes, at a later time so you can pick up where you left off.

Get ready to . . .

Activate Siri

Siri is a very useful feature for interacting with your iPad and getting information. You can use Siri to ask for a map to a nearby restaurant, send an email, or tell you how far the Earth is from Pluto, for example. Siri will respond with an answer, display a map, or access web resources for you; see **Figure 19-1**.

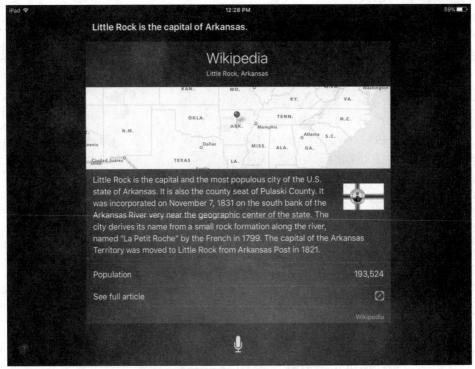

Figure 19-1

Siri should be active when you get your iPad, but if for some reason it's been deactivated, you can use Settings to turn Siri on by following these steps:

1. Tap the Settings icon on the Home screen.

2. Tap General to display the General settings (see **Figure 19-2**) and then tap Siri.

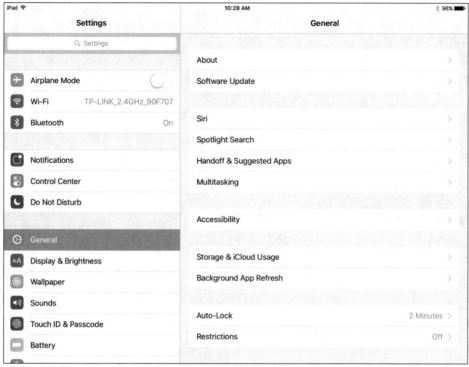

iPad ⚡		10:28 AM	⚡ 96% 🔋
Settings		**General**	

Q Settings

✈️ Airplane Mode	⚪
📶 Wi-Fi	TP-LINK_2.4GHz_90F707
🅱️ Bluetooth	On

| 🔔 Notifications |
| 🎛️ Control Center |
| 🌙 Do Not Disturb |

| ⚙️ General |
| 🔠 Display & Brightness |
| 🖼️ Wallpaper |
| 🔊 Sounds |
| 👆 Touch ID & Passcode |
| 🔋 Battery |

About	›
Software Update	›
Siri	›
Spotlight Search	›
Handoff & Suggested Apps	›
Multitasking	›
Accessibility	›
Storage & iCloud Usage	›
Background App Refresh	›
Auto-Lock	2 Minutes ›
Restrictions	Off ›

Figure 19-2

3. In the screen that appears (see **Figure 19-3**), tap the On/Off switch to turn Siri on.

4. If you want to change the language Siri uses, tap Language and choose a different language from the list that appears.

5. To change the nationality or gender of Siri's voice from female to male or American to British or Australian, tap Siri Voice and then make your selections.

 If you buy a car with the new Car Play feature, you can interact with your car using your voice and Siri. These cars are just now being manufactured, so stay tuned to Apple.com for news about how they'll work.

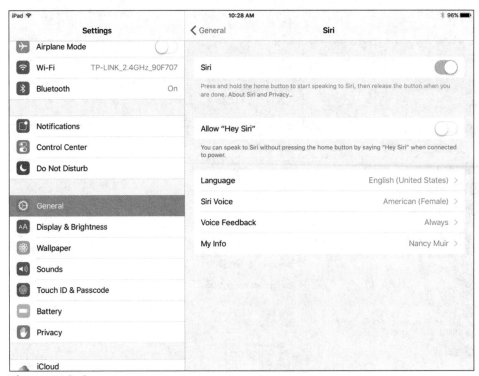

Figure 19-3

 If you want Siri to respond to your verbal requests only when the iPad isn't in your hands, tap Voice Feedback and choose Hands-Free Only. Here's how this setting works and why you may want to use it: In general, if you're holding your iPad, you can read responses on the screen, so you may not want to have your tablet talk to you. But if you're puttering with, say, an electronics project, you may want to speak requests for mathematical calculations and hear the answers rather than having to read them. In such a situation, Hands-Free Only is a useful setting.

 Siri is available on the iPad only when you have Internet access, but remember that cellular data charges may apply when Siri checks online sources if that Internet connection is via 3G/4G. In addition, Apple warns that available features may vary by area.

Understand All That Siri Can Do

Siri allows you to interact with many apps on your iPad by voice. You can pose questions or ask to do something like make a FaceTime call or add an appointment to your calendar, for example. Siri can also search the Internet or use an informational database called Wolfram|Alpha to provide information on just about any topic. You don't have to be in an app to make a request involving that app.

Siri also checks Wikipedia, Bing, and Twitter to get you the information you ask for. In addition, you can use Siri to tell the iPad to work with more features, such as opening and searching the App Store and controlling iTunes Radio playback.

Siri is the technology behind the iPad's Dictation feature. When you have the onscreen keyboard open, note that it contains a microphone key that you can tap to begin or end dictation. This feature works in any app that uses the onscreen keyboard.

Siri requires no preset structure for your questions; you can phrase things in several ways. You might ask, "Where am I?" to see a map of your current location, or you could ask "What is my current location?" or "What address is this?" and get the same results.

If you ask a question about, say, the weather, Siri responds to you verbally; with text information; in a form, as with email (see **Figure 19-4**); or by opening a graphic display for some items, such as maps. When a result appears, you can tap it to make a choice or open a related app.

Siri knows what app you're using, though you don't have to have that app open to make a request involving it. However, if you are in the Messages app, you can make a statement like "Tell Susan I'll be late," and Siri knows that you want to send a message. You can also ask Siri to remind you about what you're working on and Siri notes what you're working on, in which app, and reminds you about it at a time you specify.

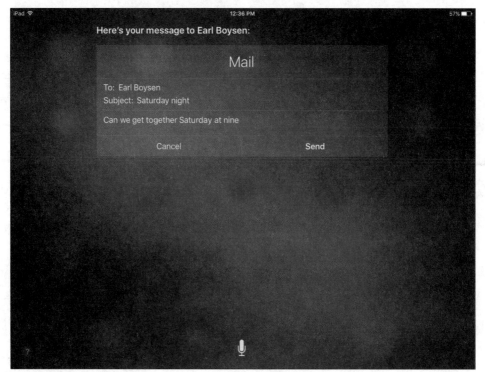

Figure 19-4

Siri works with FaceTime, the App Store, Music, Messages, Reminders, Calendar, Maps, Mail, Clock, Contacts, Notes, and Safari, as well as with several third-party apps. In the following tasks, I provide a quick guide to some of the most useful ways you can use Siri.

Note that no matter what kind of action you want to perform, first press and hold the Home button until Siri opens (see **Figure 19-5**). The rest of this chapter assumes that you're working with an iPad running iOS 9.

Figure 19-5

You can activate Siri hands-free. With your iPad plugged into an outlet, car, or computer, just say "Hey Siri" and Siri opens up ready for a command. In addition, with streaming voice recognition, Siri displays in text what she's hearing as you speak, so you can verify she's understood you instantly. This streaming feature makes the whole process of interacting with Siri faster.

Siri supports more than 30 languages, so you can finally show off those language lessons you took in high school.

Get Suggestions

With iOS 9, your iPad anticipates your needs by making suggestions when you swipe from left to right on the initial Home screen. You'll see a list of contacts you've communicated with recently, apps you've used, and nearby businesses such as restaurants, gas stations, or coffee spots (see **Figure 19-6**). If you tap on an app in the suggestions, it will open displaying the last viewed or listened to item.

In addition, you'll see news stories that may be of interest to you based on items you've viewed before.

Call Contacts via FaceTime

1. Make sure that the people you want to call are entered in your Contacts app and that you've included their phone numbers in their records. If you want to call somebody by stating your relationship to her, such as "Call sister," be sure to enter that relationship in the Related field of her contact record, and make sure that the settings for Siri (refer to Figure 19-3) include your contact name in the My Info field. (See Chapter 18 for more about creating contact records.)

Figure 19-6

2. Press and hold the Home button until Siri appears.

3. Speak a command such as "Make a FaceTime call to Earl" or "FaceTime Mom." Siri initiates the call. If you have two contacts who might match a spoken name, Siri responds with a list of possible matches. Tap one in the list or state the correct contact's name to proceed.

4. To end the call before it completes, you can press the Home button and then tap End.

 To cancel any spoken request, you have four options: Say "Cancel," tap the Dictation key on the Siri screen, press the Home button, or tap anywhere on the screen outside the Siri panel.

Create Reminders and Alerts

1. You can also use Siri with the Reminders app. To create a reminder, press and hold the Home button and then speak a command, such as "Remind me about dentist appointment on Thursday at 12 p.m." A preview of the reminder is displayed (see **Figure 19-7**).

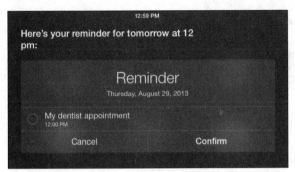

Figure 19-7

2. Tap or say, "Remove" if you change your mind.

3. If you want a reminder ahead of the event you created, activate Siri and speak a command such as "Remind me tonight about the play on Thursday at 8 p.m." Siri creates a second reminder, which you can confirm or cancel if you change your mind.

Add Tasks to Your Calendar

1. You can also set up events on your Calendar by using Siri. Press and hold the Home button and then speak a phrase such as "Set up meeting at 5 p.m. on July 23rd." A sample calendar entry appears. Tap the Confirm button to save it.

2. If there's a conflict, Siri tells you there's already an appointment at that time (see **Figure 19-8**) and asks whether you still want to set up the new appointment. You can say, "Yes" or "Cancel" at that point or tap the Yes or Cancel button.

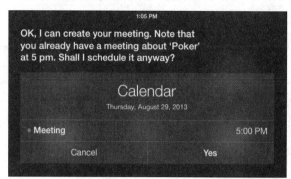

Figure 19-8

Play and Identify Music

1. You can use Siri to play music from the Music app and iTunes Radio. Press and hold the Home button until Siri appears.

2. To play music, speak a command, such as "Play music" or "Play 'As Time Goes By'" to play a specific song or album.

3. When music is playing, use commands such as "Pause music," "Next track," and "Stop music" to control playback.

4. To identify music that's playing, simply activate Siri and say something like "What song is playing?" Siri tells you and may even make the item available for purchase through iTunes.

One of the beauties of Siri is that you don't have to follow a specific command format, as you do with some other voice-command apps. You could say "Play the next track," "Next track," or "Jump to the next track on this album," and Siri will get your meaning.

If you're listening to music or a podcast with earphones plugged in, and stop midstream, the next time you plug in earphones, Siri recognizes that you might want to continue with the same item.

Get Directions

You can use the Maps app and Siri to find your current location, get directions, find nearby businesses (such as restaurants or banks), or get a map of another location. Be sure to turn on Location Services to allow Siri to know your current location (tap Settings ⇨ Privacy ⇨ Location Services, and make sure the Location Services switch is set to on and that Siri & Dictation is turned on farther down in that same pane).

Here are some of the commands you can try to get directions or a list of nearby businesses:

⟶ **"Where am I?"**

   Siri displays a map of your current location. If you have a Wi-Fi–only iPad, this location may be approximate.

⟶ **"Where is Apache Junction, Arizona?"**

   Siri displays a map of that city.

⟶ **"Find restaurants."**

   Siri displays a list of restaurants near your current location, as in **Figure 19-9**; tap one to display a map of its location.

⟶ **"Find a nearby bank."**

   Siri displays a map indicating the location of that business (or, in some cases, several nearby locations, such as a bank branch and all ATMs).

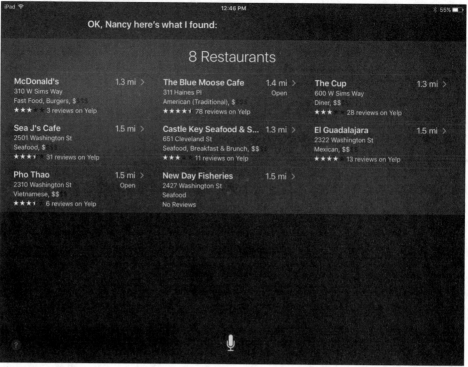

Figure 19-9

➠ **Get directions to the Empire State Building.**

Loads a map with a route drawn and provides a narration of directions to the site from your current location.

 After a location is displayed in a map, tap the Information button on the location's label to view its address, phone number, and website address, if available.

Ask for Facts

Wolfram|Alpha is a self-professed online computational knowledge engine, which means that it's more than a search engine because it provides specific information about a search term rather than multiple search results. If you want facts without having to spend time browsing websites to find those facts, Wolfram|Alpha is a very good resource.

Siri uses Wolfram|Alpha and sources such as Wikipedia and Bing to look up facts in response to questions, such as "What is the capital of Kansas?", "What is the square root of 2003?", and "How large is Mars?" Just press and hold the Home button, and ask your question; Siri consults its resources and returns a set of relevant facts.

You can also get information about many things, such as the weather, stocks, or the time. Just say a phrase like one of these to get what you need:

➡ **"What is the weather?"**

Siri shows the weather report for your current location. If you want weather in another location, just specify the location in your question.

➡ **"What is the price of Apple stock?"**

Siri tells you the current price of the stock or the price of the stock when the stock market last closed. (Let's hope that you own some.)

➡ **"What time is it?"**

Siri tells you the time in your time zone and displays a clock (see **Figure 19-10**).

Figure 19-10

Search the Web

Siri can use various resources to respond to specific requests, such as "Who is the Queen of England?", but it searches the web if you ask more general requests for information. Siri can also search Twitter for comments related to your search.

If you speak a phrase such as "Find a website about birds" or "Find information about the World Series," Siri can respond in a couple of ways. The app can simply display a list of search results by using the default search engine specified in your settings for Safari, or it can say "If you like, I can search the web for such-and-such." In the first instance, just tap a result to go to that website. In the second instance, you can confirm that you want to search the web or cancel.

Send Email, Tweets, or Messages

You can create an email or an instant message with Siri and existing contacts. If you say "Email Jack Wilkes," a form already addressed to that contact opens. Siri asks you what the subject is and what to say in the message. Speak your message and then say, "Send" to speed your message on its way.

Siri also works with the iMessage feature. Tap Siri and say "Message Sarah." Siri creates a message and asks what you want to say. Say "Tell Sarah I'll call soon," and Siri creates a message for you to approve and send.

 It's hard to stump Siri. Siri can't tweet unless you've downloaded and set up the Twitter or Facebook app, for example. But if you speak a tweet without having Twitter installed, she gives you a link to tap to install the app! After you install these apps, you can say things to Siri such as "Post tweet" or "Post to Facebook" and Siri asks what you want to say, lets you review it, and posts it. Siri can also connect you with Flickr and Vimeo with those apps installed.

Get Helpful Tips

I know that you're going to have a wonderful time learning the ins and outs of Siri, but before I close this chapter, here are some tips to get you going:

➡ **Making corrections if Siri doesn't understand you:** With iOS 9, improvements have been made to how accurately Siri recognizes your voice. However, it's not perfect. When you speak a command and Siri displays what it thought you said but misses the mark, you have a few options:

- To correct a request that you've made, you can quickly tap the Edit button below the command Siri heard; then edit the question by typing or tapping the microphone key on the onscreen keyboard and then dictating the correct information.

- If a word is underlined in blue, that word is a possible error. Tap the word and then tap an alternative that Siri suggests.

- You can also simply speak to Siri and say something like "I meant Sri Lanka" or "No, send it to Sally."

  If even corrections aren't working, you may need to restart your iPad to reset the software.

➡ **Using a headset or earphones:** If you're using the iPad with earphones or use a Bluetooth headset to activate Siri, instead of pressing the Home button, press and hold the center button (the little button on the headset that starts and stops a call).

➡ **Using Find My Friends:** You can download a free app from the App Store called Find My Friends that allows you to ask Siri to locate your friends geographically, if they're carrying devices with GPS and Location Services turned on.

➡ **Getting help with Siri:** To get help with Siri features, just press and hold the Home button, and ask Siri "What can you do?"

➡ **Joking around:** If you need a good laugh, ask Siri to tell you a joke. She has quite the sense of humor . . .

Making Notes

*N*otes is the pre-installed app that you can use to do everything from jotting down notes at meetings to keeping to-do lists. It isn't a robust word processor (such as Apple Pages or Microsoft Word) by any means, but for taking notes on the fly, jotting down to-do lists, or dictating a poem with the Dictation feature while you sit and sip a cup of tea on your deck, it's a useful option.

In this chapter, you see how to enter and edit text in Notes, as well as how to manage notes by navigating among them; searching for content; and sharing, deleting, and printing notes. I also help you to explore the new shortcut menu that allows you to create bulleted checklists, add pictures to notes, add drawings to notes, and apply styles to text in a note.

Open Notes

1. To get started with Notes, tap the Notes app on the Home screen. If you've never used Notes, it opens with a blank Notes list displayed. (If you've used Notes, it opens to the last note you were working on. If that's the case, you might want to jump to the next task to create a new, note.) Depending on how your iPad is oriented, you see the screen shown in **Figure 20-1** (landscape) or **Figure 20-2** (portrait).

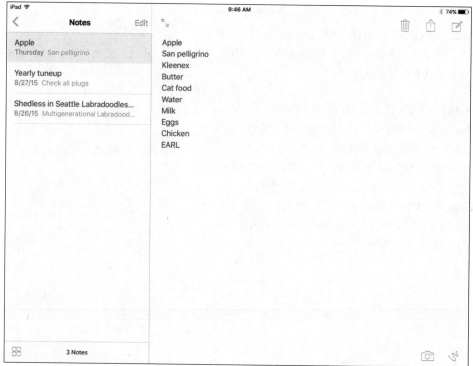

Figure 20-1

2. Tap the New button in the top-right corner of the open note — the one that looks like a small page with a pen hovering over it. The onscreen keyboard, shown in **Figure 20-3**, appears.

Figure 20-2

3. Tap keys on the keyboard to enter text (or tap the Dictation key to speak your text; the first time you do this, you will be asked to enable Dictation).

4. If you want to enter numbers or symbols, tap either of the keys labeled .?123. The numerical keyboard, shown in **Figure 20-4,** appears. Whenever you want to return to the alphabetic keyboard, tap either of the keys labeled ABC.

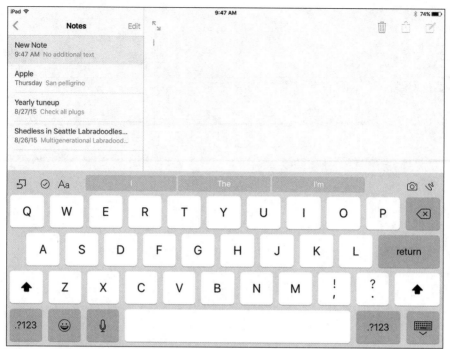

Figure 20-3

Figure 20-4

5. To capitalize a letter, tap a Shift key (one with the upward-pointing arrow on it) at the same time as you tap the letter.

6. When you want to start a new paragraph or a new item in a list, tap the Return key.

7. To edit text, tap to the right of the text you want to edit and then either use the Delete key to delete text to the left of the cursor or enter new text. No need to save a note — it's kept automatically until you delete it.

 If you use the Dictation feature, everything you say is sent to Apple to be converted into text. If you're not comfortable with that, you may want to disable the Dictation feature. For more about Dictation, see Chapter 2.

 When you have the numerical keyboard displayed (refer to Figure 20-4), you can tap either of the keys labeled #+= to access more symbols, such as the percentage sign or the euro symbol, or additional bracket styles. Pressing and holding certain keys displays alternative characters.

 You can activate the Enable Caps Lock feature in the General Keyboard settings so that you can then turn Caps Lock on by double-tapping the Shift key (this upward-pointing arrow is available only on the letter keyboard).

Create a New Note

1. With one note open, to create a new note, tap the New Note icon in the top-right corner. The current note is saved and a new blank note appears.

2. Enter and edit text as described in the preceding task.

Notes can be shared among Apple devices via iCloud. In Settings, both devices must have Notes turned on under iCloud. New notes are shared instantaneously if both devices are connected to the Internet.

 If your iPad is in portrait orientation and you want to display the list of saved notes beside the current note, tap the Notes button to see a drop-down list of notes.

Use Copy and Paste

1. The Notes app includes two essential editing tools that you're probably familiar with from using word processors: Copy and Paste. With a note displayed, press and hold your finger on a word.

2. Tap Select or Select All in the pop-up menu shown in **Figure 20-5**. Tap the Copy button in the pop-up menu or tap the Edit button in the top-left corner of the onscreen keyboard and tap the Copy button.

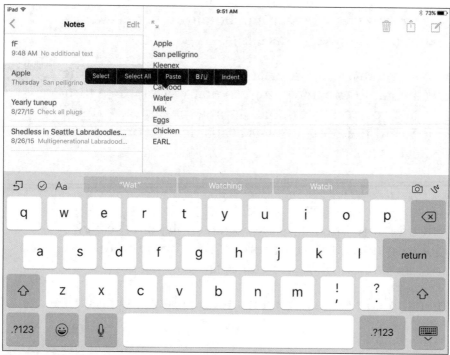

3. Press and hold the spot in the document where you want to place the copied text.

4. On the pop-up menu that appears (see **Figure 20-6**), tap the Paste button. The copied text appears.

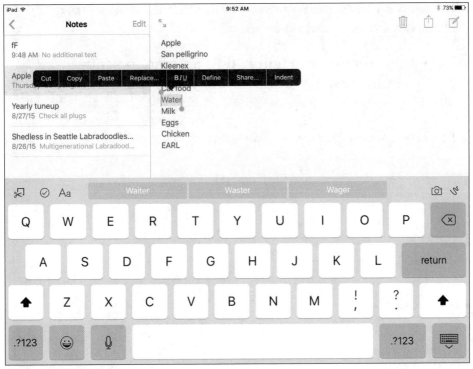

Figure 20-6

 If you want to select all text in a note to either delete or copy it, tap the Select All button on the toolbar shown in Figure 20-5. All text is selected and you can then select commands from the toolbar that appears to cut, copy, or paste text.

 To extend a selection to adjacent words, press one of the little handles that extend from the edge of a selection and drag to the left or right or up or down.

To delete text, you can also choose text by using the Select or Select All command and then tapping the Delete key on the onscreen keyboard.

Insert a Picture

1. To insert a photo into a note, tap the Picture icon shaped like a camera above the keyboard.

2. Tap Photo Library (see **Figure 20-7**) to insert a picture you've already taken and choose the photo you want to insert.

3. Tap Use and the photo is inserted into your note.

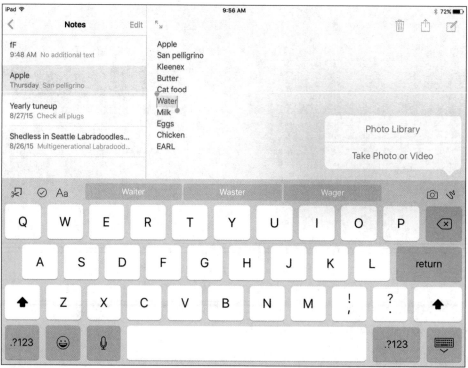

Figure 20-7

 If you want to take a photo or video, tap Take Photo or Video in Step 2 and take a new photo or video. Tap Use Photo to insert it in your note.

Add a Drawing

1. With the latest version of Notes, you can create a drawing to add to your note. With a note open, tap in the note to display the keyboard.

2. Click the Drawing tool (a squiggle near the right side of the top of the keyboard). The drawing tools shown in **Figure 20-8** appear.

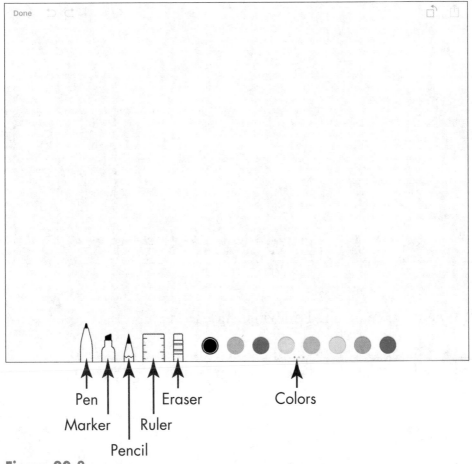

Pen

Marker

Pencil

Ruler

Eraser

Colors

Figure 20-8

3. Tap a drawing tool (Pen, Marker, or Pencil).

4. Tap a color in the color palette that appears.

5. Draw on the screen using your finger, as shown in
Figure 20-9.

Figure 20-9

6. When you've finished drawing, click Done.

 Clicking the Ruler tool places a ruler-shaped item on
screen that you can use to help you to draw straight
lines.

Apply a Text Style

Text styles, including Title, Heading, Body, Bulleted List, Dashed List,
and Numbered List, are available on the new shortcut toolbar above
the onscreen keyboard. With a note open and the shortcut toolbar
displayed, press on text and choose Select or Select All.

Tap the Text Style (labelled Aa) and then tap a style on the list that's shown in **Figure 20-10.** Click Done and the style is applied.

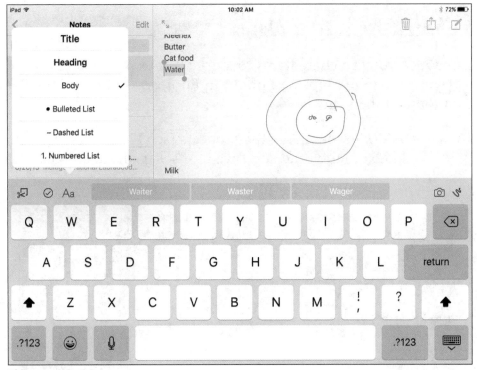

Figure 20-10

Create a Checklist

1. The new Checklist formatting feature in Notes allows you to add circular buttons in front of text and then click those buttons to check off completed items on a checklist. With a note open and the shortcut toolbar displayed, click the Checklist button.

2. Enter text and press Return on the keyboard. A second checklist bullet appears.

3. When you're done entering Checklist items, after entering the last item press Return, and then tap the Checklist button again to turn the feature off.

You can apply the Checklist formatting to existing text if you press on the text, tap Select or Select All, and then tap the Checklist button.

Add a Shared Item to a Note

In iOS 9, you can share items to a note. For example, if you are displaying a map in Maps or a photo in Photos, you can tap the Share button and then choose Notes.

When you do, in the dialog that appears (see **Figure 20-11**), you can either add text to the note and save it or select an existing note to add the item to.

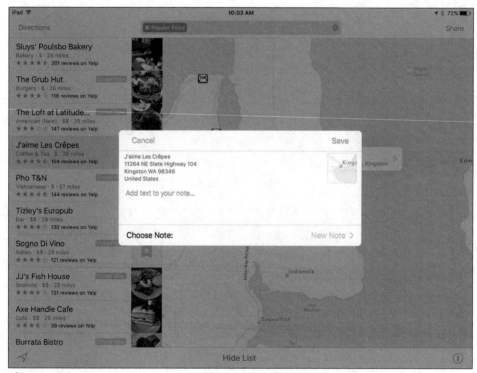

Figure 20-11

Display the Notes List

1. Tap the Notes app on the Home screen to open Notes.

2. In landscape orientation, a list of notes appears by default on the left side of the screen. In portrait orientation, you can display this list by tapping the Notes button in the top-left corner of the screen (refer to Figure 20-2); the notes list appears.

3. Tap any note in the list to display it, as shown in **Figure 20-12**.

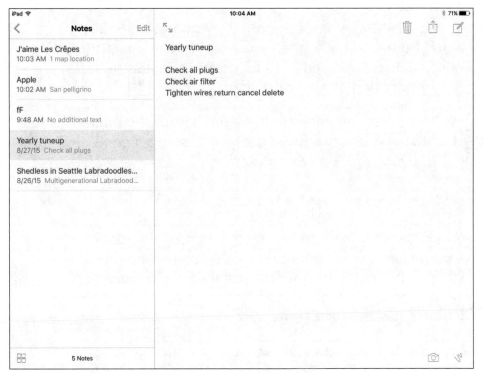

Figure 20-12

Notes names your note by using the first line of text. If you want to rename a note, display the note, tap before the current initial text, enter a new title, and press Return. This new text becomes the name of your note in the notes list.

Move among Notes

1. If you want to look for a note based on how long ago you created it, you should know that notes are stored with the most recently created or modified notes at the top of the notes list. Older notes fall toward the bottom of the list. The date and/or time you last modified a note also appear in the notes list to help you out. You have a couple of ways to move among notes you've created. Tap the Notes app on the Home screen to open Notes.

2. With the notes list displayed (see the previous task for more on viewing the notes list), tap a note to open it.

3. To move among notes in portrait orientation, tap the Notes button in the top-left corner and then tap another note in the list to open it. In landscape orientation, just tap another note in the notes list.

 Notes lets you enter multiple notes with the same title — which can cause confusion, so it's a good idea to name your notes uniquely!

Search for a Note

1. You can search for a note that contains certain text. The Search feature lists only notes that contain your search criteria and highlights the first instance of the word or words you enter in each note. Tap the Notes app on the Home screen to open Notes.

2. Either hold the iPad in landscape orientation or tap the Notes button in portrait orientation to display the notes list (refer to Figure 20-2).

3. Tap the Search field at the top of the notes list (see **Figure 20-13**); you may have to drag the panel downwards to reveal this field. The onscreen keyboard appears.

Figure 20-13

4. Begin to enter the search term (see **Figure 20-14**). All notes that contain matching words appear in the list.

5. Tap a note to display it and then locate the instance of the matching word. Tap another result in the search list to view subsequent occurrences of the search term.

Figure 20-14

Share a Note

1. If you want to share what you wrote with a friend or colleague, you can easily use AirDrop or Mail to do so. With a note displayed, tap the Share button at the top right of the screen.

2. Tap Mail.

3. In the email form that appears (see **Figure 20-15**), type one or more email addresses in the appropriate fields. At least one email address must appear in the To: field.

4. If you need to make changes in the subject or message, tap either area and make the changes by using either the onscreen keyboard or the Dictation feature (on third-generation or later iPads).

Figure 20-15

5. Tap the Send button, and your email is sent.

6. To send a note via AirDrop, tap the Share button and then tap the AirDrop-enabled device you want to send the note to (see **Figure 20-16**).

 To leave a message before sending it but save a draft so that you can finish and send it later, tap Cancel and then tap Save Draft. The next time you tap the email button with the same note displayed in Notes, your draft appears.

Figure 20-16

Delete a Note

1. There's no sense in letting your notes list become cluttered, making it harder to find the ones you need. When you're done with a note, it's time to delete it. Tap the Notes app icon on the Home screen to open Notes.

2. With the iPad in landscape orientation, tap a note in the notes list to open it.

3. Tap the Trash icon (see **Figure 20-17**).

4. In the Delete Note message that appears, tap OK. The note is deleted.

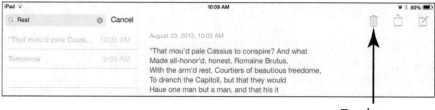

Trash icon

Figure 20-17

 Notes is a nice little application, but it's limited. It offers few formatting tools beyond preset styles or ways to print the content you enter unless you have an AirPrint-compatible printer. If you've made some notes and want to graduate to building a more robust document in a word processor, you have a few options:

⟹ You can let iCloud sync your iPad notes with the Notes app on your Mac if it uses the Mountain Lion or later version of the Mac OS and then work with the text from there.

⟹ If you bought an iPad in September 2013 or later, you get Pages free preinstalled on your iPad's second Home screen. If your iPad is older, you can buy the Pages word processor application for the iPad, which costs about $9.99, and copy your note (using the copy-and-paste feature discussed earlier in this chapter).

⟹ You can send the note to yourself in an email message. Open the email and copy and paste its text into a full-fledged word processor, and you're good to go.

Print a Note

1. If you have an AirPrint-enabled printer, you can print your notes. With Notes open and the note you want to print displayed, tap the Share button at the top right of the screen.

2. Tap the Print icon (refer to Figure 20-16).

3. In the Printer Options dialog that appears, shown in
Figure 20-18, tap Select Printer to display a list of available printers.

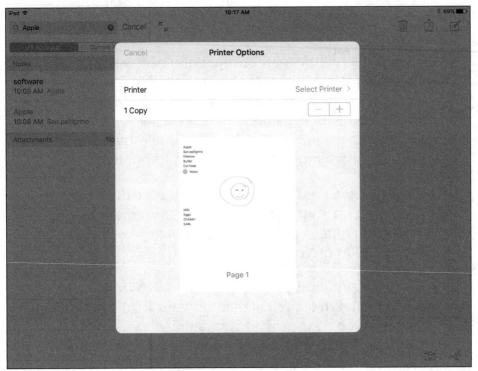

Figure 20-18

4. Tap the printer you want to use.

5. Tap the + button in the Copy field to print more than
one copy. If your printer is capable of printing two-sided,
you can also select that option.

6. Tap Print.

 See Chapter 5 for more about AirPrint-compatible
printers.

Getting the News You Need

*W*ith iOS 9 comes the News app. This so-called news aggregator gathers news stories that either match your news reading habits, or match the channels and topics you've selected. You can choose which news sites are your favorites, search for news on a particular topic, and save news stories to read later. In this chapter, you get an overview of all these features.

IIII➡ Chapter

21

Get ready to . . .

Read Your News

1. To get started with the News app, on the home screen, click the app to open it.

2. The For You tab of news stories shown in **Figure 21-1** appears by default, though whichever tab you last chose will appear next time you open the app.

3. Scroll down the page to see the news stories of the day.

4. Tap an item in the You Might Like list (see **Figure 21-2**) for more items that might be of interest to you.

Figure 21-1

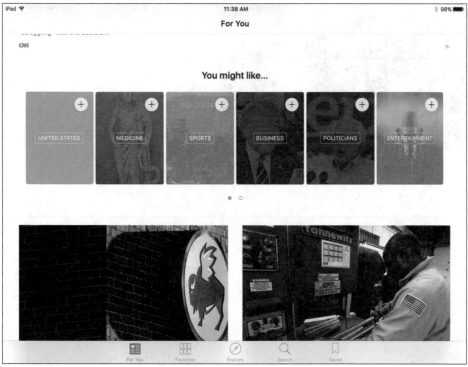

Figure 21-2

 Remember that when you're reading a story you like, you can tap the Share button at the top of the screen to share via Mail, Message, Twitter, or Facebook.

Select Favorites

1. Favorites allows you to select the topics and channels you prefer to include in Your News. With the News apps open, tap the Favorites button at the bottom of the screen. The screen shown in **Figure 21-3** appears.

2. Tap Edit.

3. Tap an item to delete it from Favorites and then tap Done (see **Figure 21-4**).

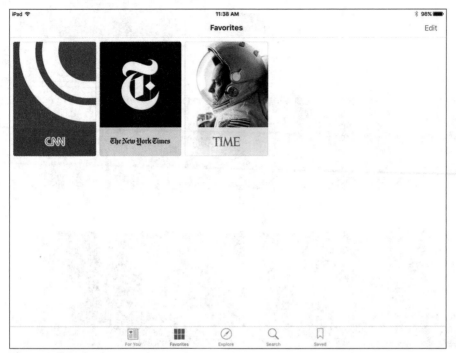

Figure 21-3

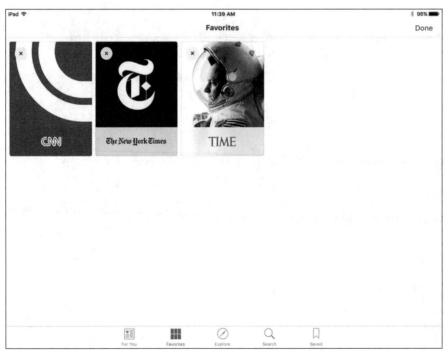

Figure 21-4

Explore Channels and Topics

1. Using the Explore feature, you can select channels to add to Favorites. With the News app open, tap Explore at the bottom of the screen. The options shown in **Figure 21-5** appear.

2. Tap a Suggested Topic to explore it.

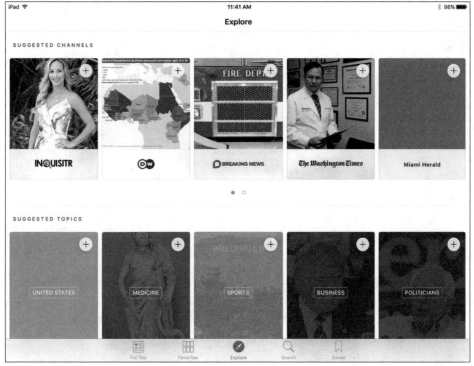

Figure 21-5

3. Tap the Back button, and then tap an item in the Browse list (see **Figure 21-6**) to display channels related to a topic. Tap a channel to add it to Favorites.

 You can preview stories before opening them, which saves some download time. In Settings, click on News and then be sure the Show Story Previews switch is set to On (which it is by default).

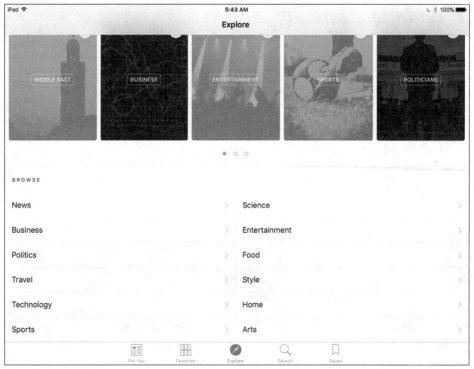

Figure 21-6

Search for News

1. If you have a particular news story you'd like to follow, you can search for it from within News. With the app open, tap the Search button at the bottom of the screen. You're presented with a Search field as well as some Suggestions (see **Figure 21-7**).

2. Enter a search term or phrase and press Enter or tap on an item in the search results (see **Figure 21-8**).

 If you don't find what you want in the results, tap the Show More Topics or Show More Channels links in the results list.

Figure 21-7

Figure 21-8

Save News Stories

1. It's handy to be able to save news stories to read offline at any time. In the News app, open a news story using any of the methods described in this chapter.

Tap the heart-shaped Save button (it looks like a ribbon) in the top right corner.

2. Tap the Back button to return to the News app and tap the Saved button at the bottom of the screen. Your saved stories are displayed (see **Figure 21-9**).

Figure 21-9

Troubleshooting and Maintaining Your iPad

*i*Pads don't grow on trees; they cost a pretty penny, especially with phone equipment subsidies and two-year contracts disappearing. That's why you should learn how to take care of your iPad and troubleshoot any problems it might have so that you get the most out of it.

In this chapter, I provide some advice about the care and maintenance of your iPad, as well as tips about how to solve common problems, update iPad system software, and even reset the iPad if something goes seriously wrong. In case you lose your iPad, I even tell you about a feature that helps you find it, activate it remotely, or even disable it if it has fallen into the wrong hands. Finally, you get information about backing up your iPad settings and content by using iCloud.

Get ready to . . .

Keep the iPad Screen Clean

If you've been playing with your iPad, you know that it's a fingerprint magnet (despite Apple's claim that the iPad has a fingerprint-resistant screen). Here are some tips for avoiding fingerprint marks and cleaning your iPad screen:

→ **Use a stylus instead of your fingers.** You can buy a stylus for about $1 (or even less) and use it to tap the screen. You may even find that a stylus is more accurate than your fingers when you're using the onscreen keyboard.

→ **Use a dry, soft cloth.** You can get most fingerprints off with a dry, soft cloth, such as the one you use to clean your eyeglasses or a cleaning tissue that's lint- and chemical-free. Or try products used to clean lenses in labs, such as Kimwipes or Kaydry, which you can get from several major retailers, such as Amazon.

→ **Use a stand or dock to hold your iPad.** With a stand or dock, you spend less time picking up your tablet, which cuts down on finger smudges.

→ **Remove the cables.** Turn off your iPad and unplug any cables from it before cleaning the screen with a moistened cloth.

→ **Use a soft cloth.** To get the surface even cleaner, *very* slightly moisten the cloth (moisture can damage your iPad if you overdo it). A microfiber cleaning cloth can be a good option. Again, make sure that whatever cloth material you use is free of lint.

→ **Avoid too much moisture.** Avoid getting too much moisture around the edges of the screen, where it can seep into the unit. Although the iPad Air 2 and later models have their glass, LCD, and touch sensor bonded together to avoid any air gaps, they can be at risk from too much moisture.

⟹ **Never use household cleaners.** They can degrade the coating that keeps the iPad screen from absorbing oil from your fingers.

 Do *not* use premoistened lens-cleaning tissues to clean your iPad screen. Most wipe brands contain alcohol, which can damage the screen's coating.

Protect Your Gadget with a Case

Your screen isn't the only element on the iPad that can be damaged, so consider getting a case for it so you can carry it around the house or around town safely. Besides providing a bit of padding if you drop the device, a case makes the iPad less slippery in your hands, offering a better grip when you're working with it.

Several types of cases are available for the iPad Air 2, iPad Pro, and iPad mini 4, and more are showing up all the time. You can choose the Smart Cover, from Apple, for example ($39 for polyurethane), which covers the screen only; the Smart Case from Apple, which covers both the front and back ($49 in polyurethane; $69 in leather for iPad mini 4 and $79 in leather for iPad Air 2 and later). iPad Pro, being the new kid on the block, has only a few covers available at this time but that will change. Consider a cover from another manufacturer, such as Tuff-Luv (www.tuff-luv.com) or Griffin (www.griffintechnology.com), that comes in materials ranging from leather to silicone (see **Figures 22-1** and **22-2**).

Cases range from a few dollars to $70 or more for leather, with some outrageously expensive designer cases costing upward of $500. Some provide a cover for the screen and back; others protect only the back and sides or, in the case of Smart Cover, only the screen. If you carry your iPad around much, consider a case with a screen cover to provide better protection for the screen, or use a screen overlay, such as InvisibleShield from Zagg (www.zagg.com).

Figure 22-1

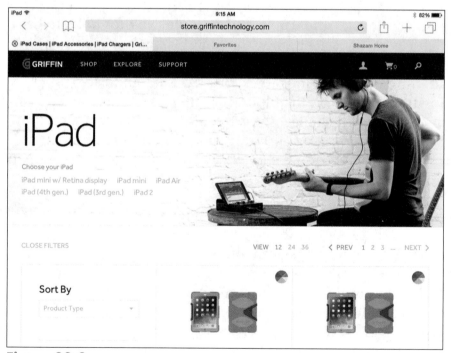

Figure 22-2

Extend Your iPad's Battery Life

The much-touted ten-hour battery life of the iPad is a wonderful feature, but you can do some things to extend it even further. Here are a few tips to consider:

⟹ **Keep tabs on remaining battery life.** You can estimate the amount of remaining battery life by looking at the Battery icon at the far-right end of the Status bar, at the top of your screen.

⟹ **Use standard accessories to charge your iPad most effectively.** When connected to a recent model Mac or Windows computer, the iPad will charge slowly; charging the iPad on certain PC connections, on the other hand, *drains* the battery slowly. The most effective way to charge your iPad is to plug it into a wall outlet by using the Lightning-to-USB cable and the 10W USB Power Adapter that comes with your iPad (see **Figure 22-3**).

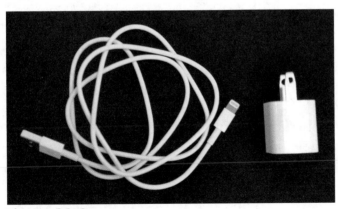

Figure 22-3

➠ The fastest way to charge the iPad is to turn it off while charging it.

➠ Your battery may *lose* power if you leave it connected to the USB port on an external keyboard.

➠ The Battery icon on the status bar indicates when charging is complete.

 Your iPad battery is sealed in the unit, so you can't replace it, as you can many laptop or cellphone batteries. If the battery is out of warranty, you may have to fork over more than $100 to get a new one with AppleCare coverage (see next tip). See the "Get Support" task, later in this chapter, to find out where to get a replacement battery.

 Apple offers AppleCare+. For $99, you get two years of coverage, which protects you even if you drop or spill liquids on your iPad. (Apple covers up to two incidents of accidental damage.) If your iPad has to be replaced, it will cost you only $49, rather than the $250 it used to cost with garden-variety AppleCare. That means $148 versus the $299 price Apple offered me to replace my iPad when it died 14 months into its life (and Apple advised me that the company couldn't service it). You can purchase AppleCare+ when you buy your iPad or within 60 days of the date of purchase. See www.apple.com/support/products/ipad.html for more details.

What to Do with a Nonresponsive iPad

If your iPad goes dead on you, the problem is most likely to be a power issue, so the first thing to do is plug the Lightning-to-USB cable (or Dock Connector-to-USB cable) into the 10W USB Power Adapter, plug the 10W USB Power Adapter into a wall outlet, plug the other end of the Lightning-to-USB cable (or Dock Connector-to-USB cable) into your iPad, and charge the battery.

Another thing to try — if you believe that an app is hanging up the iPad — is to press the Sleep/Wake button for a couple of seconds. Then press and hold the Home button. The app you were using should close.

You can always try the tried-and-true reboot procedure. On the iPad, press the Sleep/Wake button on the right top until a red slider appears. Drag the slider to the right to turn off your iPad. After a few moments, press the Sleep/Wake button to boot up the little guy again.

If the situation seems to be drastic and none of these ideas works, try to reset your iPad. To do this, press the Sleep/Wake button and the Home button at the same time until the Apple logo appears onscreen.

Make the Keyboard Reappear

When you're using a Bluetooth keyboard, your onscreen keyboard doesn't appear. The physical keyboard has in essence co-opted keyboard control of your device.

To use your onscreen keyboard after connecting a Bluetooth keyboard, you can turn off your connection to the Bluetooth keyboard by turning off Bluetooth in the iPad's Settings app or Control Center, by moving the keyboard out of range, or by switching the keyboard off. Your onscreen keyboard should reappear.

Update Software

1. Apple occasionally updates the iPad system software to fix problems or offer enhanced features. You can also tap Settings ⇨ General ⇨ Software Update to update your software. If you're not using the iCloud feature, which updates your iOS automatically, or if you prefer to look for updates yourself in iTunes, you should start by connecting your iPad to your computer.

2. On your computer, open the iTunes software that you installed. (See Chapter 3 for more about this topic.)

3. Click your iPad in the iTunes Source list on the left (in iTunes 12, click the Devices button at the upper left and select your device there).

4. Click the Summary tab, shown in **Figure 22-4**.

5. Click the Check for Update button. iTunes displays a message telling you whether a new update is available.

6. Click the Update button to install the newest version.

 If you're having problems with your iPad, you can use the Update feature to try to restore the current version of the software. Follow the preceding set of steps, but click the Restore button instead of the Update button in Step 6.

You can also use the iTunes Wi-Fi Sync feature (tap Settings ⇨ General) to sync wirelessly to a computer that has iTunes installed.

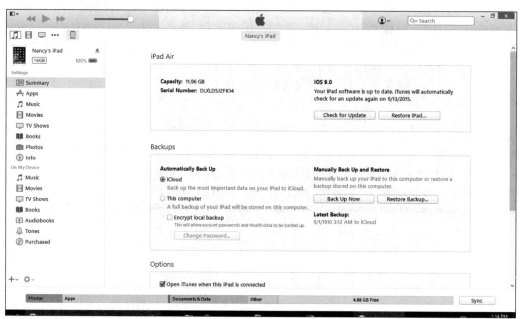

Figure 22-4

Restore the Sound

On the morning I wrote this chapter, as my husband puttered with our iPad, its sound suddenly (and ironically) stopped working. We gave ourselves a quick course in sound recovery, so now I can share some tips with you. Make sure that

→ **You haven't touched the volume-control keys on a physical keyboard connected to your iPad via Bluetooth.** They're usually on the right side of the top row. Be sure not to touch one and inadvertently mute the sound.

→ **You haven't flipped the Side Switch.** If you have an older iPad model with a side switch, and the Side Switch is set up for the Silent feature, moving the switch mutes sound on the iPad.

→ **The speakers aren't covered up.** It may be covered in a way that muffles the sound.

→ **A headset isn't plugged in.** Sound won't play over the speaker and the headset at the same time.

→ **The volume limit isn't set to Off.** You can set up the volume limit in the Music settings to control how loudly your music can play (which is useful if you have teenagers around). Tap the Settings icon on the Home screen; then tap Music on the left side. Tap the Volume Limit control (see **Figure 22-5**), and move the slider to adjust the volume limit.

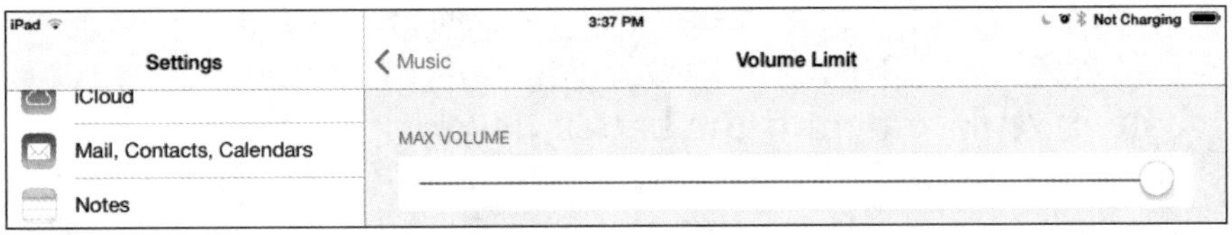

Figure 22-5

When all else fails, reboot. (This strategy worked for us.) Just press the Sleep/Wake button until the red slider appears; then press and drag the slider to the right. After the iPad turns off, press the Sleep/Wake button again until the Apple logo appears, and you may find yourself back in business, sound-wise.

Get Support

Every new iPad comes with a year's coverage for repair of the hardware and 90 days of free technical support. Apple is known for its helpful customer support, so if you're stuck, I definitely recommend that you try it out. Here are a few options you can explore for getting help:

⟹ **The Apple Store:** Go to your local Apple Store (if one is handy) to see what the folks there may know about your problem. It's best to make an appointment beforehand to avoid long lines.

⟹ **The Apple support website:** Visit www.apple.com/support/ipad (see **Figure 22-6**). You can find online manuals, discussion forums, and downloads, and you can use the Apple Expert feature to contact a live support person by phone.

⟹ **The *iPad User Guide:*** You can use the manual online at httpds://help.apple.com/ipad/9/ to visit the online version. You can also access the user guide through iBooks Store for free.

⟹ **The Apple battery replacement service:** If you need repair or service for your battery, visit www.apple.com/batteries/replacement-and-recycling/. Note that your warranty provides free battery replacement if the battery level dips below 50 percent and won't go any higher during the first year you own it. If you purchase the AppleCare service agreement, this service is extended to two years.

Figure 22-6

 Apple recommends that you have your iPad battery replaced only by an Apple Authorized Service Provider.

Find a Missing iPad

You can take advantage of the Find My iPad feature to pinpoint the location of your iPad. This feature is extremely handy if you forget where you left your iPad or someone walks away with it. Find My iPad not only lets you track down the critter, but also lets you wipe out the data contained in it if you have no way to get the iPad back.

 If you're using Family Sharing, someone in your family can find your device and play a sound. This works even if the sound on the iPad is turned off. See Chapter 8 for more about Family Sharing.

Follow these steps to set up the Find My iPad feature:

1. Tap the Settings icon on the Home screen.

2. In the Settings app, tap iCloud.

3. In the iCloud settings that appear, tap Find My iPad.

4. Tap the On/Off switch in the Find My iPad pane that appears (see **Figure 22-7**) if the feature isn't already turned on. Tap the Send Last Location On/Off switch so that iPad sends your iPad's location to Apple if your battery is almost out of juice, if you like. From now on, if your iPad is lost or stolen, you can locate it on your computer or from another iOS device using the free Find My iPad app from the App Store.

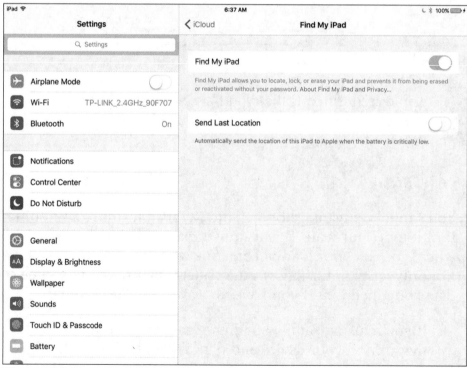

Figure 22-7

5. To use Find My iPad, go to `http://icloud.com` on your computer's browser and then enter your ID and password. Tap on Find My iPad and the Find My iPad screen appears. If you have more than one Apple device, click the All Devices drop-down list and select your iPad.

6. Click the Find My iPad button to display a map of its location and some helpful tools (see **Figure 22-8**).

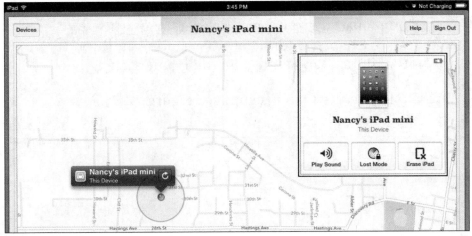

Figure 22-8

7. Click the circle representing your iPad, and then click the Information button (the *i* icon). In the toolbar that appears, to erase all information from the iPad in a process called *wiping*, click the Erase iPad button. Remember that this process will erase all content — contacts, music, notes, and so on — for good.

8. To lock the iPad against access by others, click the Lost Mode button.

 You can also click Play Sound to help you find your iPad if you've left it nearby. If you choose this option, the sound plays for two minutes, helping you track down anybody who's holding your iPad within earshot.

Back Up to iCloud

You used to be able to back up your iPad content only via iTunes, but with Apple iCloud, you can back up via a Wi-Fi network to your iCloud storage. You get 5GB of storage for free (not including iTunes-bought music, video, apps, and electronic books or music you've copied to the cloud via the paid subscription service, iTunes Match), or you can pay for increased levels of storage (50GB for .99 cents a month, 200GB for $2.99 a month, or 1 TB for $9.99 a month).

1. To perform a backup to iCloud, first set up an iCloud account (see Chapter 3 for details on creating an iCloud account) and then tap Settings on the Home screen.

2. Tap iCloud and then tap Backup (see **Figure 22-9**).

Figure 22-9

3. In the pane that appears (see **Figure** 22-10), tap the iCloud Backup On/Off switch to on to enable automatic backups.

4. To perform a manual backup, tap Back Up Now. A progress bar shows how your backup is moving along.

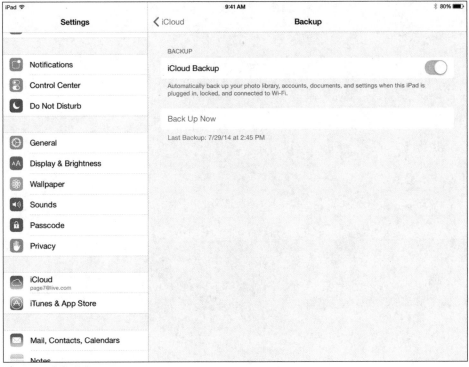

Figure 22-10

Index

• C •

About the Author

Nancy C. Muir is the owner of a writing and consulting company that specializes in business and technology topics. She has authored more than 100 books, including *Computers For Seniors For Dummies* and *iPhone For Seniors For Dummies*. Nancy holds a certificate in Distance Learning Design and has taught Internet safety at the college level.

Dedication

To my husband Earl for going above and beyond in supporting me while writing these books. Honey, you're the best.

Author's Acknowledgments

Thanks to Amy Fandrei, my loyal and supportive acquisitions editor. Also my gratitude to Brian Walls, book juggler supreme. Thanks to Lisa Bucki for tech editing the book to keep me on track.

Publisher's Acknowledgments

Acquisitions Editor: Amy Fandrei

Project Editor: Brian H. Walls

Technical Editor: Lisa Bucki

Sr. Editorial Assistant: Cherie Case

Cover Image: ©Lorena Fernandez/Shutterstock

Production Editor: Kumar Chellappan